THE BOOK OF PROPS

by Mark Juran and Fran Donato

Credits

Authors: Mark Juran and Fran Donato
Development: Ian Lemke
Editing: Erin Kelly
Art Direction: Richard Thomas
Layout and Typesetting: Kathleen Ryan
Cover Design: Robert Dixon and Lawrence Snelly
Interior Art: Hillary Miller
Photographer: J. Lank Hancock
Models: Megan Walters, D. J. McBride, Seth Hancock, Kalina Mercer, Paul Mercer, Heidi Pritchett, Reyer Withrow, and Geoffrey Fortier

We would also like to acknowledge the models from The Masquerade, Second Edition who were left out: Omar Miller, David Clark, Susie Wiggins and Lee Anne McCullough.

Special Thanks to:

Rich "Top Secret" **Thomas,** for keeping Ventrue under wraps.
Josh "Dark Stalker" **Timbrook,** for succumbing to his vices.
Chris "Corporal Hicks" **McDonough,** for his late-night antics with the intercom system.
Aileen "Night Owl" **Miles,** for becoming one of us.
Larry "Itchy" **Snelly,** for finally callin' the Orkin man.
Kathy "XX" **Ryan,** for the impending slumber party.
Rob "Born in a Barn" **Dixon,** for doing the wrong thing too many times and getting his desk toilet-papered.

GAME STUDIO

4598 STONEGATE IND. BLVD.
STONE MTN., GA 30083
U.S.A.

Sanctioning Information

If you would like to run a **Mind's Eye Theatre** game at a convention or similar large venue, you need to obtain sanctioning from us in advance. Our support materials are top-notch, and our costs are low. Recently, Night Owl Productions became an official subsidiary of White Wolf Game Studio. Night Owl is the place to inquire concerning sanctioning for **Mind's Eye Theatre** games. We can be reached at:

Night Owl Productions
4598 Stonegate Industrial Blvd.
Stone Mountain, GA 30083

THE BOOK OF PROPS

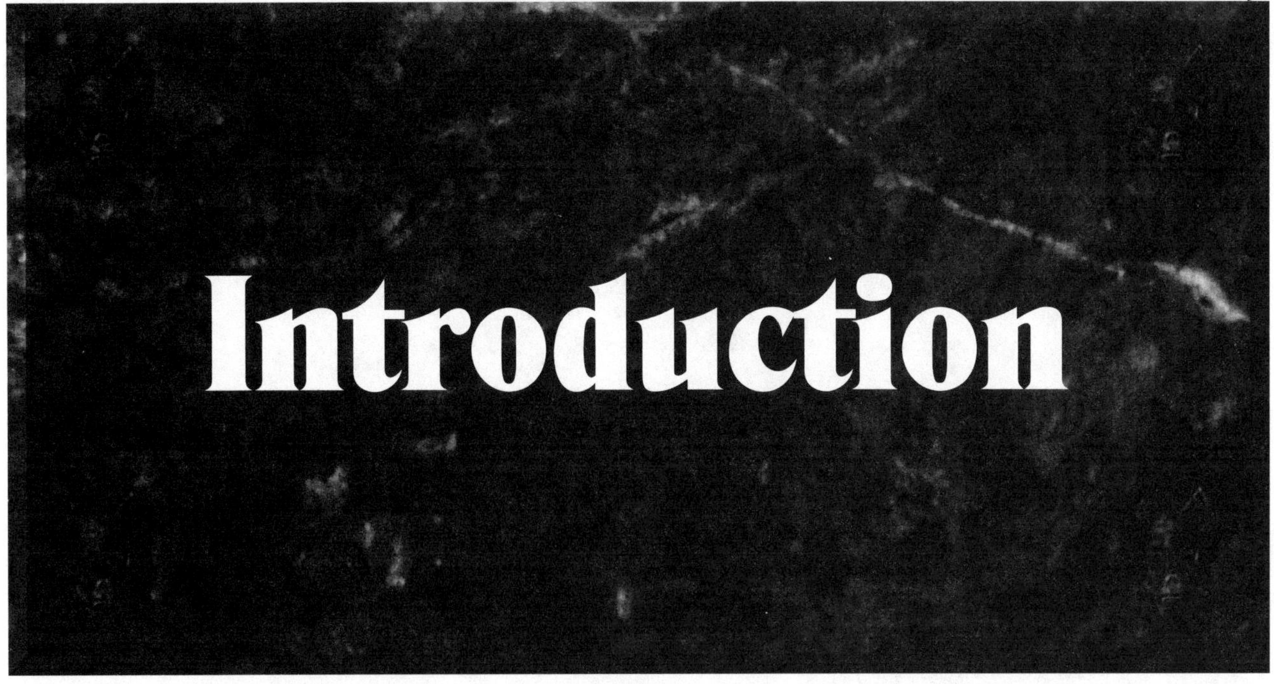

Introduction

The powerful play goes on,
and you may contribute a verse...
— Walt Whitman

Since the dawn of history, people have performed, taking their audiences away to other places as the plot unfolds. However, the plot does not always come out the way we want it to, and we often wish that there was some way we could affect the story as it takes place. So often the protagonist will overlook obvious clues, or the sidekick, who has become your favorite character, gets senselessly killed off. All of us have wished that we could step onto the stage and become the protagonist whom we so much admire or have become frustrated with. **Mind's Eye Theatre** gives you that chance; the ability to become the protagonist of a story and call the shots yourself.

Mind's Eye Theatre is the perfect release for those of you who have begun to tire of traditional forms of passive entertainment: television, movies and theatre. Even playing board games, or going over to the mall and plunking quarters into a machine to battle the oppression of that dreaded foe we call boredom, have lost their appeal. While these diversions all provide a temporary escape, they are almost entirely passive. Any decisions you make probably won't go too far beyond, "I'm gonna beat M. Bison if it's the last thing I ever do!" Even in traditional tabletop roleplaying games, you are one of a group of people living in a world ruled by one person. After a while, even the best, most experienced gamemaster falls into a rut. Regardless of how dynamic the game is, it still comes down to the same old thing: find the problem, correct the problem and kill or arrest anything that gets in your way.

Mind's Eye Theatre allows you to play a game on an entirely different, elevated level. The gamemaster does not have sole control of the plot, because you have become the protagonist in your own story. True, the plot was created in the mind of one or more people, but as soon as the action starts, the story takes on a life of its own. Winning is no longer the most significant objective here: Roleplaying and telling a good story become your primary objectives. Your character, your adopted persona, has a chance to become as "real" as possible within the confines of the game and achieve her goals and the goals you create for her as a consequence of the plot. The game pieces are living, breathing people. Your character has a destiny you can control and influence. That fuzzy, little, electronic, blinking character on the TV screen that you manipulate with the push of a button, or that sheet

of statistics you play once a week with your friends is transformed within the mind's eye into a more realistic personality. Here, your character has a past, and you get to control her future. As you learn more about her, the world she lives in, and the other characters she knows, you begin to develop how she looks, walks, talks, and every other little aspect and mannerism she has. You manipulate a distinctive figure that interacts in a virtual society by physically and mentally portraying her as a part in a dynamic play, rather than directing a piece of molded lead skidding around a tabletop, having its existence dictated by stats on a sheet.

There are some who play just to see what it's all about, or just to keep in touch with other players, treating the game more as an opportunity to socialize than as a means of escape. Most players, however, want to step out of the grind and become a fictional character who is as far-removed from their everyday existences as they can get. For that one evening or more, you can be a mover and shaker, a subversive underground figure, a hero who saves the day, or anything your imagination can conjure up. for that one night, you want to live the part, dress the part, alter your look for it, and breathe life into it. But, it's not always that easy. There is only so much time you can devote to developing a character you will be playing for only one night or weekend. Even if you are playing a character in an ongoing chronicle, there is only so much you can do. So, for those of you who want to do more than just socialize, we offer a starting point for developing your character into a living, breathing persona without having to devote too much time to the endeavor.

This book is also intended to offer assistance to Storytellers who wish to breath a little more life and realism into their story or chronicle. Though not necessary to a good story, just a few minor props or sets help stimulate players' imaginations and make the experience all the more real for everyone. Each Storyteller has to decide how much time and money he wishes to invest into providing props and sets for his story.

There are many tricks of the trade, tools actually, that actors and set designers have used for years to portray characters in as "real" a way as possible. Ancient Greeks and Romans used masks held before their faces to signify emotions. In the Middle Ages, traveling bands of performers entertained from the backs of wagons or on whatever relatively flat surface they could find, oftentimes using the crudest of props to suggest their surroundings. It wasn't until 1576 when The Theatre, the first permanent structure built for the purpose of producing stage plays, was opened, so that performers could organize events using a familiar stage area and develop elaborate props (and occasionally sets). For the first time, an acting troupe knew beforehand what physical space the scenes were to take place in, and from what view they would be seen by the audience. In 1599, The Theatre was dismantled and shipped to the South Bank of the Thames in one of Elizabethan society's attempts to rid London of creative types. There, James Burbage rebuilt it and called it The Globe, which later became known worldwide for the productions of William Shakespeare's works, and served as a pattern for the creation of other theatres. In these theatres, props became more elaborate and numerous, because now there were places to store them, and their construction could be justified by their reuse in other productions. Sets, such as they were, were also used more extensively to convey the surroundings of the play. Costumes became more elaborate and expensive, and a few years later, makeup began to be used. It was at this time that modern theatre techniques developed, and they continue to evolve today with every recent advance in technology.

In this book, we will touch upon many of these tricks of the trade used by actors and stagehands to give you ideas for developing your own **Mind's Eye Theatre** stories and characters into exactly what you want them to be. We will discuss professional theatrical techniques for character development, costume design and construction, personal props, makeup, as well as set design and construction. In each section, we will consider budgets: the easily affordable to the more expensive and time-consuming. To cover all the techniques employed by the theatre would be next to impossible, because the human imagination is limitless. Volumes could be written on any one of the topics covered herein. Finally, in the back of this book you will find many different types of cards, which can be used to enhance your story by providing a quick reference for players. These cards include: weapon and item cards, Blood Trait cards, Status cards, and Animal cards. The aim and hope of this book is that it will give you some ideas to start with, so that you can help to make every **Mind's Eye Theatre** event you are involved with a memorable experience, whether you be a player or a Storyteller.

Chapter One: Character Development

Behold, I show you a mystery; we shall not all sleep.
But we shall be changed.
In a moment, in the twinkling of an eye, at the last trump;
for the trumpet shall sound, and the dead shall be raised
incorruptible, and we shall be changed.
— 1 Corinthians 15:51-52

This chapter discusses ways to add believability and realism to your character portrayal, whether you are playing a protagonist or a narrator character. You will learn the importance of preparation and relaxation, and how to maintain a character throughout the length of a story.

The single most important aspect of a **Mind's Eye Theatre** story is your character. The Storyteller can provide props and sets to create a realistic setting. You can use clothing, makeup, and movement to create a physical image for your character, but you cannot successfully portray her without first understanding what it is that motivates her, what her strengths and weaknesses are, and how she feels about the world around her. The ability to immerse yourself in your character for the duration of the story, and the ability to set it aside afterward, requires the type of discipline actors have been using for decades. You are, in essence, performing in a fluid, dynamic, improvisational play whenever you participate in a **Mind's Eye Theatre** story. Like improvisational theatre, there is no script for you to follow and no set outcome. All you have to work with are the plot, the setting, and the goals your character was given, or has developed. You, as your character, write the script, and ultimately contribute to the outcome of the story. For this reason, it is important to establish a strong and sustainable character. Ultimately, you are responsible for the actions of your character and the enjoyment derived from playing her.

Unlike a tabletop roleplaying game, character development for a **Mind's Eye Theatre** story goes far beyond the simple balancing of equations and assigning abilities to a character. You have to take a step beyond and understand the character's motivations, needs, desires, and morals. In these stories, you actually assume the persona of your character when interacting with other characters, and in everything you do. It is important for you to be able to maintain that adopted persona, and not become bored with it and lose its essence as the story or chronicle goes on. Remember, you have a responsibility to yourself, and to the other players, to keep yourself immersed in the persona you've adopted. If the others should falter, you could be the one who carries the story through to its end.

Character creation is when you decide the basics of who your character will be. At this stage you can delve into the possibilities of your character and create a truly unique person; go beyond your initial assumptions of what you perceive as a logical background for your character and look for things that could add spice and interest to the story. Oftentimes, the first ideas that come to your mind for your character's background are based on preconceptions that you are comfortably familiar with. Though this isn't necessarily bad, it can detract from the dynamic nature and individualism of your character. Make your character your own, with tenets and goals that are realistic in terms of her clan or tribe and that reflect her own unique views. Once you have your background complete, always ask your Storyteller if she wants to review it to assure compatibility with the plot of her story.

A **Mind's Eye Theatre** story should always be a team effort where the goal is the enjoyment of everyone involved. Your character may be socially independent of everyone else in the game, but you must still contend with your fellow players to achieve your objectives. Alienating a fellow player or group of players for no particular reason will set a precedent to be alienated in return. Even your character's enemies play an important role in furthering the plot and should not be overlooked. Every hero and villain needs an enemy to make his existence meaningful. By developing a solid concept of your own character and adhering to that concept, you should never feel the need to set yourself apart from the other players in the game. You should be able to project an image of solitude, if that is your character choice, without imposing that solitude on others. In the end, it is your responsibility to create a character that can function within the parameters of the story as well as she can relate to other characters.

In the following sections of this chapter, you will find a host of concepts to give you a starting point and a direction to follow for creating a well-rounded character. Some of the concepts discussed may seem odd, or even trivial, at first. However, they are all exercises and concepts used by actors to help define a character portrayal. You will learn the importance of focus and how to maintain it throughout the length of a story. You will understand the need to remain relaxed and ready for any contingency as well as how to maintain your physical well-being throughout the length of your character portrayal. You will come to realize how seemingly irrelevant concepts can help you derive maximum enjoyment from an evening of playing in a **Mind's Eye Theatre** game. Hopefully, all the information imparted hereafter will give you something to contemplate and leave you with an understanding of the true depth and nature of the game.

Understanding the Genre

Before you reach the point of developing a character for a **Mind's Eye Theatre** story, you should explore the premise of the various character genres, or types, you might play. On the most basic level, there are two: mortal and immortal. Each has a unique perspective of the world, and their own motivations for what they do. From these two primary outlooks springs forth a myriad of variables representing the various character types. Vampires, mummies, and wraiths represent all those who do not fear time, and have developed or have begun to develop attitudes accordingly. Humans, Garou, and even mages must always be aware of the ticking of the clock, as it marks the passage of their lives, and they will most likely act on this premise consciously or subconsciously. Effective portrayal of a character in a **Mind's Eye Theatre** game requires understanding the scope of each of these premises.

What Price Eternity? – The Immortal

How does immortality affect the mind? True immortality is not necessarily infinite life, but rather a life so long that it is beyond our comprehension. Try to imagine every day of your life in the short period of time you have been in existence: the things you have learned, that you will always remember, and that you wish to forget. Take every experience that you have had, and think about how each one has affected you in this short period of time you call your life. Now, take all of these experiences and multiply them by a factor of 10, 20, 30 times, or more. With such vast amounts of time available, you could spend a mortal's lifetime contemplating one single aspect of your existence that you find intriguing, or you could move on, trying to find meaning in all things. You could perfect training in any skill and attain vast knowledge in any number of subjects. However, such pursuits would doubtless become tedious after a time, and it is extremely possible that you would succumb to an eventual state of ennui, where nothing fazes you. Your life might well become a struggle against stagnation, though surely the 20th century has given some amusement to the ancient immortal. Imagine what life was like a mere hundred years ago; then imagine it a thousand years ago. Customs, language and technology would evolve tremendously over your immortal lifetime. You would witness the folly of humankind as they forgot their past and repeated their mistakes over and over again. How would this affect your perspective? You can never know. However, you can attempt to emulate that which you cannot truly understand, and hope to do it some form of justice.

There are many aspects to consider when playing a long-lived or immortal character. Beyond the obvious, each character has her own peculiar outlook, separating her from all others. As mentioned before, it is important to look beyond the obvious. Think of the differences between what we take for granted every day and the meaning such things have for someone bound by a set of different physical rules. (The sweetness of the air or the smell of perfume have no relevance to a creature that has to remember to breathe.) The purpose of this contemplation and the following observations is to help you challenge your view of each genre and find new aspects to integrate into your character.

The Kindred

Certainly, the Kindred are among the most common immortals played in a **Mind's Eye Theatre** story. Yet few take the time to think about what it really means to be a vampire. When attempting to portray one of the Kindred, you must imagine your life as one continuous line, centuries in length, rather than as a series of fragmented memories developed for your character background. Many events throughout the ages have influenced your conduct and your perceptions of the world. You have witnessed the death of many mortals, friend and foe alike, changing how you interact with others. Would you admire a sworn mortal enemy such as a Garou for her persistent, yet misguided, ways? Would you let her live if the choice were left to you, knowing that she would be but a memory in your not-so-distant future? Or would you take the safe route and slay her so as to remove the threat that she represents? You live an existence as far removed from mortal life as can be imagined. Yet, you are forced to watch and take part in the affairs of mortals every day of your existence. Your emotions are ruled by a force alien to human nature and, as time wears on, you begin to adapt to it, making yourself alien in turn to the humanity you once knew. All the while, you have to abide by the rules of the Kindred and maintain the Masquerade of appearing mortal. The physical concerns that plagued you daily as a mortal are no longer a concern to you. There are no little aches and pains, or limbs that fall asleep and cramp up on you if you stay in one position for too long. Gone are all the little sensations that give you the subconscious comfort of being human.

Of course there are those Kindred who have spent a portion of their existence in torpor, whether self-imposed or forced upon them. Centuries may pass as you remain in limbo, completely unaware of the events shaping the world outside. If you are playing such a character, you must take into account the shock of awakening in a world drastically changed from the one you knew. You have to decide how such an occurrence will affect the manner in which you portray your character. How long has your character been in torpor and how long has it been since you awoke? These are questions you must ask yourself. Is your character quick to adapt to the new experiences around him or does he tenaciously cling to the past? If your torpor was enforced by an enemy, vengeance may very well be a motivating factor for your character. Or is vengeance even possible, given the passage of time? By the time you awaken, your age-old enemy may no longer exist.

Finally, there is the neonate's perspective. As a neonate, you are not far removed from the humanity you have forsaken for your new existence, and your actions may still be influenced by it. You must decide how much of your humanity you are willing to surrender to the new influences in your life. How you were Embraced should have a great deal of influence on your new perspective. Were you Embraced against your will, thrust suddenly into a never-ending night? Or were you offered the chance of immortality? Just because you chose to accept it does not mean that you are ready for the power that it represents. The age at which you were Embraced is certainly an important factor. Those Embraced while still youthful often become wildly overconfident in their newfound powers, while those Embraced at an older age often cherish their renewed youth, but are more conservative, not wishing to risk losing their immortality by making a stupid mistake. This is the time of your character's greatest vulnerability, for he is still adapting mentally to this new aspect of his existence.

The Fleeting Days of Spring – The Mortal

Mortals are perhaps the easiest of all character types to understand. At least, they should be. However, even after centuries of researching and philosophizing human behavior, why we are what we are remains a mystery. The human mind is capable of creating the means to deal with almost any situation. The unpredictability of these reactions makes each of us a unique individual. True, there are generalizations you could make to predict reactions to specific events, but in the end you are the result of the multitude of environmental influences you've been exposed to since birth. Some argue that heredity plays an important role in determining our dispositions. However, this is no excuse for not taking responsibility for our actions. Our consciousness ultimately controls all our actions. Whether we rule it, or allow it to rule us is a decision we must learn to make.

The Human

Humans have so many variables influencing and preoccupying them that they may actually be the hardest characters to portray well in a **Mind's Eye Theatre** story. Too many players consider them fodder when played in a game with Kindred or Garou. As a result, many people don't take them seriously. This might be partially due to the fact that mortals' power (or lack thereof) is not threatening. On the other hand, where in the rules does it state that you have to take on any of these creatures face to face? If your human character is in a bind, try to imagine how you, yourself, would respond to it. Then, take your character's restrictions and Abilities, and impose them on those responses. If you were alone in a dark alley, unarmed, would you try to take on a raving lunatic with an ax? Hopefully, you would apply a little thought to the situation and respond to the best of your ability. The important thing to remember is not to assume your human character has as great a knowledge of the supernatural as you, the portrayer, does. If you impose those limits on the knowledge you would use to solve a problem, you might begin to see some interesting roleplaying opportunities.

You are playing Stiletto, a street-smart girl of 18 who thinks she has seen it all. Stiletto's knowledge of life is limited to what she has to know in order to survive. She has no knowledge of the supernatural, aside from the bogeyman stories she heard while growing up, which she quickly forgot in the reality of the streets. You, having adopted Stiletto as your persona for the game, must forget all you may know of the various entities that inhabit the world of **Mind's Eye Theatre** and impose a threshold of acceptance for her, deciding how far she will go in initially accepting the supernatural as an explanation for the events that will shortly come to pass. Anyhow, Stiletto is on her way to visit some friends when a dazzling, charming man tries to lure her into an alley for some "fun." You, as Stiletto, decide that he can't be all that dangerous; besides, his words confuse and beguile you to the point where you decide that some cheap thrills aren't such a bad idea. You head into the alley when the creep tries to pull some sick prank on you and lunges at you sporting a cheap set of plastic fangs. He's fast and strong, but you've dealt with his type before and land a couple of good jabs to his eyes and shower him with pepper spray, just for the heck of it. Later that night, you feel as though you are being followed. You've learned to depend on your street-smarts to sense danger, and call in some favors from your friends to check things out. Sure enough, the creep is back. You and your friends get the jump on him and intend to teach him a lesson he'll never forget. However, you soon end up learning a thing or two yourselves. Those fangs were real, and this guy is some type of monster. After taking a few losses on your side, you eventually finish off the fang dude, and you and your friends are now aware of a new threat to contend with on the streets. Suddenly, the world seems even a bit more unfair.

To play Stiletto effectively, you had to suspend your knowledge of the supernatural in order to give her a chance to grow and experience new things in her life. Part of the enjoyment of participating in a **Mind's Eye Theatre** event is watching your character grow in the short time that you play her. The reward is even greater when you play that character in a chronicled event. Stiletto may never learn about Kindred, Garou, or any other genre in the game. She only knows that there are threats to her and her friends and that they must be dealt with accordingly by a typical instinctive reaction — destroy the threat. To play Stiletto while imposing your beliefs and actions upon her would be doing the plot and yourself an injustice. If after the initial attack, Stiletto suddenly became an expert on all things supernatural because you, the portrayer, bought all the reference material and spent hours looking it over, then playing her would lose all meaning, and you and your fellow players would lose out on an opportunity for a fun, in-game learning experience. Human characters have the greatest potential for growth, because they come into the game with a clean slate, ready to learn and experience new things. As a human, you have the potential to become something totally different from what you started out as.

Some plot lines are entirely based on humans and human problems. For a while, you have no direct threat of encountering some exotic entity intent on disrupting your otherwise normal life. Regardless of how nice this sounds, you must still be willing to play your character within the framework that you have created for her. She must still have levels of acceptance, a moral code, and goals that she wishes to achieve. The addition or lack of supernatural entities is incidental to your effective portrayal of the part. You have to believe in your character and give her a chance to grow in order to maximize the opportunities presented in the plot.

The Garou

Of all the lycanthropes in the **World of Darkness**, the Garou are the most prevalent and well-documented. They are the true werewolves, the noble beasts. To portray a Garou, you must first understand their plight and cause. For the most part, they believe in their duty to combat the Wyrm, which represents entropy and the destruction of nature. They truly love this world, which they call Gaia, and the potential that it represents. Garou feel most comfortable in the wild, close to nature. However, time has taken its toll on the structure of their society, and the Garou blood grows weak and their numbers grow fewer. Some of the 13 tribes, such as the Bone Gnawers and Glass Walkers, have even adapted to life in the artificial world of the city. Others, such as the Black Spiral Dancers, have become tainted by the Wyrm, and have deigned to serve its needs as it endeavors to consume Gaia. What was once a proud and powerful force that preyed upon evil has itself fallen prey to the trappings of the modern world. The Garou are most like us, save for the fact that they are aware of their plight and are actively trying to stop its progression.

To prepare to portray a Garou, you should first determine the nature of her birth. Was your character born homid (human), lupus (wolf), or metis (interbred)? How did her rearing affect her outlook? If she was born homid, you must determine how being a part of humanity during her developmental years affected her acceptance of all the ideals that the Garou represent. Perhaps the influence of the modern world renders her more susceptible to the influence of the Wyrm. Or maybe it has left a bad taste in her mouth for the irreverent way that humanity has treated the planet. The same considerations must also be taken into account if she is lupus or metis. Metis are particularly demanding to play, for they belong to neither lupus nor homid, and are scorned by both for the deformities that their birth bequeathed them. Yet, as a metis you are

"allowed" to remain a part of Garou society because of your value as a fighter. How would such an existence influence your character's outlook on life? Would he grow to hate his tribe for their attitude toward him or his parents for their indiscretion? Or, would he be grateful to be a part of the Garou and enjoy the opportunity to defend Gaia? The point of this discussion is to make you aware of how deeply you can develop the attitudes and feelings of your character based upon what is known of the Garou. As with all the character types in this chapter, you must look deep within at the motivations and driving influences of your character, and not just at the surface factors. Regardless of the path you choose for your character, her origin will have some effect on her outlook and the direction she takes during the story.

For the most part, Garou are as messed-up as humans when it comes to making decisions, and have to deal with many of the same day-to-day issues as the rest of us. As a Garou, you would suffer from the same disadvantages as all mortals. However, you would also have advantages that humans don't have, mainly: unity among your pack, an understanding of its hierarchy, rapid healing, a common purpose, and a sense of spirituality through your contact with the Umbra and your spirit Totem. All Garou, for the most part, share in the song of ages, the Litany, which offers them a history and tradition. You should become familiar with the tenets expressed within the Litany, even if you belong to a tribe that does not actively enforce them. The Litany offers insight into the behavior of all Garou and is all too often overlooked in the heat of roleplaying. The Litany and tribal history are important influences in your character's existence and should not be forgotten.

Variations on an Old Theme

Before going into more character development, we would like to discuss a few ways to vary some of the more traditional views of certain character types, thus adding more flavor to your character and ultimately, the story. Remember, how you portray a character is, in the end, up to you. It is your interpretation of the genre that gives the game a life of its own. However, a well-developed and strong character will be able to give clear and concise arguments for his actions using the history of his clan, tribe, or the appropriate tenets of his kind. This ability to defend yourself against criticism lends power to even the least-imposing character you portray.

One of the most potentially enjoyable, yet least-understood of the Kindred are the Malkavians. Often, they are played as children set loose in a manic playground. Whenever things get out of hand, they tend to run off to entertain themselves and hide from the dilemma at hand. If you undertake the portrayal of a Malkavian, you should do so with Malkav's original intent in mind. He wished for his progeny to open their eyes to the endless variables of the universe by looking upon it with the altered insight he bestowed upon them. (At least this is what we would like to think he had in mind.) However, it would be wrong to assume that he was merely insane, and thus any Malkavian is an uncontrollable idiot with little or no capacity for reasoning. There should always be a method to your madness. Malkavians can be a truly formidable force to deal with when played to their full potential. The gift of the prank should be delivered with a definite lesson in mind for those on the receiving end, and used to further lend credibility to such a misunderstood group.

Another clan of the Kindred often played short of full potential is the Brujah. Members are frequently portrayed as rough and tough gang members who want nothing more than to party. You should keep in mind that the Brujah originated from philosophers. You would be safe in assuming that there are some Brujah old enough to remember these days of glory. You would not necessarily be changing the scope of the game if you explored this original premise and tried to revive the ways of the past. Brujah have always been known as the rebels of their time. Rebellion can take on many forms, as Gandhi showed by developing the ultimate form of rebellion, passive resistance. Violence is not always the key, and often begets more violence. If your character survives her attempt to establish her own beliefs, she could initiate an interesting revolution which could result in a new direction for the story.

Garou are sometimes portrayed as irrationally aggressive individuals who wish to take on all comers. In the wild, the only animals that act in this manner are the ones frothing at the mouth. A part of survival is finding joy in existence and avoiding unnecessary conflict. Even when hunting, an animal may spend hours observing his intended victim before pouncing. Animals have found a common median of existence amongst themselves and other creatures. Lions do not constantly go rampaging for the joy of it. If they did, there would soon be no resources left for survival. Only humans slaughter for the sheer enjoyment of it. Animals only act aggressively in response to a threat to their survival, whether real or imagined. Aggression in these situations is normal and expected. Acting like a rabid war machine all the time quickly grows old to everyone else participating in the game.

These observations are offered as examples of how people's perceptions of each character type can become unmalleable and stale. All the literature developed for **Mind's Eye Theatre** contains a wealth of clues and information about the rich history of the creatures that inhabit it. There are many ideas for your adopted persona to explore. Take the time to look beyond the obvious and see if you can find some aspect of your character's nature that has not been developed as thoroughly as it could be, then add it to your character.

The Discipline of Pretend

Keep it quiet
Go slow
Need to know
Stamp the date upon your file.
Masquerade, but well worthwhile

Wear an air of casual indifference
Careful how you go about your usual business.
I'll tell you when — (not yet). Soon the great unveiling
Bless my boots! Upon my soul! Secrecy, it is my failing.
— Jethro Tull, "Under Wraps"

In developing your character for a **Mind's Eye Theatre** story, it is important that you familiarize yourself with and understand the nuances of each creature in the game. Try to find overlooked aspects and use these to give a greater sense of sustainable realism to the persona you are creating. This adopted persona is what the other players in the game will see and respond to when they engage you in play. Your adopted persona should reflect all the aspects and nuances of your character and communicate that information to the other participants. If you have a well-developed persona, you should be able to reveal exactly what you wish to other players at all times throughout an entire event. A strongly developed character can command attention without even uttering a word, or manipulate a situation without leaving a trace of his machinations.

In theatre, actors employ various disciplines to achieve a realistic and sustainable adoption of a character persona. These disciplines have been fine-tuned over the centuries and are evolving to this day. Acting is more grueling than most people realize. Good acting involves years of study and training in the nature and origin of emotion, movement, speech, and voice. It is an ongoing process of learning and skill development that, as a participant in a **Mind's Eye Theatre** story, you will experience to some degree. Regardless of how many of these skills you use in a game, however, you can benefit from the disciplines actors have developed to project a strong portrayal of your character.

Focus Pocus

Chief among the disciplines employed by actors is focus. Focus goes beyond the mere definition of the word; it is a vital concept that allows you to give and take, share your energy, retain information, maintain your adopted persona and draw strength from it when you grow weary as the game goes on. Think of focus as something beyond a concept, something that each of us possesses, but in varying degrees. Some people have great reserves, others only a trickle. An interesting aspect about focus is that you can draw it from other people and imbue yourself with it or bestow others with it. Regardless of how little focus you have, you can create all you need to carry you through the story, if you know how. The important thing is knowing how to properly use focus in a positive manner, as it is a discipline with many facets and uses. By controlling focus and understanding its power, you can convince anyone of the validity of your character and will have absolutely no problem conveying your intent

To understand the positive nature of focus, you should first understand its negative aspect. One part of focus is the ability to draw attention to yourself. It also has a bit to due with your inner concept of your character. Calling "Fire!" in a theatre is one way, albeit an incredibly stupid one, to draw attention to yourself. The negative energy created by demanding focus in such a way can only harm you in the end. It reflects poorly on your self-image if you have to resort to such obvious and potentially harmful pranks to put yourself in the limelight. The same applies in a **Mind's Eye Theatre** game. Calling negative focus to yourself disrupts the flow of the game and diminishes the enjoyment of it. Sometimes you may feel that you are absolutely right in your convictions and that the other players must come around to your point of view, or that you have a really cool character and you just have to show everyone how great you are. There are ways of doing this without causing conflict. Interrupting other players, acting aggressively beyond what is necessary for your character, ignoring the signals sent by your fellow players, and disregarding other players' goals for the sake of expediting your own, are all example of negative focus. Hogging focus and denying it to others bogs down the action and creates a negative backlash toward you. The entire plot would dissolve into a mire of groups battling and arguing among themselves if each person were to lose sight of her objective and characterization. By being positive with your focus and your goals, regardless of how diabolical and plot-twisting they may be, you can help reverse this negative slide in an event and make the game a positive experience for everyone.

A player that has a good grasp of his characterization and has confidence portraying it often garners a lot of attention. This is a part of the positive nature of focus that you can emulate to draw attention to your adopted persona without interrupting the flow of the plot. Remember, the plot is mutable and does not rely exclusively on any one player, regardless of how much attention that character may be receiving. In the end, being envious of the attention another player is receiving without first deciding why you feel the way you do can only lead to the generation of negative energy, which translates to the way you portray your character, defeating his intent and lessening his effectiveness. This can happen without conscious thought on your part, and this is why it is so important to keep your goals and motivations in mind.

Exercising the Right to Relax

The first stage in developing a good basis for positive focus begins with the simple concept of relaxation. You cannot begin to bring all the myriad factors of your character's persona together if you are distracted by the tensions and stresses of the day. To begin, find a place where you feel comfortable and lie down on your back. If you want, play some music that is not demanding or distracting. Breathe from the diaphragm in a slow and steady manner. Too many people have learned to breathe from the chest, and this builds tension and constricts airflow, which causes more tension. Good oxygen flow is important to ensure proper metabolic functions and to help the body burn off tiring toxins. For those of you asking where the diaphragm is, it is the area between your pelvis and your lower ribs, essentially the stomach area. Breathe in and out from the diaphragm, slowly and naturally through your nose, and feel the rhythm of your chest as it goes up and down. Continue this way for a while, until the focus of your attention is on the rhythm. Avoid distractions and keep your eyes closed. Now, beginning with the feet, tense each area of your body, one part at a time, as hard as you can, hold it for a few seconds, then let it go. First the feet, tense and let go; then the calves, thighs, pelvic area, stomach, chest, arms, neck, face, in that order, until you have tensed and relaxed each area of your body. As you tense, feel all the tension already present in that area, how you held it there, and how it affected the way you hold yourself. Then feel how the new tension you are applying adds to it. When you relax, let all of the tension go from that area, including that which you had originally stored there. It may take a while to become aware of the tension that exists in your frame. When you do find that tension, let it go and try to relax the area in question. By adding more tension to each area of your body, you become aware of how it reacts physically to stress and how stress influences your natural bearing. The purpose of this exercise is to relax you and release the tensions that currently exist in your frame so that you are ready, physically and mentally, to assume a new bearing and demeanor.

Now that you have completed this first exercise, stay in this position and relax. Become aware of each area of your body that has residual tension in it and play with ways of removing it. Proper breathing techniques are important when dealing with tension. Notice the areas of your body that still contain tension and internally direct your breath to these areas. Imagine the air from your lungs filling the trouble spot and gently kneading it and pulling apart the knots and pushing the stress from your body. Remember, breath is important. It powers your body and is required continuously. You may never consider how much the way we breathe affects our behavior and vice versa, but it is a significant link. At another time, explore the ways that you breathe in different situations and what those methods of breathing mean. If you are suddenly overcome with the need to yawn, go with it. Yawning is a natural response that indicates you are entering a relaxed state, and it also helps stretch the vocal cords. (Vocal exercises will be touched upon later in this chapter.) At this point in the exercise, continue to relax and maintain position.

You may have to repeat this particular exercise a few times until you have reached a state of total or near-total relaxation. Once you have achieved this state without falling asleep, move on to the next stage. Keeping your eyes closed the whole while, slowly let your attention drift to the sensations around you. At first, become aware of the closest things to you, the feel of the floor on your back, the draft that is licking your face, the smell of your own body, the sound of the blood rushing in your ears. Gradually expand that awareness outward from you in stages until you sense all the things around you. If you expand your awareness far enough, you may notice little things for the first time. Try to remain in a relaxed state throughout this exploration. Expand your awareness slowly so that your mind has a chance to accept, without conflict, the input it is receiving. Take your awareness to its limit and sense all that is going on around you. Maintain this state of awareness for a while and then begin to pull back into yourself in stages, until you are once again at the starting point. At this time, you are ready to proceed to the next stage.

From the prone position, still with your eyes closed, begin to raise yourself slowly to a comfortable sitting position, all the while being aware of how you move to that position and what muscles you are using. From this sitting position, slowly raise yourself once more to a standing position, still with your eyes closed, and feel the blood as it moves through your body. This state of self-awareness can be developed so you can apply another character over your base self. Once you have explored all the aspects of your senses and body, open your eyes gently for the first time since beginning the exercise and begin to study your surroundings. What has changed about them since you started? If you are in your room, how do the objects in your "space" reflect your nature? While still in a relaxed state, contemplate this and understand how what you have chosen to adorn you room with reflects who and what you are. Understanding how your environment affects you is the first step in understanding how your adopted persona's environment affects her. If you have a character in mind at this point, it might be interesting to play with the idea of how she would feel in the space you now inhabit. How would she react to your surroundings?

The Void

The following basic exercises are used to develop a point of focus upon which to base your characterization. Almost all of the exercises involve starting from the relaxed state you created in the last exercise. From this state of relaxation can come the understanding and development of character presence, emotions, self perception, give and take with other characters, stamina, and character believability. For the purpose of simplicity, you may refer to this relaxed state as the void. From the void you can extract the material you will need when portraying a character. The void also provides focus, with which you can mold your adopted persona. Your adopted persona will become a character imbued with believability.

Into the Fray

How do you want your character to come across to other characters in the event? Do you want to be sneaky, strong, happy, angry, goofy, or perhaps something altogether odd? All the factors of your character's presence can be found reflected in nature and in the objects of your everyday environment. How many times have you said someone was stubborn as a mule, slick as an eel, strong as an ox, or thick as a brick? You begin to attribute the nature of these objects and beasts to a person's behavior without consciously making any effort to do so. Adopting attributes from objects and nature helps you to define your character's persona. Humans are just as much a part of nature as any other animal on the planet and, as such, assume traits found in nature.

Those people you hold in awe at their ability to command their adopted persona during a story may not necessarily be using these principles on a conscious level. They may just have an instinctive grasp of what it takes to subtly manipulate a situation or convey their character's intent. The point is that it is common for us to assume aspects of our environment into our personalities. The ability to pick and choose what those aspects are on a conscious level, thus affecting others on an unconscious level, is what makes for a good performance. Think of all the times that you have watched a play or a movie in which one of the characters does not seem believable to you. The reason for this is that you are subconsciously reading or "picking up" his efforts to assume the nature of his role. The actor either does not

feel comfortable with what he is doing, or does not have a good understanding of his role. You should weigh in your mind the differences between some of the truly great performances you have seen in the past and some of the truly bad ones. In a **Mind's Eye Theatre** game you can use attribute adoption to strengthen your character.

Attribute Adoption

Begin this exercise from the void. If you practiced the relaxation techniques enough, you should be able to get yourself into the void by merely counting down from 15, controlling your breathing and releasing your tension with a countdown. You do not need to be prone to achieve the void. Release the tension and achieve focus. From the void, chose an animal that you feel best represents the nature of your adopted persona. Is she noble like a lion, nimble like a monkey, nervous like a Chihuahua, slow like a sloth, or playful like a dolphin? Imagine all the various types of animals your character may share qualities with. Try not to pick obvious ones, like bat for a Kindred, owl for a mummy, or wolf for a Garou. Even a Garou of lupus descent may share many qualities with some other animal. You want to avoid such stereotypical assignments and delve into the true nature of your character. A Garou may have the strength of a gorilla, or the sneakiness of a rat. The object is to choose the animal that works best for you and relate it to your character.

Once you have selected an animal, begin to explore all you know about it. Experiment with the animal's movement and sound. Move yourself as your animal would and feel how your body adapts to these movements. At first, exaggerate the movements and really explore the full range of motions. How does it feel? Gradually tone the movements down to the point where they become more natural to the human frame, and incorporate them into your developing character. Use the sounds of the animal as a guide to the pitch and intent of your voice. Are the sounds excited? Confident? Define and exaggerate these sounds and gradually tone them down to the point where you can incorporate them into your developing character. While still in the void, think some more about your animal. Consider its eating habits and family structure. How does the animal gather its food? What consideration does the animal give as to the selection of its food? Carnivores often prey on the weak and the old, culling the herd to keep it strong. How does the animal feel about its young? The cuckoo raids another bird's nest, replacing one of that bird's eggs with one of its own for the other bird to raise, whereas a bear is very protective and loving of its young. Consider the feelings you associate with that animal and how they reflect your character's view of her accomplices, friends and even enemies. Continue this exercise until you feel comfortable adopting the attributes you desire from your animal. From the void, count out ten, back to your adopted persona, and retain the attributes you chose from the animal for your developing character.

Object Recognition

The next exercise is object recognition. Begin as usual from the void and choose an object that best suits your character. It could be a mug of ale, a hat, a memento given to him by an elder of your character's sect, or a lock of hair from a mortal he once knew. The object should be something that is important only to your developing character. This will be the object used to anchor part of your character's existence and give it meaning. It does not have to be a real object, although you may be inspired to create or find such an object after reading the chapter on props. The important thing is to specify an object. In your mind, observe the object. Look at it closely and think of what it means to your character. Are the memories happy or sad? Do they reflect love or disdain? Examine the emotions brought about by the object and what it means to your character, and try to determine how it has affected your character's existence. Maybe it represents an as-yet-unfulfilled promise to someone? Perhaps the object is something that was provided by a Storyteller as a part of the plot. You have to give this object meaning to make the plot more real to you and to others in play. Once you have acquired the object in your mind, memorize every detail of it so that you may recall it when needed during an event for a reminder of who you are and what your purpose is.

Defining Your Character

The next exercise involves combining the previous exercises while projecting yourself into a defining moment of your character's existence. Begin from the void with your eyes closed and imagine a scene in your character's life that was crucial in her development. Put your object in the scene and find a way to relate it to the moment. Imbue your character with her animal aspect. The scene should be something defining to your character. It could be the moment your character was initiated into the Sabbat, sitting at her tribe elder's feet as he told her stories of past heroes, her Embrace, or your character's greatest loss. Whatever the moment is, it should have some impact on your character's development. Replay the scene until you are comfortable with the flow of it. Take the scene forward, then backward in your mind. When the scene flows well, play it slowly forward until it reaches its climax and freeze it. Now, just like when you opened your eyes after first entering the void, open your eyes to the scene you have frozen. Open your awareness and take in the sights and sounds that surround you. Think of how your character's existence was influenced by this moment and how it continues to shape her actions to this day. Put yourself into the scene and decide how you feel by what you see, taste and smell. You might be repulsed by what your character finds comforting, or your character in turn may be repulsed by your lifestyle. The ability to divorce yourself from your adopted character and infuse her with her own set of beliefs will make your character more believable to the other players in the game. From the scene you have created, bring your character back to the void with a ten count for the last exercise.

The last exercise we will discuss is bringing your developing character from his defining moment to the here and now. From that defining moment, bring your character slowly forward to the present. If you have a long way to go, speed things up a bit and simply pause at the more interesting places. Don't dawdle too long. Bring your character to the present and place him in the spot you are. Freeze him in your mind and step back to view your creation. Look at the way he holds himself. Sense the animal. See the object and take it from your character. Study his reaction to its loss. Look at your character as someone else would and relate all the various components you have created for him to one another. Do they all work together? Do they all make sense? Ask your character all the little unconscious questions that you ask anyone you at a first meeting. Does the character you created have a sense of completeness about him? If you can answer yes to all of these questions, you have developed a character that can effectively command the game and grow as you play it, if only for one night or in a chronicled event.

Using the Disciplines of Pretend

Once you have gotten yourself to the point where you feel comfortable entering the void, you can use the exercises discussed above to help attune yourself to your character. For single night events, find a quiet spot where you can take a few minutes to quickly touch on the highlights of the character you have been given. Choose the attributes you want to give her and go through the exercises to test the character's believability and realism. Twenty minutes of preparation can prevent the feeling of being lost that can ruin an evening for you. The time you take in preparation can also allow you to find any glaring clashes in the way your character was intended to be portrayed and the reality of the plot's intent. It will give you time to find a Storyteller and iron out these problems before they get out of hand.

In an ongoing chronicle, you can use the relaxed state created in the void to generate the focus you need to maintain the character you have developed throughout the course of the chronicle. Developing a phrase that summarizes your character can be useful in helping you to tune into your character. Since you have already developed your character, you do not need to go through all the exercises every time you are involved in an event. Create a catchphrase for your character, and before an event begins, take a few moments to relax and repeat the phrase. The phrase can be anything that works to bring your character to focus in your mind. Whatever works for you is fine, so long as the phrase takes you instantly through all the exercises reviewed herein and brings you to the point of readiness to play. When the evening goes into overtime and you feel that your attention is becoming scattered, use the phrase to bring your character back into focus.

It is important to remain in control while you are in character. You want to share the stage with the other players, not dominate it all the time. Remember, this is a game for everyone to enjoy. If you see someone struggling with her character or constantly demanding attention in a way that is detrimental to the game, don't ostracize her. Instead, use the focus you have achieved with your character and help motivate her to get into the story. If you have to, signal time out and take her aside to quietly talk about the situation. You may wish to share some of what you have learned about maintaining focus. Give and take between you and another player is a measure of your understanding and respect for the concept of focus. Keep in mind that hogging focus or constantly demanding attention only creates negativity that will detract from the plot and everyone's enjoyment of the event. The reverse also holds true, in that should you find yourself faltering, you can draw from the focus of those around you to carry on. Think of the times that you have been motivated by someone else going all out on a project you are working on together. Sharing focus among everyone involved boosts the level of intensity of the plot overall.

In the end, each of the exercises touched upon should be considered a separate layer that can help you develop your character. Like a cake made for a special occasion, the character you develop for an event is something that you create with a specific idea in mind. By adding layers to your adopted personality, you create intricacies in your character appropriate for any situation. Whether you are playing the character for an evening or in a chronicled event, adding realism and believability to your character will add to the overall experience. You can develop your character to any degree and level you want by layering him as deeply or as shallowly as you wish. Staying relaxed and keeping your awareness focused on your surroundings will help you overcome any stage fright. Remember, everyone else in the game is taking the same risks as you by performing in a story before other people. The object of the game is enjoyment, and no one should be in a position to criticize another's performance if he is making a valid effort to portray his role. With that in mind, be supportive of your fellow performers, even if they are playing your enemies. By getting in touch with all the nuances of your character and being aware of your fellow gamers, you should be able to make your character an influential force in the game, regardless of her status.

When the Going Gets Tough

The environment in which an event takes place can affect your ability to maintain focus on your character over the length of the event. The air in hotels can be dry and sap your body of fluids, making your voice rough and causing you discomfort. Homes present their own special problems, with pets that cause allergies and other distractions, while playing outdoors creates an altogether different set of obstacles. Hot, humid days drain your energy, and can even prove harmful if you don't keep up your fluids and electrolytes. Cool days may give you a false security by boosting your energy level early on, but you may find yourself burned out before noon, with nothing left to give by the end of the day. You should try to anticipate any problems that could interfere with your ability to perform at your best. However, you can't anticipate every problem that you might encounter during an event. The best you can do is prepare yourself for a game by becoming aware of your limits, both physical and emotional, and how those limits relate to your ability to portray a character.

Watch What You Eat

Because some games last an entire day, or even more than one day, it can be difficult to maintain your character. It is not always possible to get a good night's rest prior to participating in a story. You can partially compensate for a lack of rest by eating properly. By keeping the body nourished, you maintain your reserves and stamina. Don't load up on carbohydrates without also taking in some foods that contain protein. Eating only foods high in carbohydrates can give you a temporary boost, but you will eventually tire more quickly unless you take in protein to slow down and regulate how the body consumes the carbohydrates. If at all possible, try to avoid sugary food, since sugar is the most refined and simplest of the carbohydrates. Slow and steady is how you want to maintain your energy level during a long story line. Basic common sense in selecting the types of food you eat will go a long way in achieving this goal. Also, drink plenty of fluids to help your body flush out toxins that can cause you to tire more quickly. Avoid caffeinated drinks in excess and any alcoholic beverages. They dehydrate the body and put stress on your system. Putting some forethought into keeping yourself energized with foods that have some semblance of nourishment will help you in the long run during any game.

The Voice

Your voice is an important tool in conveying your character's presence, and you should pay some attention to it so you don't lose it during an event. Constantly straining your voice to be heard over other players', getting caught up in long negotiations with a Tremere, and the environment can all take their toll on you voice. Your voice is generated in your vocal cords and regulated by a complicated series of muscles located in your throat, mouth and diaphragm. The vocal cords are two flaps that move together as they vibrate to produce your voice. Like any other part of your body, the muscles controlling your voice can be fatigued and over-stressed if you push them too far. Actually, you probably stand a better chance of straining your voice than any other part of your body in a given day if you use it a lot. The flaps of your vocal cords are also susceptible to damage if you misuse them. The problem is that so many people take their voices for granted and don't know the warning signs; a sore throat, achiness in the throat, and tenseness in the jaw muscles are all signs that you may be beginning to strain and damage your voice. Anyone who has ever suffered from nodes on their vocal cords will tell you that it's worth learning a little to avoid getting them. Nodes are basically callous-like scar tissue buildup on the vocal cords (flaps) that can become a problem if left untreated. They are found most often in people who use their voices a lot for singing, public speaking, etc., and who have little knowledge of the proper care necessary to keep their voices fit and strong.

The good news is that like any other muscle group, the voice can be maintained through proper care. Prior to participating in an event, there are some simple exercises that you can do to ready your voice and keep it limber for whatever you may demand from it. The exercises that follow are the most basic, and can be helpful to you in preparing for an event. If you are serious about developing a strong voice, find someone with experience in vocal training and get advice from her on what you can do to achieve your goal.

Begin by controlling your breathing as when you are entering the void. If you haven't guessed by now, relaxation is an important aspect of any acting exercise. Breathe through your nose. The nose is the body's natural air-conditioning system and warms and moistens the air as it enters the body. Dry vocal cords cause damage as they rub together, and warm, moist air prevents this. Breathe from the diaphragm and avoid breathing from the chest. You generate more power in your voice from the diaphragm while reducing the stress you put on your vocal cords. Breathing from up high in your chest causes tension which translates into your voice, again possibly causing damage.

Warm up your voice before you use it in an event, just like you would warm up your other muscles before a good workout. In the case of the voice, begin to hum softly and start chewing as though you had a wad of gum in your mouth. Make the wad as big as you can and work it around in your mouth. As you chew, massage your cheek muscle and the area under your ears where the hinge to your jawbone is located. Continue this way for a couple of minutes until you feel as though you have sufficiently loosened up your face. Stop this first phase and open your mouth as wide as possible. Stretch your jaw wide and stick out your tongue as far as it will go. Stretch your tongue to the right, then left, up and down. Move it around like this a few times. Put your tongue back in your mouth and close it. Next, begin to gently work your voice from the highest it will go to the lowest you can get it and back again. Feel where your voice changes between high, middle, and low ranges. You should feel definite points of change. Familiarize yourself with these points and learn where they are generated. They will help you define a comfortable speaking level. Now, begin to repeat the alphabet, carefully enunciating each letter. Play with the range of your voice gently. Always remember never to force any sound. Let it come out in a relaxed manner. Even if you are projecting as loud as you can, you should never force the sound from your throat. Spend a good 15 to 30 minutes gently working these exercises. Don't overdo it; warm-ups are meant to prepare you for an event, not wear you out. Warming up your vocal cords prior to a game, keeping them relaxed, and keeping them moist by drinking plenty of water are all things you can do to prepare your voice for a long event and keep it healthy.

Important Things to Remember About Your Voice

- Avoid dairy-based products before an event, as they can cause phlegm to form in the throat and impede the function of the vocal cords.
- Drink plenty of fluids to keep your vocal cords moist. Cool, clear water is best for this purpose. Caffeinated drinks and alcohol can dry your vocal cords.
- Always try to project your voice from the diaphragm and keep it relaxed.
- If you feel any discomfort in your throat, rest it for a few moments and hum softly while pretending to chew gum. This will loosen up the vocal cords and neck muscles.
- Yawning is good in that it stretches the vocal cords and helps to relieve any tension in them.

• Never push your voice if you are feeling continued discomfort. If the discomfort doesn't go away after a while, see a doctor. It could be something as simple as an allergy, or something that should be taken care of with treatment.

• Avoid coughing and clearing your throat. Coughing and throat-clearing slam the vocal cords together and can damage them if done too often. If your throat is feeling phlegmy, swallow or drink water to clear it.

• Avoid smoking or anything that may irritate your vocal cords.

• Avoid speaking from the middle portion of your throat. Public speakers often speak a little higher or a little lower to avoid stressing the vocal cords.

Last-Minute Hints

There is a lot more that you can do to add depth to your character. You are limited only by the amount of time that you have. A visit to your local library can give you some interesting historical information, which you can use as part of your character's life experiences. You could develop a dialect or accent of her native language. Perhaps you could experiment and combine different accents to represent some of the different languages your character knows. Dialect tapes are available at better book stores that specialize in theatrical literature. As a matter of fact, such bookstores can be a treasure trove of information and ideas about portraying your character. Research is the key to fleshing out your character. The longer your character has lived, the farther back you should look for interesting tidbits of trivia your character may know. So much vitality can be generated with just a little effort; all it takes is some ingenuity on your part.

Conclusion

All the topics and exercises covered in this section represent only a fraction of the disciplines utilized by actors to develop believability and presence in their portrayals of various roles. However, there are enough of them included here to get you started and let you develop the character you want to play for an event. The ideas are presented as beginning points for further exploration into the discipline of acting, ideas that you can employ in creating a persona of a depth and complexity beyond what you are used to creating for a game. They are to be used as examples to expand your awareness of your adopted persona. You must keep in mind that the learning process you embark on is ongoing and always changing, as is life. It will add vitality and a sense of realism to the supernatural and fantastic nature of the game. Vitality is essential to keep the plot alive and moving forward. You can go beyond the apparently obvious in any event you participate in and find new inspiration to motivate your character. Exploration is the key to preventing stagnation.

In the end, acting may not be as easy as it appears, for there are so many disciplines and so much knowledge to retain. However, all you have to do is remember to remain relaxed and ready, be aware of your surroundings, and understand your character's motivations and the motivations of the other characters in the game, and you should have no problems achieving the goals of your character. By playing in a **Mind's Eye Theatre** story, you have made a decision to take on the role of a performer for a short period of time, if only for your own entertainment and enjoyment. You have made the decision to try to propel yourself into a new realm of experience that puts you in control of the ebb and flow of the story, instead of sitting back and watching it unfold before you. Hopefully, you can use what you have learned here as a starting point to increase your ability to take control of your character. Remember, the keys are in your hands, so go out and have some fun.

Chapter Two: Costuming

Tiss not alone my inky cloak, good mother,
Nor customary suits of solemn black...
For they are actions that a man might play:
But I have that within which poseth show;
These, but the trappings and suits of woe.
— William Shakespeare, *Hamlet*

In this chapter we will discuss how choosing an effective costume for your character can help to reinforce her portrayal and believability. Considerations for putting together an ensemble, and where and what to look for in the way of clothing will be discussed. We will also address the basics of costume design, materials, fabrics, equipment, and construction techniques. This information should provide a good foundation for developing your own character wardrobe.

Costumes and costume design are an important part of modern theatre. They help give credence to a character portrayal and lend the audience insight into the character's nature and purpose. Clothing can convey a character's wealth or poverty, her station in life, her vocation, her cultural background, and many more little insights into who she is. It can also reflect the mood of the plot and the time period in which the scene is set. In all, it is a powerful, yet subtle, tool for expressing the unspoken.

Costumes can serve a very similar purpose in a **Mind's Eye Theatre** story. The dynamic nature of **Mind's Eye Theatre** lends itself to infinite possibilities for you to explore. In a one-shot event, you can convey quite a lot about the character you portray, just from the clothes you wear. You can say, "Beware my evil nature," by dressing in dark and sinister clothing. You can influence other players by revealing certain aspects of your nature through your clothing. In an ongoing story line, your character may develop a reputation for his style. You can develop a whole separate wardrobe for him to wear on special occasions. Whatever the attire you choose for, clothing can be very effective in helping you to portray your character.

The Costumes of Everyday Life

The clothes you wear every day speak volumes about your personality and station in life. One of the first things you notice about someone, aside from the way they keep themselves, is the clothing they're wearing. In your mind, you begin to construct an image of their personality based upon the clothing they choose to wear for any given occasion. You may perceive them as being smart, uncaring, insightful, free-spirited, uptight, domineering, angry, or loving, all without actually having engaged them in conversation. We have even gone so far as to create descriptive names to delineate different styles. Punk, goth, grunge, preppy, Fifth Avenue, and sportswear are some of the names we've created in order to classify the types of styles that people wear, and each of these classifications represents a predefined personality type. The clothing you wear every day reflects your nature as well as your current mood. If you put no thought into the clothes you wear, that is an expression of your lack of concern for such matters. Likewise, the clothing your character wears should be a reflection of his true nature.

So, the topic of costume design is really one of personal choice for you and your character. There are guidelines you can use to help you choose and reinforce the image you want to project. Such things as character genre, character age, time of birth, your resources and sewing skills, and plain luck all contribute to developing your character's style. The trick is knowing where to look for clothing, what to look for, and how to go about assembling a really effective wardrobe. How do you project the nuances and tenets of a character hundreds of years old through his style? How do you determine what effect the evolution of civilization has had in influencing your character's choice of fashion, having witnessed it first-hand? The choice, in the end, is up to you. However, the more true you remain to your character's concept and genre in developing her style, the more secure you will be in projecting the believability of your character to the other players.

Aspects of Fashion

To understand how character genre affects the wardrobe you wish to create, it is important to explore the nuances of each character type. The nuances of each type of character available to **Mind's Eye Theatre** players were discussed in-depth in the last chapter. There are, however, some things not mentioned in that chapter that are very relevant to costuming and style development. These factors include the often-overlooked and little-explored physical and emotional aspects of each entity, which influence the clothing they wear. Facets that you may have dismissed as irrelevant, or don't consider pertinent, could give your character an air of reality that imposes itself upon the subconscious minds of those around you. Read over all the reference material that has been printed so far on the type of character you wish to portray and visualize the clothing ideas given therein to extremes in your mind's eye. Explore those images in detail. Think of the vast ages of some of the characters, their physical limitations, and the emotions that course through and shape each one of these creatures. Don't be afraid of how ludicrous some of the images you come up with may be, just go with whatever your imagination finds lurking in the recesses of your mind. Use those images, along with the following ideas, as starting points for your imagination to develop and fly off in new directions, away from the obvious. When you have exhausted yourself visualizing all the possible clothing any one inhabitant of the game may wear, take those images and sort through them for something that your character can use. Hopefully, you will discover some interesting possibilities.

Kindred Fashion

Kindred are a good place to start for character style development. Their accumulated life experiences open up many venues of clothing choices to explore. As a vampire, you would no longer be concerned about the convenience of your clothing. In essence, Kindred aren't concerned with the bodily functions we have to deal with every day. For a Kindred, clothing does not have to be easy to put on and remove. Tight or revealing clothing effectively exudes sensuality and thus can entice prey or make a personal statement. To the average human, it isn't worth the inconvenience unless your nature motivates you beyond such considerations. As a vampire, the inconvenience is negated by your supernatural strength and endurance. Weather conditions are also of little concern to you. You aren't limited by your body's discomfort at how hot, cool, or wet it is. Your only limitations are self-imposed and rely on how deeply you wish to maintain the Masquerade.

Try to imagine what type of clothing you would wear in a world inhabited solely by Kindred, where image is everything. Clothing is truly nothing more than a prop for you to bolster your presence and personality. This is by no means to suggest that you should ignore such considerations of comfort in your all-too-human self. However, when you are creating an image for your Kindred character, you should not necessarily take into account what would be most convenient for you to wear at first, but instead stress more the image that you wish to create as a vampire. Part of the challenge when creating an effective look for an unliving character is determining how far you are willing to go in emphasizing your supernatural image. Of course, these are examples of the extreme ideas that you can explore when preparing a style for your character. You should choose a look that you are comfortable with.

An important decision to make regarding your character is to what degree time and life experience affect your vampire character's fashion choice. The older your adopted persona, the more variations in human fashion she has experienced over the decades or even centuries. Perhaps she has become fond of a particular look, believing that it flatters her more than the current fashion trends. The image she develops for her modern self may incorporate aspects of the attire she enjoyed wearing so many centuries ago. It would be interesting to see what elements of past fashion ideas can be successfully integrated into modern fashion. You can look at any era for inspiration. Perhaps a 16th-century doublet could be transformed into a modern leather coat or a 1920s flapper gown could be incorporated into a modern gown design. The ideas you include do not need to be obvious. A hint of the past is all you may need to convey the effect you are looking for. Just a little something that will give your character a reassurance of his identity and a tie to his past. For the most part, Kindred wear what the moment calls for, just as anyone else would.

Garou Fashion

Though there are many tribes among the Garou, there are certainly strong similarities among the clothes that each would wear. Most Garou would undoubtedly find it important to wear clothing that is not restrictive to movement and that is made of natural substances. Cotton flannels, leather, fur, and down-filled, naturally fibered, coats are probably preferred materials. It's true that the processing of these materials may imbue them with some aspect of artificiality, but they are still more natural than not. Fluidity of movement is something else to keep in mind when creating a wardrobe for a Garou. While it's true that a Garou's clothing disappears during the change, you have to consider your character's origins when thinking about her clothing preferences. Lupus were born of wolf form, and animals do not like to have physical restrictions placed upon them. Perhaps a lupus would balk at even wearing clothing, but gives in to her human nature for the sake of conformity. Homids may enjoy whatever fashions they wore before the change took them for the first time. The character's tribe should also have a lot of influence on the type of clothing she wears. Bone Gnawers and Glass Walkers both embrace modern civilization. One survives in the streets, scorned and rejected, and the other survives through the use of technology. For these creatures, you must look to your character development as a guide for creating their tastes in clothing. Both Uktena and Wendigo may garb themselves in vestiges of their American Indian heritage. Regardless, all Garou likely still feel the need to include some aspect of nature in their attire.

Those Garou tainted by the Wyrm, the Black Spiral Dancers, are the exception to this idea. They love to flaunt their disregard for nature, and may wear clothing reflective of their twisted natures. As with Kindred, they are more concerned with image and the effect they can generate in others. Intimidation plays a big factor in the look they are trying to develop. They are like rabid animals; dazed by the infection of the Wyrm and mostly aggressive. Their clothing should reflect this rebellion against nature. It can be fun dressing up as someone so fear-inspiring, and watching other people's reaction to you.

Building an Effective Wardrobe

Finding clothing suitable for your character and the fashion image you envision for her depends directly on the amount of effort you are willing to put into your search. Surprisingly enough, clothing of different eras — dating all the way back to the early 1940s — can be found lurking on the dusty shelves of used clothing shops across the nation. The best place to start is at your local Goodwill store and thrift shops. People tend to hang onto old clothes long after they have gone out of style, and it isn't until they clean out their closets that they give them away, giving you the opportunity to find something unique for your adopted persona to wear. Flea markets, garage sales and classified ads also provide good opportunities for you to increase your character's wardrobe. Old suit jackets with tails, zoot suits, flapper gowns, tuxedos, shoes, and boots from all eras are just some of the goodies you can find if you look hard enough. Even if the clothing that you find is not in the best shape, you can still use it to make patterns from which you can make your own version to wear. If you don't mind paying a little more money, look through vintage clothing stores and boutiques. Keep searching and don't be afraid to try out a new look for yourself.

One way to ensure that you find the clothes you're looking for is to shop in yard sales that reflect the nature of your character. Shop for well-to-do characters in expensive neighborhoods, where you can find some remarkable articles of clothing for sale at very reasonable prices. Clothing found in such areas is often very chic for the time period it represents and can be just the right thing to wear for that special meeting you have with some "old" friends. Some truly amazing bargains can be found if you look hard enough. For middle-of-the-road characters, find shops and yard sales in everyday suburbia. Use your imagination in finding places to shop for your clothing and have fun. All it takes is a little effort and some spare time.

Considering the many character types that you can portray in a story, it is likely that you will play more than one over the course of time. You might want to set aside a trunk and fill it with odds and ends from your forays into the world of thrift shopping. If you see something that you like, but aren't sure what to do with it, buy it anyway and throw it in your trunk. You will always have something to wear for an impromptu event or the occasional costume party. Having a lot of little articles of clothing tucked away will help you assume almost any character rather easily. A simple accent piece such as a bandanna, an old hat, or a scarf can add to your character's image. The more little things that you can find, the better. Look for things that you like and barter the price down. There is no need to go overboard and spend a lot just to have some fun.

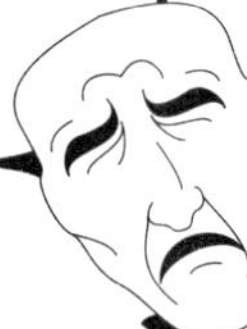

If You Can't Find It, Make It

As mentioned before, if you find something during one of your forays that you really like, but find it is too worn to wear, or that it can't be made to fit you, keep it to use as a pattern for making your own version. Constructing your own costumes from scratch is always an option, and can provide you with a lot of satisfaction. Yes, now you too can partake in the joy of creating fashion from nothing, just like they do on Fifth Avenue and other famous fashion walkways the world over. Grab the measuring tape, all you would-be tailors and designers, we are going to try and get through the basics of Sewing 101.

True, this section requires a little technical know-how on your part. Those of you who have experience making clothing have the initial advantage and can use the information presented here as a springboard to explore more ideas in making costumes for a character. For those of you with little or no experience sewing, this section will give you a good starting point from which you can go on to develop your own abilities. Don't worry, if you can change the oil in your car, you should probably be able to figure out the technical complexities of the average sewing machine. Never feel intimidated by the prospect of making your own costumes. The rewards, in the end, far outweigh any disappointments you may experience during your first attempts at sewing. Remember the first rule of costume making, "If someone is close enough to you to notice flaws in your workmanship, you let him get too close." Seriously though, making a good costume is not very difficult. A little effort and experimentation will reward you with results you can be proud of.

So, why bother going to all the trouble to make a costume for an event? Why not just find what you need at the local thrift shop like we just discussed? Well, some people do it because they enjoy making their own clothing. Others, because they want something unique for their character. Also, there is no other source of clothing for many of the time periods your character may be familiar with. No matter how long you look, you are not going to find a 16th-century nobleman's coat at someone's yard sale. Wearable clothing can survive for only so long, regardless of how well it's preserved. If you want the look of bygone days, you have one of two choices: You are either going to have to find someone who can make the clothing for you, or you'll have to take the plunge and do it yourself. Your character can be truly unique in his style if you take the time to learn the basics of costume construction. Also, you aren't reliant on someone else's skill and time. You are bound only to your schedule, and you control the quality and care that goes into your outfit. Finally, when your work receives praise from others, you will feel well-deserved pride in your construction.

The Equipment

A sewing machine is a required piece of equipment for any attempt at costume making. Unless, of course, you really want to re-create the look of older styles and spend the rest of your free time for the next year stitching together an outfit by hand. Trust someone who knows from experience: Though rewarding, hand-sewing is not an enjoyable way to pass time. The best places to find sewing machines for reasonable prices are flea markets and garage sales. As for the type and make of machine to purchase, the manufacturer is not as important as the quality of the machine. Make sure that you will have no trouble finding parts for it. A good way to do this is by checking the yellow pages for the type of machines serviced in your area. If the machine you're looking at is listed, odds are that they will have parts to repair it if the need arises. It is a good idea to take this list of machines with you when you begin your search and use it as a reference. Look for a machine that can handle heavy materials and is durable in construction. They are often labeled "heavy duty," but be wary. Manufacturers seem to have different ideas of what "heavy duty" means. Some machines are still going strong after 20 years or more of service, while some new ones give up the ghost on two plies of denim material. If you are handy with machines you should be able to spot a well-made one and judge its value. For really heavy-duty leather work, one money-saving idea is to find an old foot treadle machine in good working order. You can keep it as a foot-operated machine or convert it to electric power. Converting it to electric power requires knowledge about electrical wiring and machinery,

however. Old treadle-type machines are overly engineered marvels of a time long past and can handle very heavy leather stock easily. If you wish to do a lot of work with leather, your only other alternative is to buy a heavy-duty industrial sewing machine, which usually costs $200, used. On average, you should not have to spend more than $40 to $50 to get a good, old, heavy-duty sewing machine, whereas treadle machines are found mostly by luck. Buying one from an antique shop will negate any savings you would get over finding a heavy-duty electric leather machine.

Another requirement for costume making is space to lay out all your supplies and the material when the time comes to start cutting. Make sure the work area you choose is out of the way and that it will remain undisturbed by others during the construction of the outfit. Choosing the living room as your set-up area is not a good idea, because of the traffic that continually streams through. Other requirements include a good pair of shears (scissors), a measuring tape, tons of pins, lots of spare needles for the sewing machine, marking chalk, and duct tape. Besides being the universal fix-it tool, duct tape is helpful in making patterns, holding heavy material, you name it. Pattern making will be discussed a little later on. For now, just gather all of your things together and get your space organized. Look over the manual for the sewing machine and make sure you have it threaded correctly and oiled, and prepare for the next step: choosing the materials for your outfit.

The Material World

When creating an outfit from a specific era, the materials you choose should match the original materials as closely as possible. There is a reason that those materials were used in the first place, and it has a lot to do with what fabrics were available at the time. Synthetic materials did not come into being until later in the 20th century and have become a part of almost everything we wear because of their convenience and durability. However, they may not work well with fashions from past eras. If you have ever had the sad pleasure of seeing a 1920s flapper gown re-created out of shiny, yellow lame or seen a 16th-century ladies' gown with polyester trim work, you realize some of the problems associated with using modern materials in older patterns. This is not to say that all modern materials are bad for re-creating past fashions. There are many modern, synthetic, durable fabrics and materials that are good matches for the textures, patterns, and colors of long ago. Study the influence each era had in fabric construction and color choice, then find a modern substitute that closely resembles this material. Those of you who are purists and want every aspect of your costume to be authentic should be prepared to spend more time and money to find and re-create the materials you need. Regrettably, not all materials can be re-created. Modern manufacturing techniques are replacing old, and mass production limits the unique patterns that were possible in older, more personal manufacturing processes. However, you should not be dissuaded from looking for them. You will probably have to find substitutes for most of your ideas, but the challenge of the search can be very rewarding in the knowledge you gain.

From Past to Present

A brief history of clothing might be useful in helping you to decide on the type of fabrics to choose in making your outfit. In the beginning, humans used animal hides and fur as a means to protect themselves from the elements. This could be significant if your character just awoke from torpor after a couple of millennia. A major turning point occurred when cotton was first used in the making of cloth. Cotton became the material of choice in ancient Egypt, and remains a popular fabric even today. It is easy to harvest, breathes well and wicks moisture away from the body, helping to keep it cool and protect it from the sun. Its only drawback is that it doesn't provide protection from the cold when it gets wet. This was not a great concern in Egypt, but in the colder northern regions, the ability to remain warm under harsh conditions was necessary for survival. The inhabitants of these northern regions used wool, the most logical choice of material, to make their garments. A natural fiber, wool provides excellent protection from the cold, even when wet. Ancient humans saw that it worked for the animals, and adopted it for their own use. You begin to see a trend of humans using fabric materials based upon natural elements and by observing what worked best in nature.

The colors you choose in making your outfit can help to relay the era on which it is based. At first, fabrics were left to their natural colors: usually cotton was off-white, and wool ranged from white to black, beige to brown. It didn't take long before individualism drove people to experiment adding color through the use of dyes found in nature. Berries, seeds, barks, flowers, and a host of other natural plant products were tested as sources for dye colors. Dyes were used to create patterns in clothing with religious significance and personal meaning to the wearer. These colors were normally not as vibrant or durable as dyes we use today. They would often fade like an old pair of jeans after only a few months of use. If you could afford it, you could have your clothing re-dyed to bring back its vivacity. Hence, bright, unnatural colors are a poor choice for an old style.

Eventually, different colors evolved to indicate position in society. Queen Elizabeth I claimed purple as her favorite color and dictated that no one else could wear it. Anyone who was caught wearing purple had heavy fines levied against them or found themselves imprisoned if they were insistent on sharing the queen's color. Black was another significant color back in the Renaissance era. It was such a hard color to create and maintain that only the very wealthy could afford any great amount of it. The nobility often used black as an accent color. Anyone dressed entirely in black during that time would have been respected for her wealth. As time progressed and new and more durable dyes were created from chemical sources, more color choices became available at a much lower cost. Color came to reflect simply the personal choice of the wearer.

Embroidery and decorative stitching began to be used to add significance to an individual's attire. The more an article of clothing was enhanced with decorative stitching, the more important the person wearing the outfit. Of course, there were exceptions. Merchants who became wealthy through their trade would pay good money to emulate people of noble birth. They hoped the clothing they wore would cause people to treat them with the respect often reserved for the upper class. It can be fun to determine what social strata your character came from and then playing it up as someone trying to be something he's not.

Finding Materials

Fabric material is sold at any cloth store. However, if you want to find the best deals, check out fabric outlets. Usually, they have good prices on bulk material. If you intend to do a lot of costuming, this might be cost effective. Again, however, yard sales can offer good accent material. Old linen drapes, especially embroidered ones, make very good accent material and can be found reasonably priced at any thrift shop or yard sale. One advantage of salvaging old fabrics, besides reducing waste, is that a lot of old materials were made with patterns that may no longer be available because of modern production techniques. What a shame to let them go to waste and rot away in some dark landfill, when they could gain new life in your own creation. Such material adds a sense of authenticity and uniqueness to your outfit, increasing its value and meaning to you. Trim materials can also be found rather inexpensively at outlet shops dedicated to selling trim work. The point is to look around before spending an outrageous amount of money on fabric and trim materials. There are so many potentially good sources for material, and so many different types of materials to look for, that an overview of the different material types is in order.

Material Types

Materials and fabrics research has advanced tremendously over the last few decades. Every day chemical companies create and manufacture new, more durable fabrics for use in industry, the military, space and the home. Materials have advanced to the point where their applications are almost limitless. Luckily, you will not have to study chemical engineering to become a costume designer. The types of fabrics you will be using are, for the most part, ones you are familiar with, and are more or less easily worked on, depending on your skill. The following list presents some of the material types and fabrics you may use in constructing an outfit for your character and some terms to use when asking for information about availability of materials.

Cotton — A natural plant fiber used for thousands of years to make clothing. Cotton wicks sweat from the body, keeping it cool. It is inexpensive and readily available. Cotton shrinks in hot water and should be washed and dried to pre-shrink prior to cutting your patterns from it. It holds dye very well, and is extremely versatile because of this. You can buy cheap white fabric and dye it any color you want.

Wool — A natural fiber made from animal fleece. Wool is excellent at maintaining warmth in cold, wet environments. Used often for cloaks and gowns, it can become too hot to wear indoors for long periods of time. Wool is more costly than cotton and some people experience an allergic reaction when wearing it. Wool comes in many colors and patterns, and is not usually found undyed. Wool must be dry-cleaned.

Silk — A natural fiber derived from the cocoons of silkworms. Silk has a luxurious and smooth feel to it and has always represented wealth. Modern technology has made silk more affordable. Generally, it requires more care than cotton or wool due to its delicate nature. Silk can be found undyed and readily accepts new colors. It usually requires dry-cleaning, but some silk products can be hand-washed.

Satin — A manmade fabric that emulates silk. Satin is relatively inexpensive, but doesn't have the luxurious feel of silk.

Leather — A material derived from the skins of various animals. Leather is durable and has come to represent high fashion on one end and sensuality on another. It can be difficult and unforgiving to work with and can only be cleaned by a qualified cleaner. Leather can be bought unfinished and colored with special dyes to just about any color and finish. Leather is an expensive material to work with and requires a heavy-duty sewing machine and special tools.

Suede — Leather buffed into a nap. Suede is softer and more pliable than regular leather. It has the same benefits and restrictions as leather, except that it is harder to keep clean due to its rough texture. Because of its special texture, suede is very hard to dye, but usually can be found in a good range of colors.

Ultra-Suede — A manmade material that closely resembles suede in texture and appearance. Ultra-Suede can be machine-washed and is easy to work with due to its consistent nature. Ultra-Suede is very costly and cannot be dyed.

Suede Cloth — A manmade material that emulates suede, but not as closely as does Ultra-Suede. Suede cloth is machine washable and relatively inexpensive. Suede cloth has a tendency to fray if the edges are not stitch finished. Dyeing suede cloth is not recommended.

Polyester — A manmade fiber, polymeric resin, derived from chemical reactions. Polyester is readily available and inexpensive. It doesn't breathe or wick moisture away as well as cotton. It is machine washable, easy to work with, and accepts dye well.

Rayon — A manmade material made from cellulose. Rayon is readily available and inexpensive. It doesn't breathe or wick moisture away as well as cotton, but is machine washable, easy to work with, and accepts dye well. It is considered more "natural" than polyester.

Velour — A velvet-like material with a soft nap. Velour represents wealth and is costly. It must be dry-cleaned. It is recommended that you do not attempt to dye velour.

Patterns

Dressmakers Velvet — A rich fabric of silk, rayon, etc. with a soft, thick pile. Velvet represents wealth and is used a lot in 16th — 18th century clothing. Dressmakers velvet must be dry-cleaned. It is recommended that you do not attempt to dye dressmakers velvet.

Upholstery Velvet — A durable velvet used for upholstering furniture. It is heavier than dressmakers velvet and it holds up a lot better for certain clothing. Some types of upholstery velvet can be machine-washed and spot-cleaned with carpet cleaner. It is recommended that you do not attempt to dye upholstery velvet.

Upholstery Fabric — Any durable fabric used in upholstering furniture. The patterns available in upholstery fabric sometimes closely resemble patterns used in 15th — 18th century outfits. It can be machine washed. It is recommended that you do not attempt to dye upholstery fabric.

Latex — Artificial rubber sheeting which can be used to make clothing. Latex is almost impossible to work with unless you have access to some very special tools and adhesives, and it does not allow the body to breathe. As such, it is not a very practical material to consider when choosing a material to make an outfit. It comes in a variety of pre-manufactured colors and cannot be dyed.

Once you've decided on the type of outfit you wish to make for your character, you're going to need some kind of direction in assembling it. Patterns are essential, because they act as a guide from which to construct your idea. They also will save you money when you are using expensive fabric to make your outfit. They are the blueprints for the construction of your clothing and thus allow you to maximize each piece of material you use. Depending on the outfit you want to make, you may be able to find patterns already available on the market. The other alternative is to make your patterns from scratch. Whichever the project calls for, there are things you need to keep in mind.

Most fabric stores carry patterns for just about any type of outfit you could make. If you cannot find the specific pattern your are looking for, find a pattern similar to the style you want and modify it. Patterns for certain gowns can be adapted for gowns worn centuries ago. Gentlemen's attire can be derived from modern patterns just as readily. The advantage of using store-bought patterns is that they already have the tucks, folds and cuts marked to conform to the human body. They have allowances for movement built-in, which takes the guess work out of it. The disadvantage is that most patterns are based upon a standard human frame, and require modifications for larger or smaller frames. So, not only do you have to modify the pattern to match your character's style or era, you'll have to adapt it to your frame as well. Store-bought patterns are valuable because they give you the opportunity to study how professional designers solved the problems they encountered while making the patterns.

Believe it or not, duct tape or masking tape can be used to make patterns for articles of clothing that fit tightly to the body. Moccasins, corsets, or any article of clothing that is required to conform closely to the contours of the body can benefit from this form of pattern-making. Duct tape is more durable and will hold up better during the construction of your project than masking tape. When using tape to make a pattern, always use a separator to keep it from adhering to the skin. Even the smallest amount of exposure to the adhesive in tape can cause reactions in sensitive people, and removing the tape from exposed skin can be painful. Be careful not to let the tape remain in contact with the skin for prolonged periods of time. You can use old T-shirts, socks, or even plastic sheets cut from garbage bags as separators. Once the area of the body that you want to make a pattern from is fully encased, determine where you want the seams to be and mark them with a magic marker. Carefully, very carefully, cut along those lines with your shears to get the separate pieces for your pattern. Transfer those pieces to butcher paper, which can be found at office supply or paper goods stores. To transfer the patterns, take the pieces that you cut from the taped form and lay them atop the paper. Trace around the pieces and add a little room for movement, liner, and seams.

When making any type of outfit that fits snugly, make sure you understand the nature of the material you are using and allow for as much freedom of movement as possible.

Another important pattern-making technique is the drape method. This technique involves wrapping the material around the person you wish to make an outfit for, then manipulating the material until you achieve the effect you want. You then pin the material into place and trim it, or mark it with a magic marker and cut the patterns later. Always use great care when using any sharp object near the body. You do not want to accidentally hurt someone. The only drawback of the drape method is that you may end up wasting a lot of material until you understand how to make your patterns work. Once you get used to the drape method, you may find that it is the best for most of your projects.

One of the best and easiest ways to make an effective pattern for a project is to have the actual piece of clothing you wish to re-create available for study. Of course, this is not always possible. However, if you do happen to chance upon an article of clothing that you like at a thrift shop, and it is too small or badly worn but closely resembles the outfit you had in mind, buy it anyway as a pattern. This idea was mentioned earlier in this chapter and will be explained further here. Carefully disassemble the article of clothing that you wish to reproduce and lay the pieces on the table. Some old fabrics become frail with age, so be gentle. The fabric may be warped as a result of being stitched together for years, and you may have to iron the individual pieces flat. Transfer the pieces to butcher paper and adjust them to fit you. There is no substitute for actually having an article of clothing to study when you are trying to reproduce it.

A good way to avoid using up all your expensive materials while learning the art of pattern making is to use inexpensive muslin to construct mock-ups of the piece you are working on. Muslin is an inexpensive material, usually lightweight cotton, that is used for lining and can be sacrificed to make a pattern. Use any of the methods described above to make your pattern. Then use the muslin to make a complete mock-up of your project, including all the tucks, folds, and seams of the intended finished piece. If something doesn't work out the way you thought it would, you can tear it apart and start over again, or throw the whole thing out and come up with a new idea. All that has been lost is a little time and some spare change, rather than your expensive material stock.

Before you begin choosing patterns to modify or making patterns from scratch, you must have a well-developed idea of what you want your finished project to look like. Making sketches is an effective means to visualize your ideas. This is where you can save the most money, by going over each and every aspect of your outfit in detail. Use a copying machine to make a few copies of your sketch and use colored felt-tipped pens to try out the different color schemes you are considering. Try many different combinations of colors, one for each copy you've made. Once you have decided on a color scheme, you can use your sketch as a guide when you go hunting for material. Refer to the sketch often during your assembly period to keep yourself attuned to your vision. This will help you stick to your budget goals by keeping you focused on your original concept.

A Note on Nap

When using velvet, velour, or any material that has a definite nap to it, you have to be very careful that you cut your pattern pieces from the material so that the direction of the nap is the same over the entire finished project. The nap is the direction of the lay of the fabric, much like a dog's fur coat. If you brush in one direction, it is smooth. In another, it is rough. The nap of your finished project should always be down, so that you can rub from the top of your sleeve or vest to the bottom and feel smoothness. Naps that are not aligned properly throughout a project will reflect light differently. This will cause the outfit to look splotchy and poorly constructed, regardless of the effort you put into it. Always check your patterns before cutting them out of the fabric to make sure the nap is oriented correctly. Mark your pattern's top with a "T" and the bottom with a "B." It's one of those little things that can cause big headaches if you forget about it when cutting your patterns from the material.

Making Outfits

Okay, you have your area all set up; you found a sewing machine, figured out how to thread it, sharpened the shears and studied your stress relief manual. So, what are you going to make? Well, keep in mind all that has been discussed so far concerning the style, age, and genre of your character. Go to the library or local bookstore to find inspiration for choosing your attire. Remember, research is important.

The rest of the chapter will go through the basic step-by-step procedures involved in the construction of various articles of clothing. As with all of the topics covered in this book, use what is presented here as a starting point to expand your knowledge on the topic of costume making.

A Ladies' Gown

Of all the eras to explore for inspiration, the 16th century had some of the most incredibly detailed and extravagant clothing for those who had the privilege of belonging to its upper class. Women wore beautiful gowns and cloaks. Men wore doublets of intricate design to denote their rank and wealth. Because of the complexity of the clothing of this era, many people re-create their own versions today for use in historic reenactments, costume parties, or for personal enjoyment. For the same reasons, we thought it would be a good idea to go step-by step through the construction of a gown of that time period. We'll be using a basic design and ideas to inspire you. As you become more proficient with the techniques involved, you can add more detail to your project and experiment with new construction techniques.

Getting Started

For the sake of clarity, it is assumed that you are making the following outfits for someone else. This person will be referred to as the model.

Begin the construction of your gown as you should begin the construction of all your projects, by measuring your model and noting the measurements on a sheet of paper that you can refer to later. Your model may not always be available for fitting, and it is convenient to have a reference sheet handy to verify your seam lengths. Draw a sketch similar to the one in *figure 2* or copy the page out of the book and use it to record your measurements. You can never take too many measurements, and you may be surprised at how many you miss the first time around.

After you have recorded all the measurements, begin sketching your ideas, keeping the proportions of your model in mind, and emphasize her best features. Decide on the color scheme and confer with your model for the final decision. At this point it will be beneficial to either have a good knowledge of color choices for that era or have a good talent for debate. Some people are terrible at choosing compatible colors, and your model may decide on a totally inappropriate color scheme. It is best if you have accumulated some working knowledge before you attempt to make something for someone else, so that you may present logical and convincing arguments for your ideas.

Next, make the pattern pieces using one or more of the techniques described earlier. The basic pattern for the ladies' gown is similar to that of a hooped wedding gown, which you can find at any fabric store. Be sure to leave plenty of material around the edge of your patterns to work with. It's very hard to add material to a piece that was cut too small without it looking odd. You might want to make a muslin mock-up at this point. If you are confident in your abilities, use the actual material.

A ladies' gown requires a lot of fabric to complete. You need at least 4 yards of 45-inch wide velvet for the gown alone, and another 2 yards for the bodice and the sleeves. The bodice is the top piece of the dress, minus the sleeves. You will also need 4 yards of a patterned fabric for the underskirt and trim material for accents. Four yards of white, mid- to lightweight cotton will be used for the farthingale, the bottom underskirt that contains the hoops, which in turn support the underskirt and outerskirt. Two yards of white, lightweight cotton will be required to line the bodice and sleeves. You may also want to purchase fake jewels to adorn your finished project. Remember that the fabric you buy may only be available in limited supply. Buy enough material to complete the project all at once. If you buy too little initially and go back later to purchase more, you may find that the store is sold out, permanently.

Refer to *figure 1* for the basic design of the bodice. It is based on a corset or vest type design, and, as you can see, the bodice is intended to be laced up the back. As such, you have to make allowances for a 1-inch fold on either side to reinforce the lacing buttonholes. The left side of the back requires a little extra material to allow for a placket (a piece of material under the lacing that prevents the skin from being

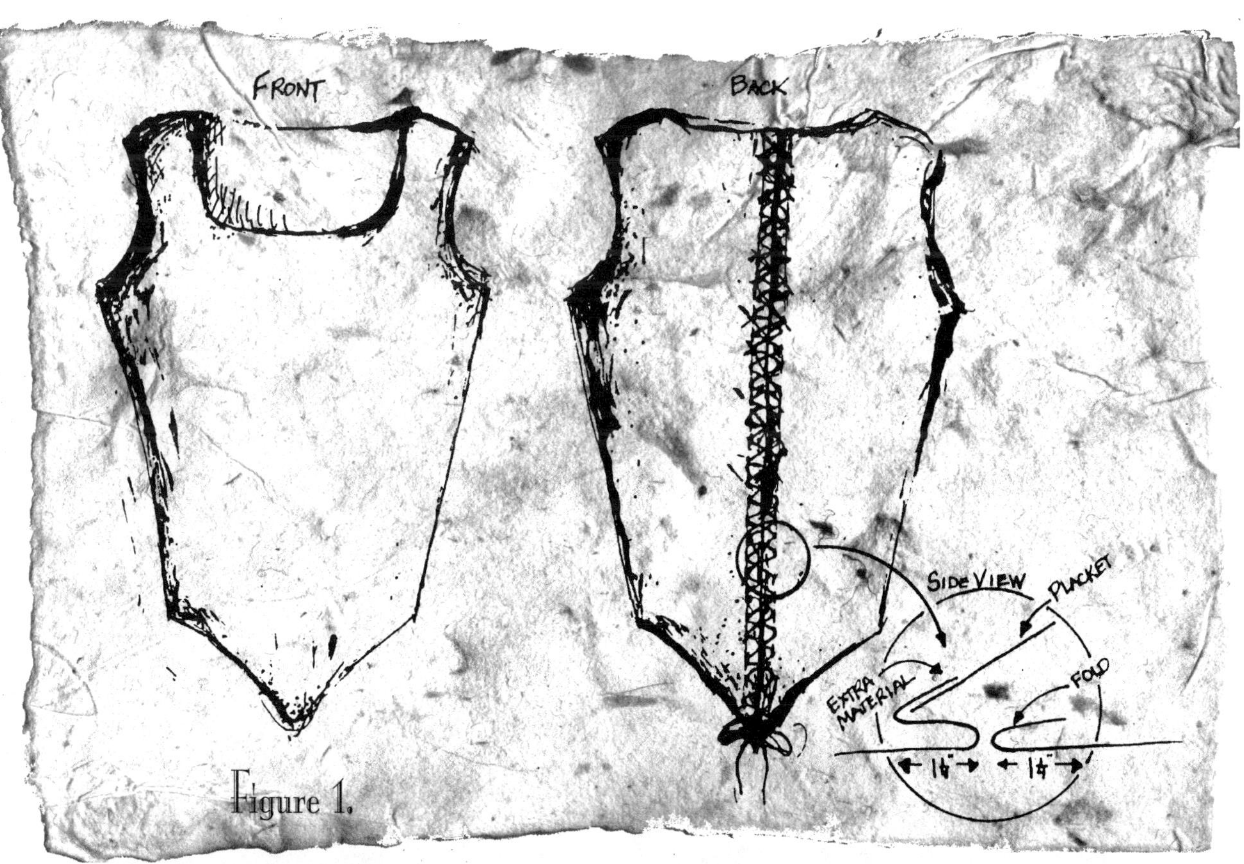

Figure 1.

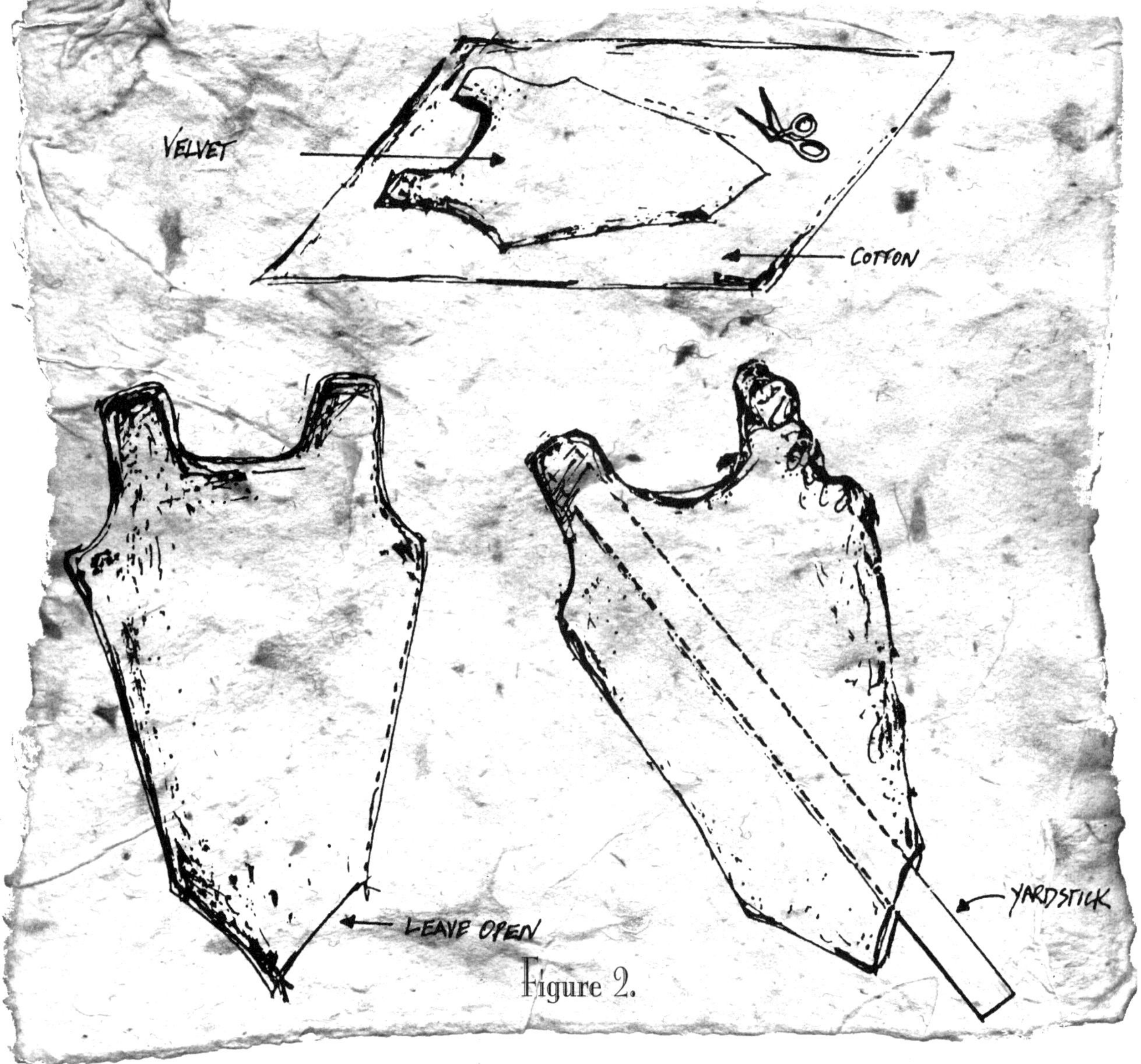

Figure 2.

exposed) to be attached. With this in mind, allow for 2 inches of additional material along the right side of the opening (facing the back), and 3 inches of additional material on the left side (also, facing back).

Lay out the material on the floor or a large table, face side up. The face refers to the finished side of the material. Upholstery velvet is recommended for the bodice. It is strong, durable, and washable. Place the patterns over the material and trace the patterns using the marking chalk. Make absolutely sure that you have the nap in the right direction and that you have the patterns correct side up. Cut the pattern pieces for the bodice first. Cut the pattern pieces for each section of the gown as you get to the section, and not before. If you cut all the pieces at the same time, you may lose a part, or worse yet, find that you have to change one part of the gown, which affects the rest of the pieces. For this reason, it is best to do one section at a time.

Now add lining to each piece you have cut for the bodice. Lining lends strength and stiffness to the completed piece and helps to wick moisture from the skin and separate it from the rough, inner surface of the upholstery velvet. Use a white, undyed light- to midweight cotton fabric. You want to try and avoid dyed fabric, because the dye may bleed through into your velvet as you perspire. There are many different ways to line a garment piece. For this project, we will stitch the lining to each piece before assembling. This method isn't used often, but it effectively seals the edge of each piece of upholstery fabric without the need of special edge-finishing machines (sergers), or a lot of over-stitching. It also allows you to easily open the seam if necessary to make modifications.

Take the cotton fabric and lay it, face up, on a table. Put each of your cut bodice pieces face down on the cotton so that the pieces are face-to-face. Cut around the pattern pieces close to the edge. Using regular-weight cotton thread in your machine, stitch around the edge of the pattern piece, 1/4 inch from the edge, leaving one short side open. Invert the piece (turn it inside out) so that the faces are out. Use a yardstick to push the edges taut, as shown in *figure 2*. Finish the open edge by tucking the lining and velvet in and stitching the opening closed. Iron the edges flat. The end result should be that the faces of both the lining and the velvet are facing out and that you have clean, tight edges. Repeat this procedure for each piece of the bodice. If you were paying attention, you should realize that you have just reduced the overall dimensions of each pattern piece by 1/2 inch. This is one of the reasons you should make allowances when working up your patterns for seams and finishes.

Using heavy-duty upholstery thread and a denim needle in your machine, stitch together the pieces of the bodice. Check the fit of the bodice and adjust the seams as required. Once you have adjusted the fit, run another line of stitching along each seam to really secure it. Looking at the back of the bodice, fold the fabric inward until a 1-inch gap will remain when the bodice is snugly fastened. Allowing for a gap will let you tighten the bodice very snugly when you lace it up. Make sure that the back pieces are symmetrical. Sew a seam along the fold, 1 inch from the edge. Insert a piece of boning along the inside of each fold to keep the lacing from bunching up when tightened. Boning can be found at any good fabric store and usually is in the form of stiff plastic. In the old days, boning was just that, whalebone. Later, steel was substituted, until plastic became prevalent. It is used to make corsets and to stiffen an article of clothing. Stitch along the top and bottom of the fold to secure the boning in place. Make buttonholes, large enough to thread heavy lacing through, 1 inch apart along each side of the fold. Cut a piece of material the length of the back opening and 5 inches wide. Apply lining to it and secure it to the leftover edge on the inside left-hand opening. This is your placket piece, which will fold back over to conceal any exposed skin between the lacing. (*see figure 3*) Hand-stitch a 2-inch piece of Velcro securely to the inside liner of the bodice at the waist. This will interface with the piece on the waistband of the outer skirt, as described later. You should now apply the trim work to your bodice and decorative lacing to the front.

Finish the bottom edge of the bodice with cut and lined pieces of fabric applied with upholstery thread in the pattern shown in *figure 4*. These trim pieces are called peplums and can be decorated using pleats, embroidery, or personalized in any manner. You can vary the size to suit you or your model's taste. During the Elizabethan era, many style variations developed in both men's and women's clothing. Have fun

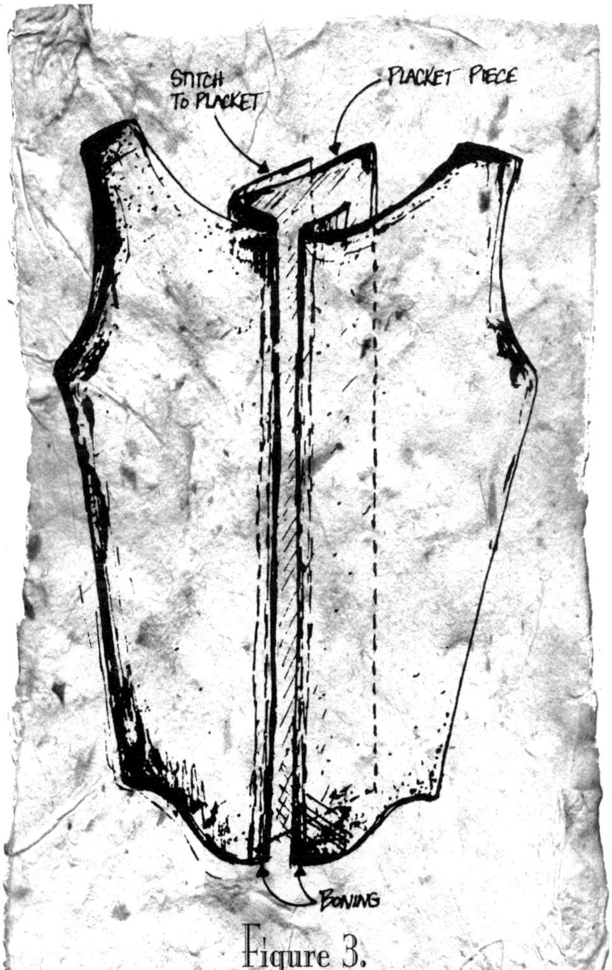

Figure 3.

Figure 4.

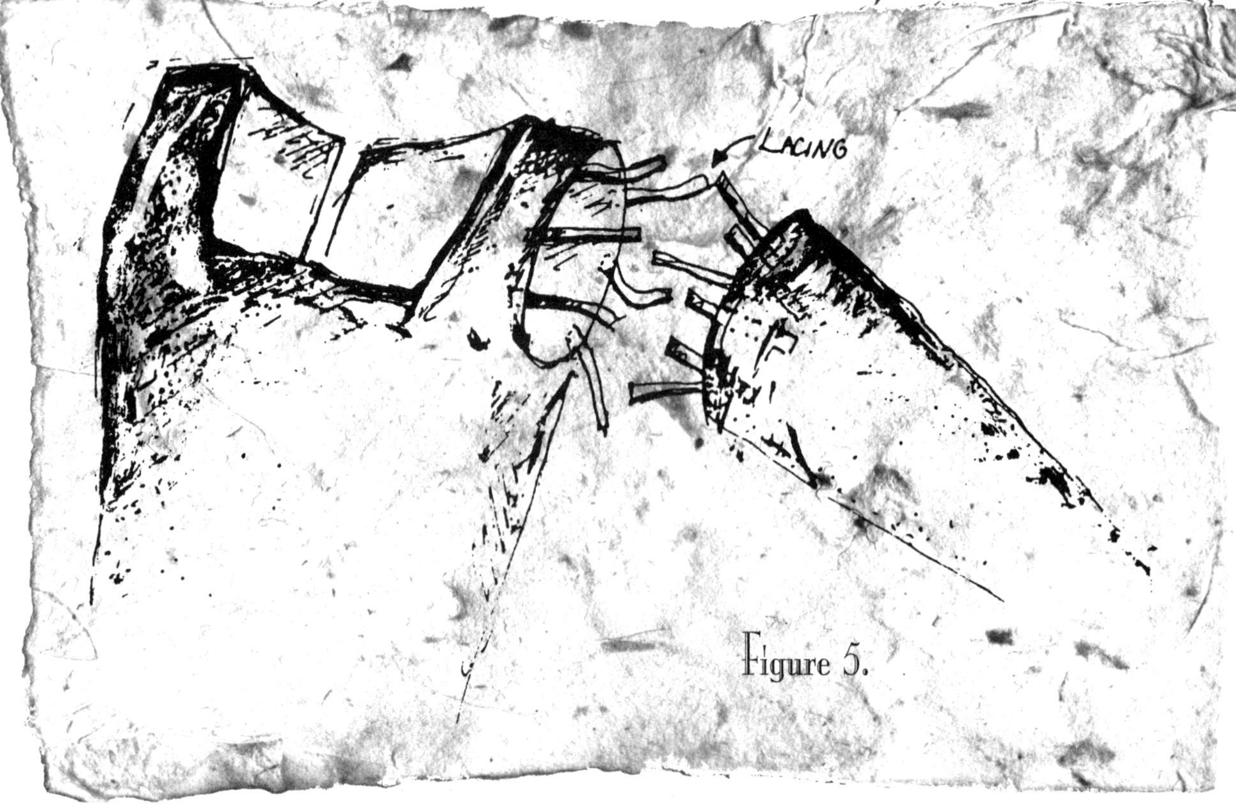

Figure 5.

and experiment. After all, you are making an outfit for a character who is re-creating an outfit from memories hundreds of years old, influenced by his or her own personal tastes. Such a costume could be pivotal in relaying a story of historical significance.

The next step is to make the sleeves. You have the option of permanently attaching the sleeves to the bodice or making the sleeves removable by using lacing attached to the sleeve and bodice, which can be laced together as shown in *figure 5*. Cut the pieces, keeping the direction of the nap in

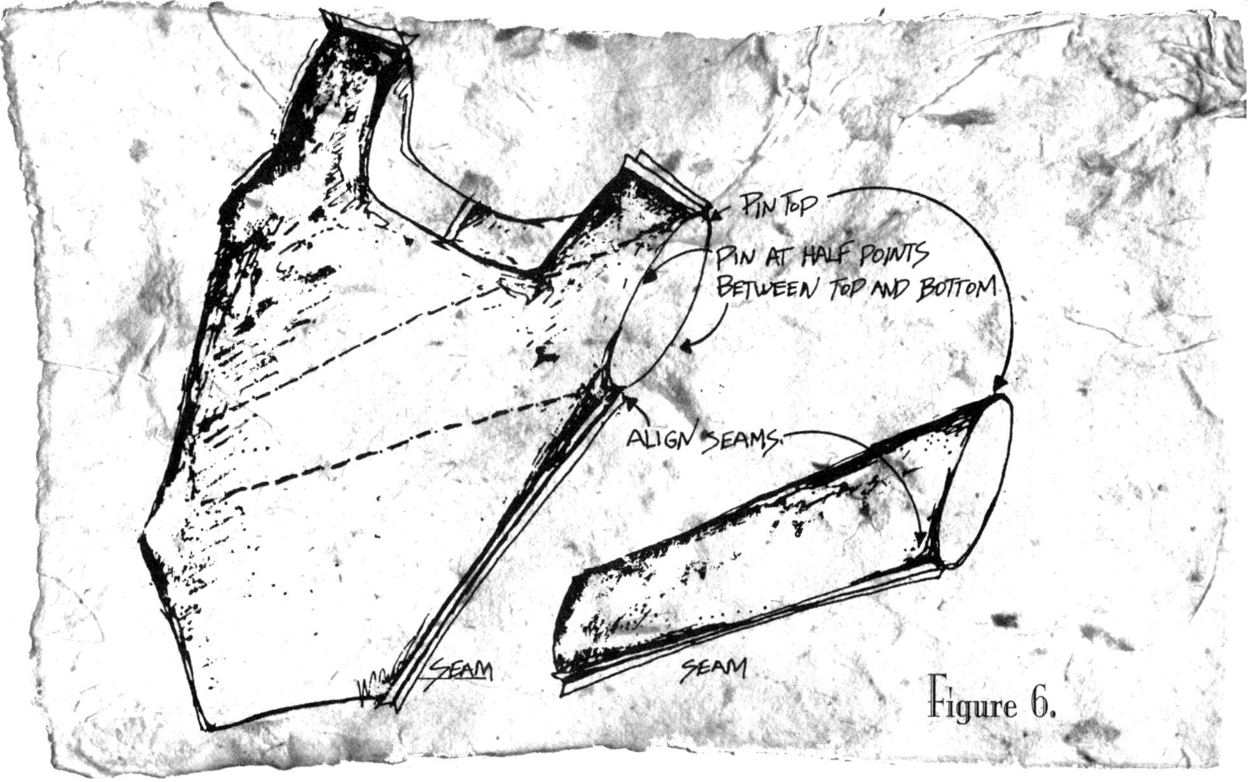

Figure 6.

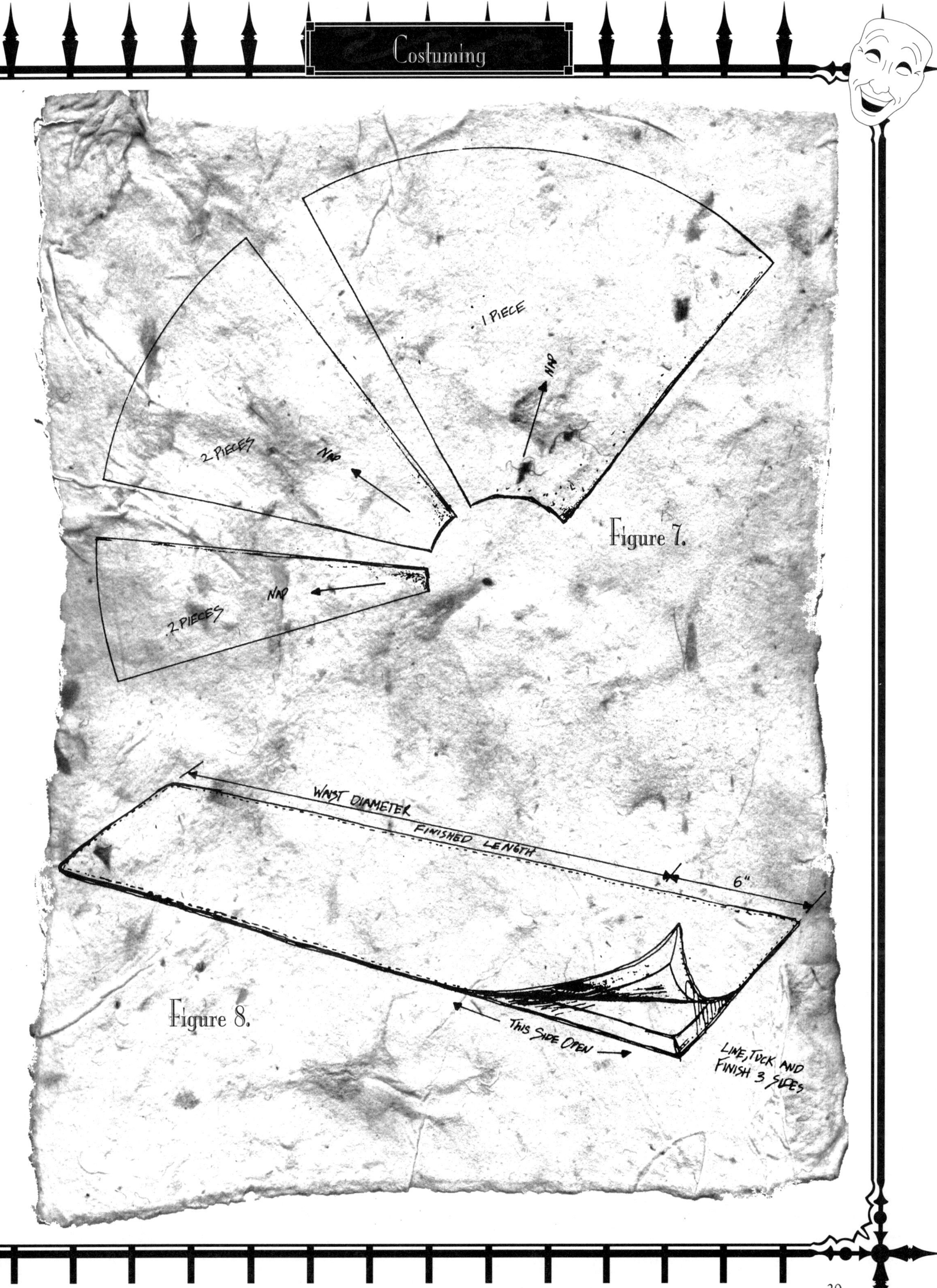

Figure 7.

Figure 8.

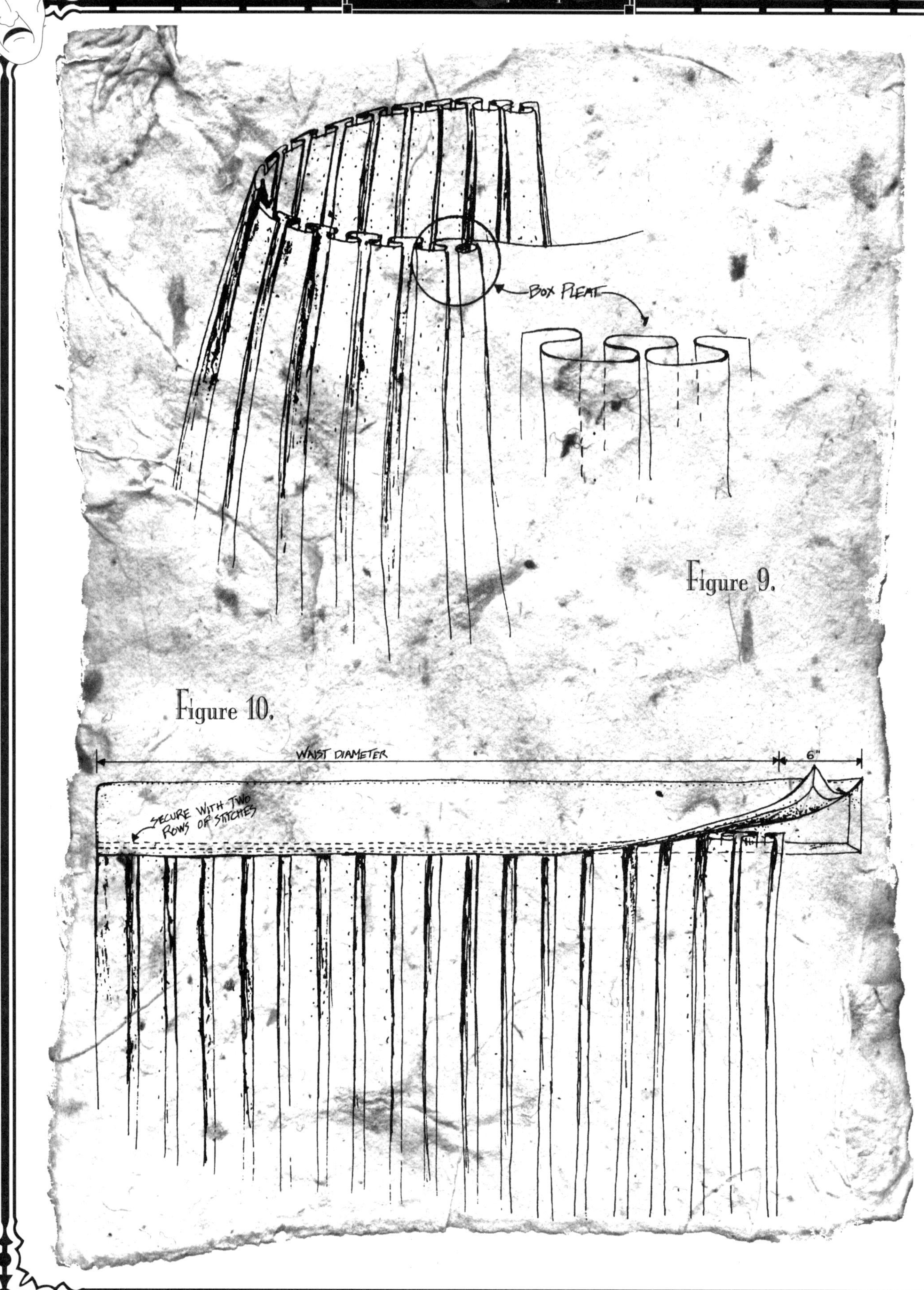

Figure 9.

Figure 10.

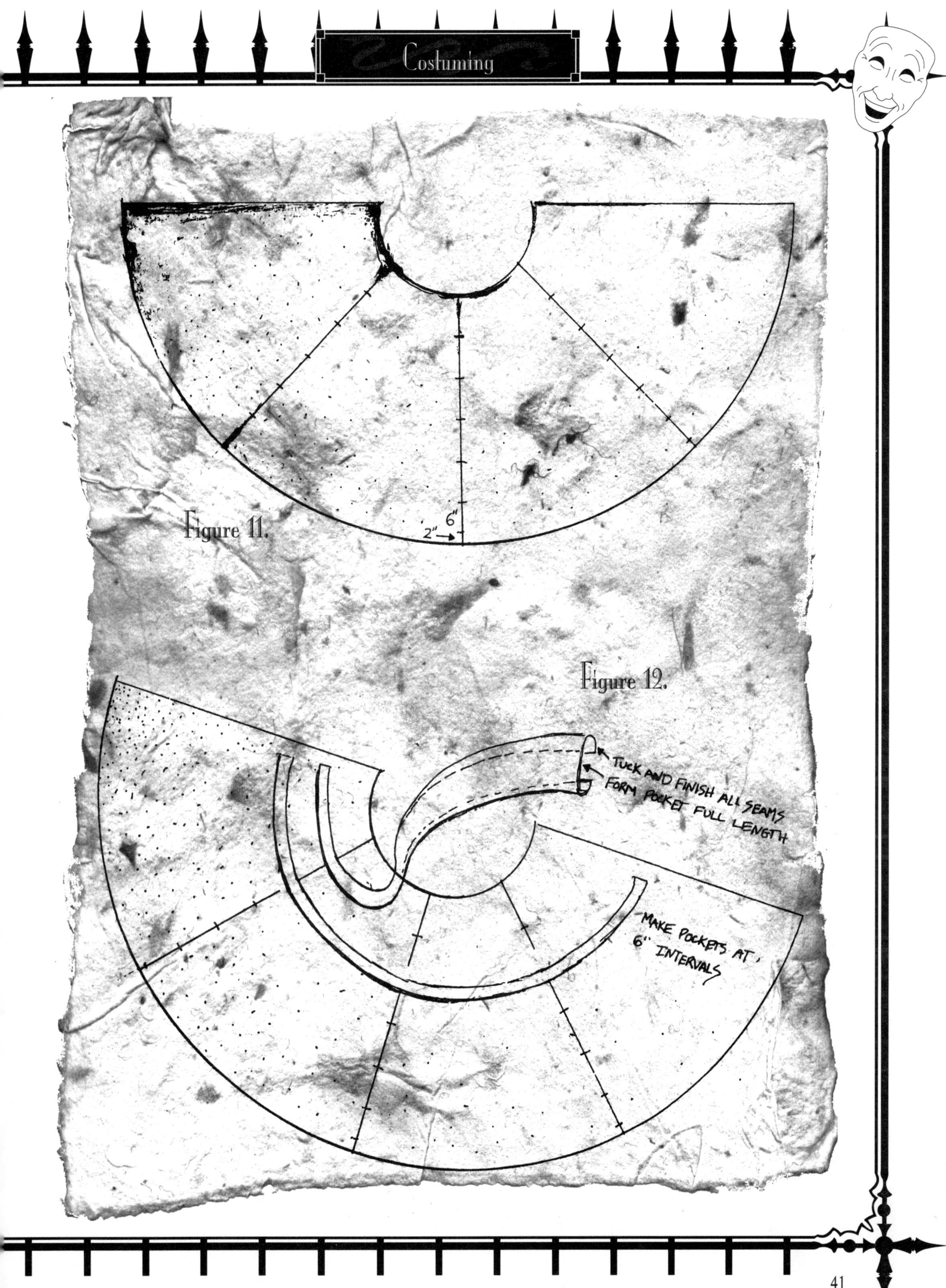

Figure 11.

Figure 12.

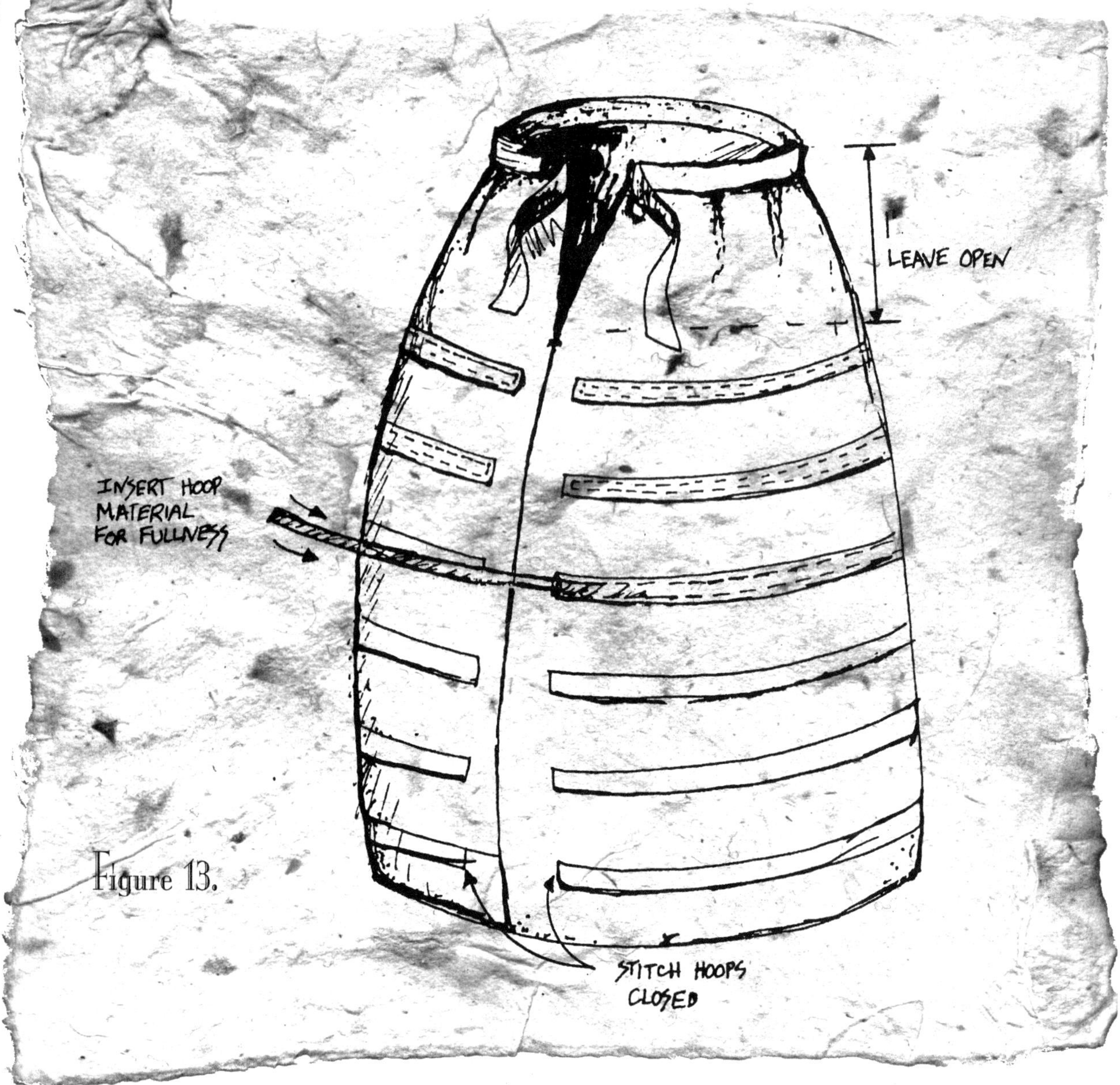

Figure 13.

mind, and apply lining to each sleeve. Unless you intend to hand-stitch your trim work and lacing onto your sleeves, apply them before assembling. It is impossible to get a finished sleeve into a regular machine for applying trim. Once the trim work and lacing are applied, assemble the sleeve with heavy-duty thread. To permanently attach the sleeves to the bodice, turn both sleeves and the bodice inside out. Place the sleeve inside the bodice as shown in *figure 6*. Align the seam at the side of the bodice and the seam of the sleeve. Pin the sleeve to the bodice at this point. Now, pin the top of the sleeve to the top of the shoulder of the bodice. If the sleeve is larger than the bodice armhole, and the armhole is the size you want, keep pinning the sleeve to the bodice at half points until you have achieved an even wrinkled effect. This will ensure that your sleeve is aligned properly.

Now comes the construction of the skirt. Use the pattern from the wedding gown, as described earlier, for the starting point. You want the gown to have a full overskirt that includes an open front, revealing the decorative underskirt material underneath. Refer to the pattern shown in *figure 7*. Cut the patterns as indicated. Run a zigzag stitch along each cut edge to keep the material from fraying. You want the inside opening of the top of the gown to be about 10 inches larger than your model's waist, and the bottom should be at least 3 yards in circumference. You do not need to put liner under the skirt. The skirt is going to be heavy enough without adding any unnecessary material. Assemble the skirt pieces and apply the decorative trim before attaching the skirt to the waist piece. Construct the waist piece from fabric cut long enough to span your model's waist plus 6 inches and with a width of about 4 inches (final dimension 3 inches after

sewing the seams). Apply lining to the waist piece and leave the bottom open (see *figure* 8). Box pleat the skirt top as shown in *figure* 9, so that it has the same diameter as your model's waist. At the back of the skirt, make a slit approximately 1 foot long and fold and finish the edges. Starting from one edge of the rear slit that you have just finished, slip the open edge of the waist piece over the top 1 inch of the skirt top, as shown in *figure 10*. Fold and tuck the lining and upholstery fabric over the skirt top and pin into place. Make sure to place the pins perpendicular to the direction you will be sewing. When you are done applying the waist section, you should have at least 4 inches of material left over. Fold and tuck the remaining material. Secure the skirt to the waistband with two lines of stitching of heavy-duty thread. Apply 2-inch Velcro all around the outside of the waist band, and apply the mated piece of the Velcro to the inside face of the overhang firmly to secure it in place. The Velcro on the outside of the waistband will interface with the Velcro piece that you applied to the inside of the bodice earlier, and will hold the two pieces firmly together. Use heavy-duty thread. This is why you should have a heavy-duty sewing machine. This project will put any machine to the test. Make buttonholes on either side of the slit so that you may lace up the back opening. Check the length of the overskirt on your model.

You do not want the overskirt to drag on the ground. Finish the edge of the underskirt with trim and apply horsehair (a stiffener found at most fabric stores) to the inside of the bottom edge to stiffen it and give it strength.

Construct the underskirt in a similar manner. However, you can use lighter weight, decorative material for this part. Since you will only be seeing the front of the skirt through the opening in the overskirt, you can "cheat" and only use your good material for the front piece that will show. Pleat the top and stitch over with binding (material used to finish open ends of a piece). You can use lacing to secure the underskirt at the top.

Construct the farthingale next. The farthingale is the hooped skirt which will give your skirt that full look you see in the movies. Begin construction of the farthingale with midweight cotton fabric, cut in a pie-shaped pattern, allowing 4 inches at the top for your model's waist and 4 yards circumference at the bottom. You want this piece to have less pleats at the waist. Before assembling the skirt, lay each cut piece out on the floor and mark lines with the chalk along the curve every 6 inches, starting 2 inches from the bottom, as shown in *figure 11*. Assemble the pieces together to form the skirt, leaving the bottom edge unfinished for now. Cut 3 inch strips of cotton fabric as long as you can and apply them to the skirt. Tuck the edges under and finish all the seams. You want to create a little pocket the full length around the skirt. After you have completed one entire circle around the skirt, finish the ends and leave them open. Repeat this procedure for each of the lines you have drawn (see *figure 12*). Insert hoop material, which may be found at theatrical supply houses, into one of the open ends of the pockets you formed and work it all the around the skirt to the other end. Hoop material is steel wire encased in a resin-type finish. Use as much hoop material as needed to create the desired fullness. Overlap the hoop material at each tier 4 inches and join them with duct tape. Do not secure the hoop material to the skirt, let it rest within the pocket you have created. The hoop material cannot be washed and must be removed from the farthingale each time you need to clean it. Repeat the insertion of hoop material at each pocket location until you are finished. Check the skirt for fullness and adjust the hoop material as needed (see *figure 13*). Apply binding to the top and leave about 8 inches at either end to act as lacing to secure it at the waist. This is your farthingale. Put it on your model to check for length and mark it. You want the farthingale to be shorter than the other two skirts. Trim and finish the bottom edge with binding.

At this point, your skirt is basically complete. You can add decorations such as jewels and pearling. Jewels, fastened to clothing, were often used to denote prestige and status among nobility. Imitation jewels can be found at most well-stocked craft stores. Any Kindred with a modicum of vanity has probably picked up some rather nice jewelry over the years. The techniques described for making this gown are the result of one person's experimentation, based on a lot of research and questioning of other costume designers. Do your own research and develop your own techniques. Be logical in your approach to

Figure 15

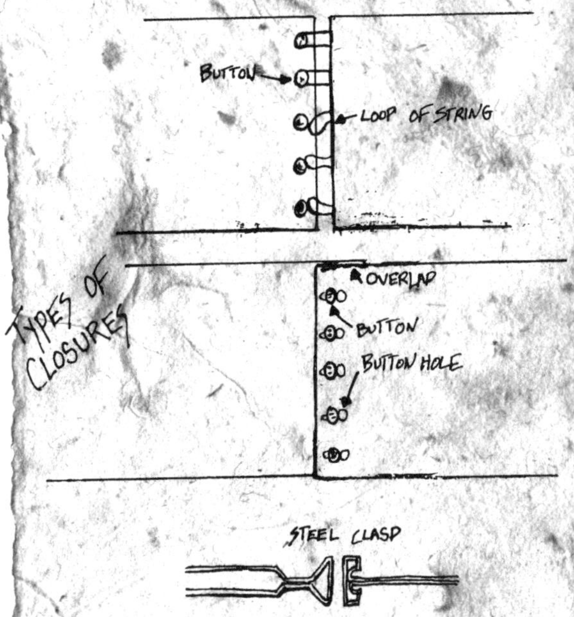

Figure 16.

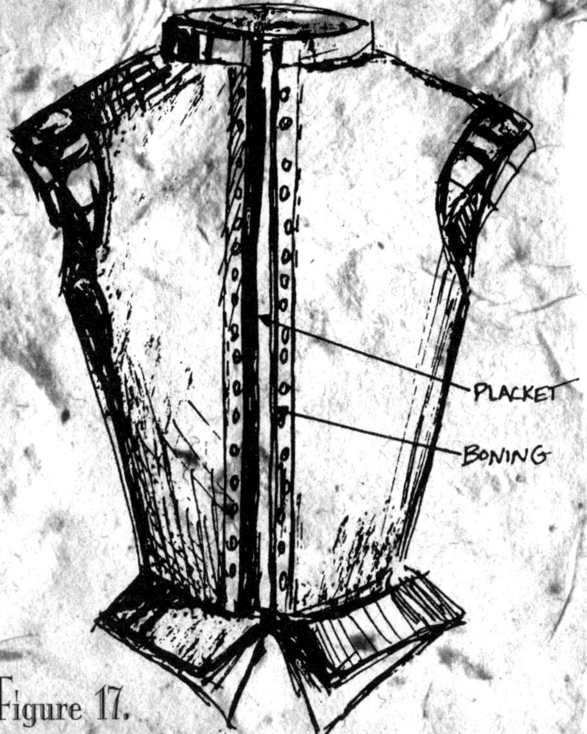

Figure 17.

any problems you encounter and be patient in developing your skills. You might want to take some sewing classes to get a good basis for developing your techniques.

A Gentlemen's Doublet

The pattern for a 16th-century men's doublet is similar to that of a modern vest pattern, which could be used as a basis for the doublet's construction. However, you will need to enlarge the armhole and neck dimensions to allow for freedom of movement. Also, modify the point of the front bottom of the doublet to more accurately reflect the style of the time period (refer to *figure 15*). Make your patterns and transfer them to your material. Upholstery velvet works well for this project. However, if you find lighter weight dressmakers velvet that you like better, you can use that, as long as you use a heavy cotton as a liner. Line all the pieces regardless. Use liner that complements the color of the material you chose to make the piece. It is possible that the inside liner of the doublet will be seen, and you don't want bright white flashing out. You will not need a placket for the doublet. The doublet is intended to be opened from the front, much the same as a modern vest.

You have a number of options on how to close your doublet front. You can use ornamental metal buttons and buttonholes as we do today; or buttons and loops, which were popular during that time; or you can use lacing to close the front. Refer to *figure 16* for some examples of closures. Dressmakers of this time were very inventive with fasteners, which were often ornamental as well as practical. Everything they used was handmade and reflected the skill of the crafter who created them. Perhaps your character has an affection for well-crafted ornaments and will use them in his attire. Whatever you decide, install the closure system you want for your doublet and check the fit of it. Adjust as necessary.

Once the torso of your doublet is complete, you can begin to assemble the sleeves. The sleeves for a doublet differ from those of the ladies' gown in that they are loose and blousy. However, this rule is subject to change, as you have many options in the design of your doublet sleeve. Create patterns from your ideas and make mock-ups to see how they work. When you have your idea worked out, cut the pieces, line them, and assemble. Apply the trim to the sleeve and finish all the edges. The sleeves of a doublet should be removable, allowing you freedom of movement if the occasion should call for it.

Attach the sleeves to the torso section of your doublet with laces installed on both pieces and tied together with bows. Before stitching the lacing into place, permanently install epaulets at the shoulders of your doublet. Epaulets are decorative flaps that serve to hide the lacing and make the shoulders look bigger. Refer to *figure 17* to see how the completed shoulder piece should look.

You now have the option of adding a collar, or any other type of accent piece appropriate for that time, to your doublet. The doublet itself was often decorated with slits placed in patterns throughout the torso.

The gentlemen's doublet is a relatively easy project to complete, compared to the ladies' gown. As stated before, it would be interesting to see how an article of clothing could be adapted to modern fashion styles. The doublet is an elegant article of clothing that any distinguished character who has memories of that time would probably remember fondly.

The Peasant Shirt

Peasant shirts are making a comeback in certain areas, and certainly any Garou would wear one for its earthy, natural feel and simple elegance. Some places are charging as much as $40 for a peasant shirt of middling quality. When you realize that the estimated cost for the 3 yards of midweight cotton required to make a peasant shirt is only about $8, you begin to see opportunities to make some spare change. With a little practice, you could make three or four a night.

Begin construction of your peasant shirt by laying the fabric on the floor, folding the fabric, and cutting four rectangles as shown. Cut the rectangles so that the combined width of any two of them is greater than the width of your chest by at least 8 inches (see *figure 18*). The pieces should be at least 3 feet long. Lay the four pieces in a cross pattern as shown in *figure 19*, face side down. Overlap the corners as shown. Two of the opposite pieces will become the sleeves

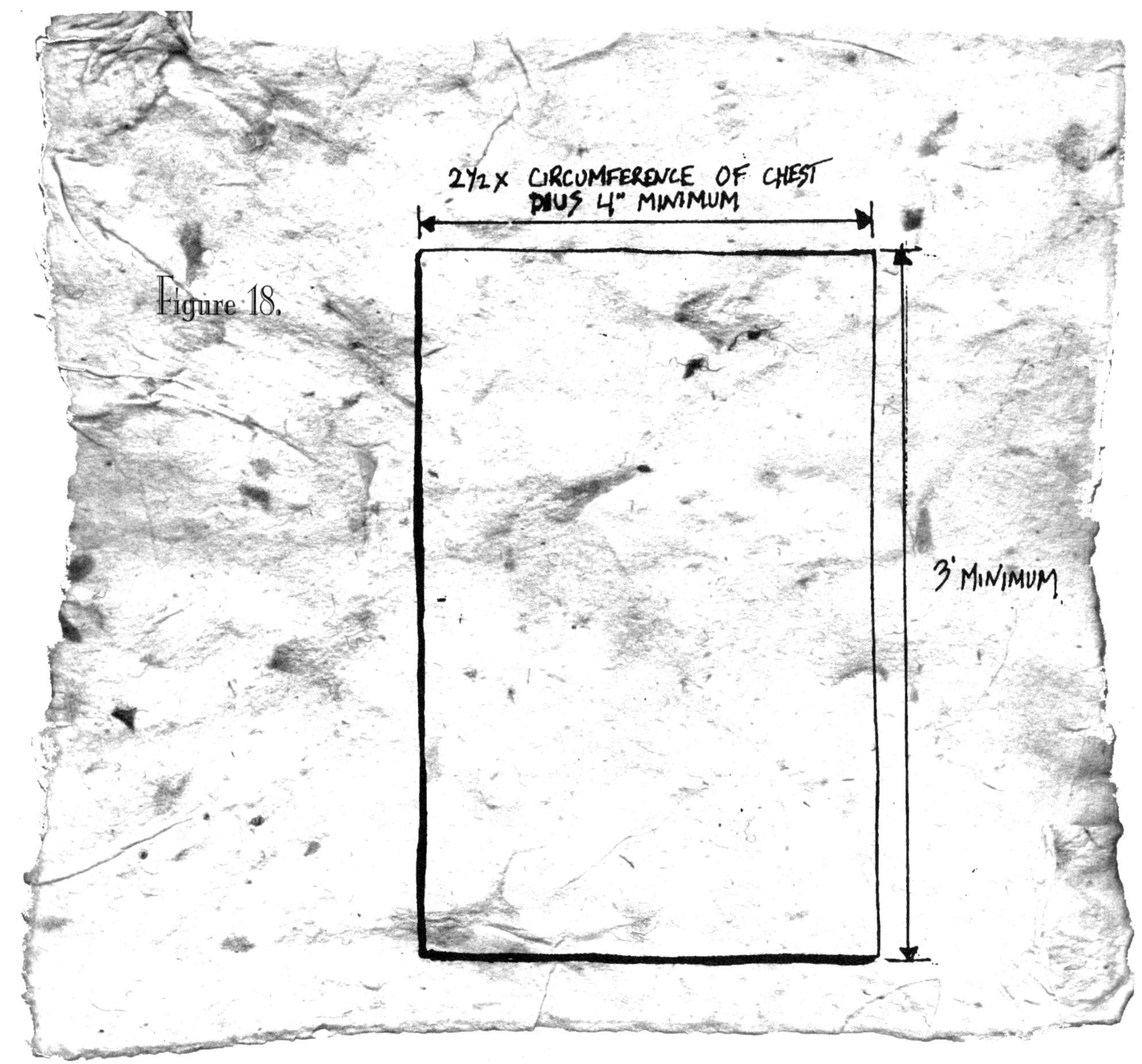

Figure 18.

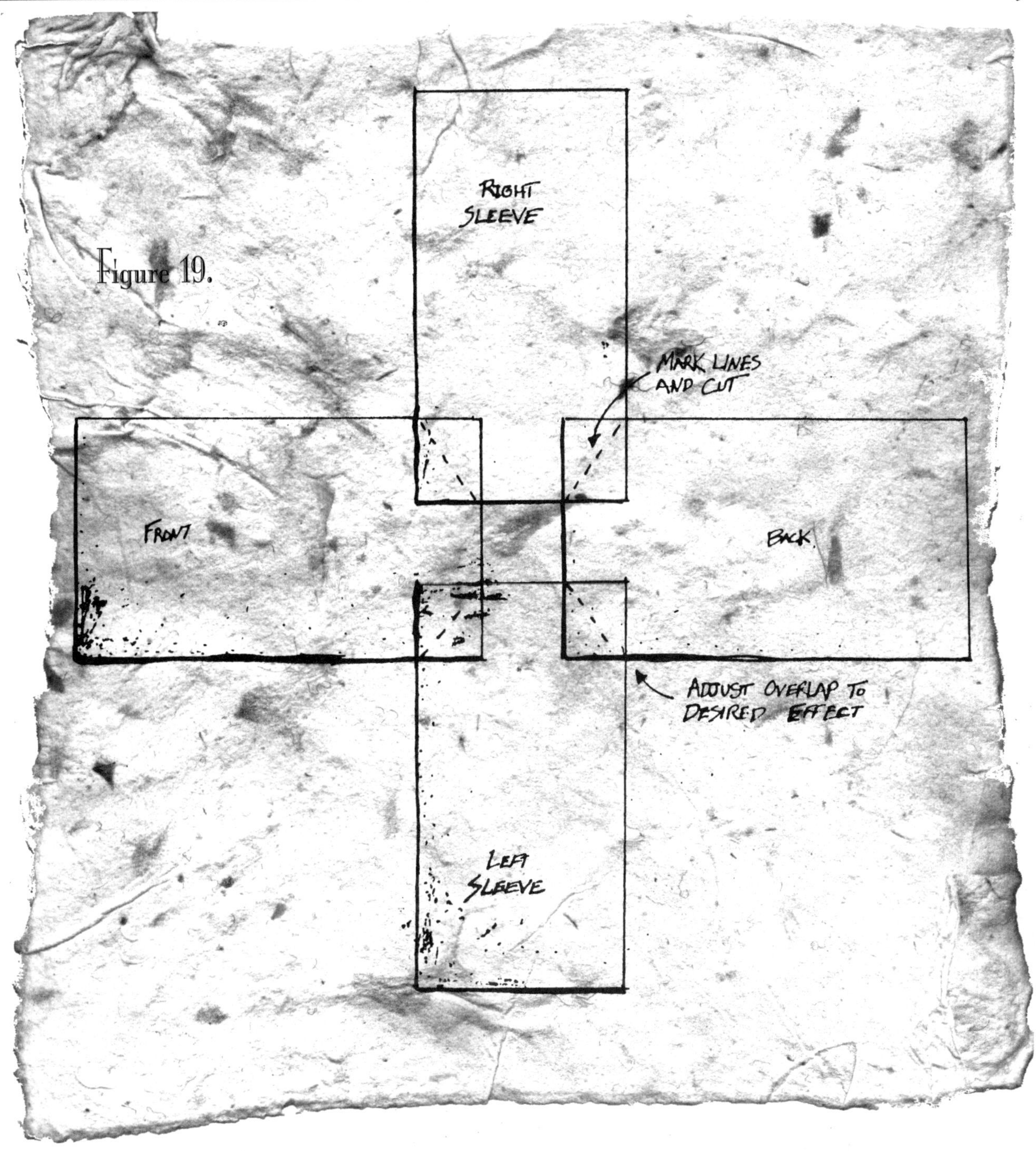

Figure 19.

and the remaining two opposite pieces will become the front and back of the torso. Mark the angles of the overlap and trim the pieces. Pin the pieces together and sew. Lay the pieces back on the floor in the original pattern, seam side down. Fold the piece to form a "T" shape as shown in *figure 20*. Pin the edges of the torso and sleeve pieces together. At the point where the sleeves intersect the torso, mark a line at an angle. Trim the fabric. Stitch the torso pieces together, then the sleeves. Finally, stitch the sleeves completely into place. You should now have a big, formless shirtlike piece with blousy sleeves (see *figure 21*).

To finish the sleeves, make cuffs from the leftover material, using *figure 22* as a guide. You want the cuffs to be at least 4 inches long and wide enough to just barely span your wrist if you are using lacing to close the sleeve. If you are using buttons, you will want the cuff to overlap at least 1 inch. Slit each sleeve end of your shirt 8 inches from the end. Tuck the edges of the slit under and finish the edge as shown in *figure 23*. Attach the cuffs to the sleeves as shown. Pleat the sleeve ends to match the diameter of your wrist. Make buttonholes for either the lacing or the installation of buttons. You can make your cuffs longer for a more dramatic look, as shown.

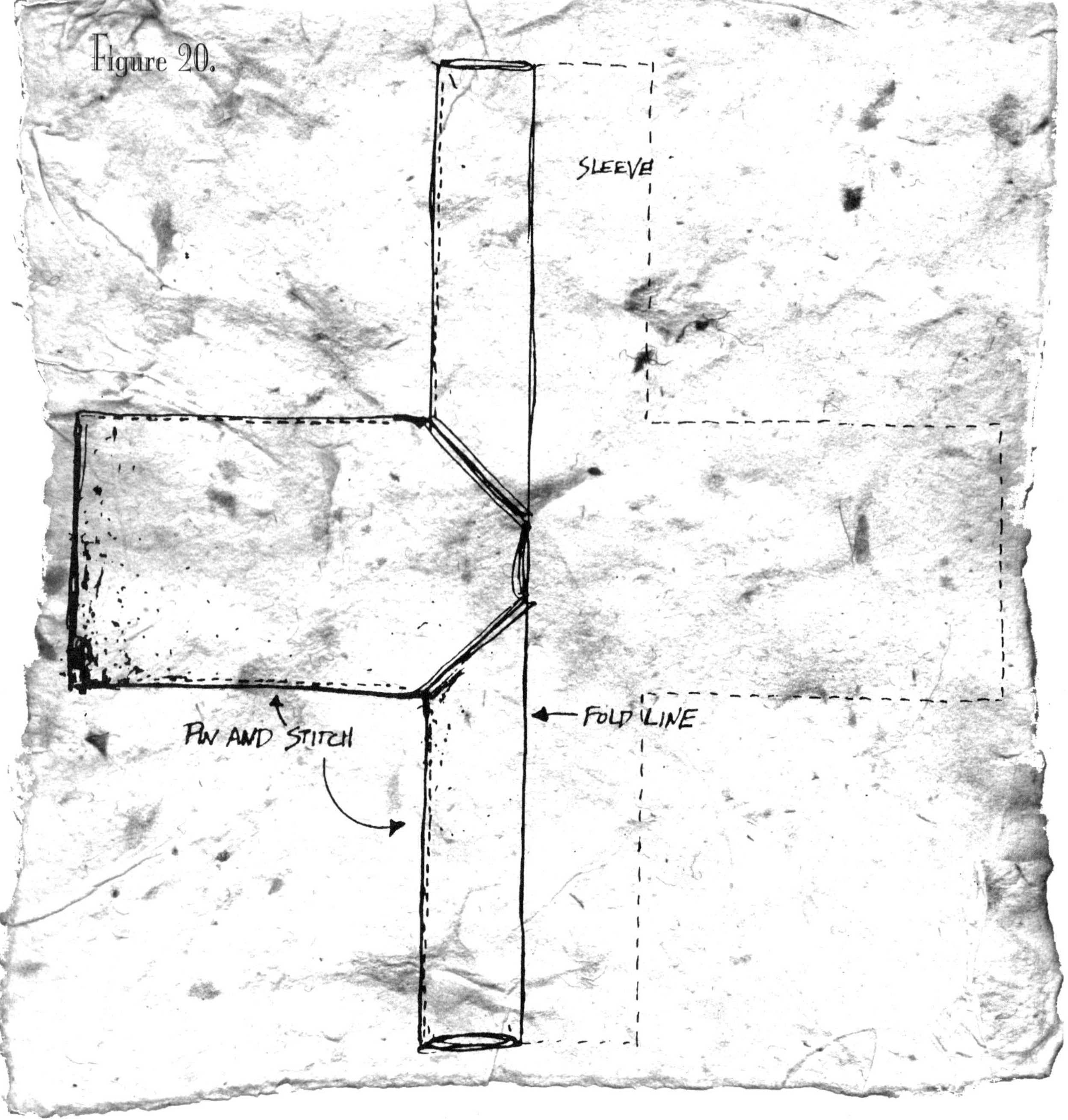

When you don your shirt, your sleeves should drape over your cuffs and hang in a dramatic fashion. If they are too long for your taste, remove the cuff, adjust the length, and reinstall the cuff.

Finish the neckline of your shirt by slitting the front of your shirt (determined by you) about 8 inches. Tuck and finish the edges of the slit edge. Apply a folded piece of fabric to the edges as shown in *figure 24*. This will strengthen the edge. Tuck the edges of the neckline under and finish the edge. Now, tuck the edge of the neckline under once more to form a 1/2 inch pocket as shown, all the way around the neckline (see *figure 25*). Thread a piece of lacing through the pocket you formed around the neckline. This will allow the drawstring to close the front securely. An alternate finish is to place buttonholes along the front opening for lacing and put a collar at the neckline as shown in *figure 26*. Use the patterns shown in *figure 27* as a guide to making your collar. Attach the collar to your shirt and you are almost done. Finish the shirt by tucking the bottom edge under all the way around and stitching the seam closed.

There you have it, a complete peasant shirt that, with a little modification, is the basis for a nobleman's shirt. You can add trim work, piping, etc., to make the shirt more prestigious. You can try different cuff and collar designs to change

Figure 21.

Figure 22.

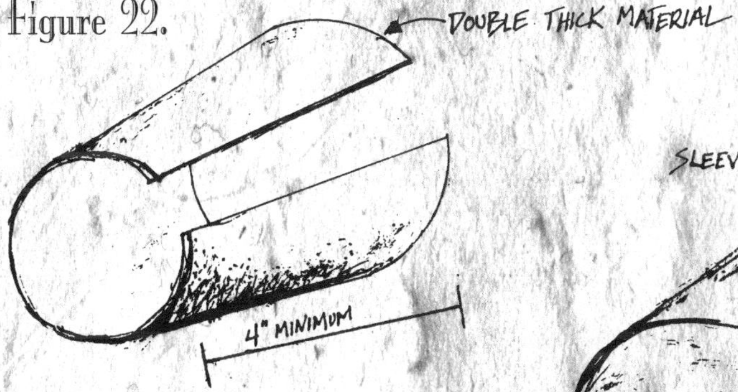

Figure 23.

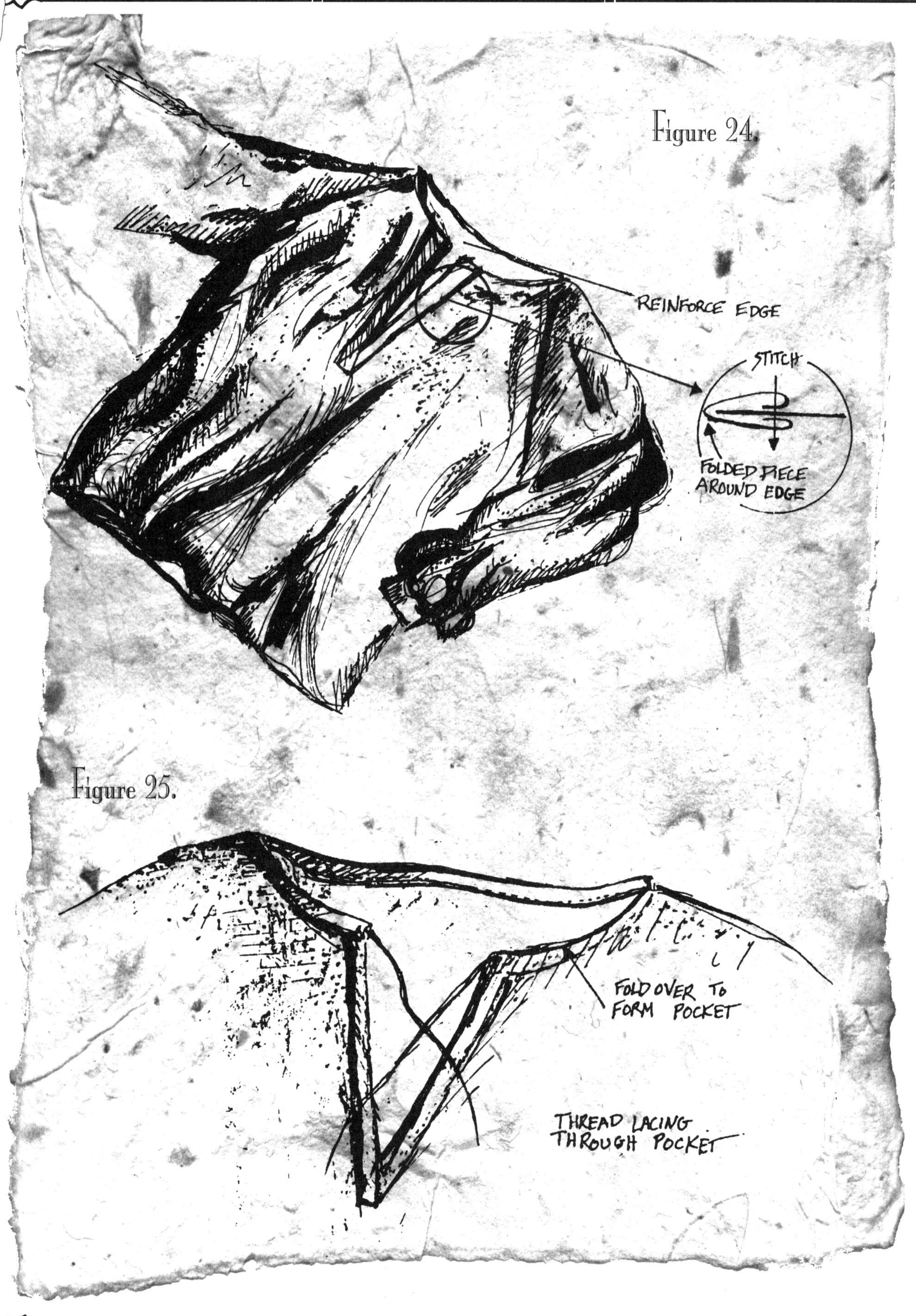
Figure 24.
REINFORCE EDGE
STITCH
FOLDED PIECE
AROUND EDGE
Figure 25.
FOLD OVER TO
FORM POCKET
THREAD LACING
THROUGH POCKET

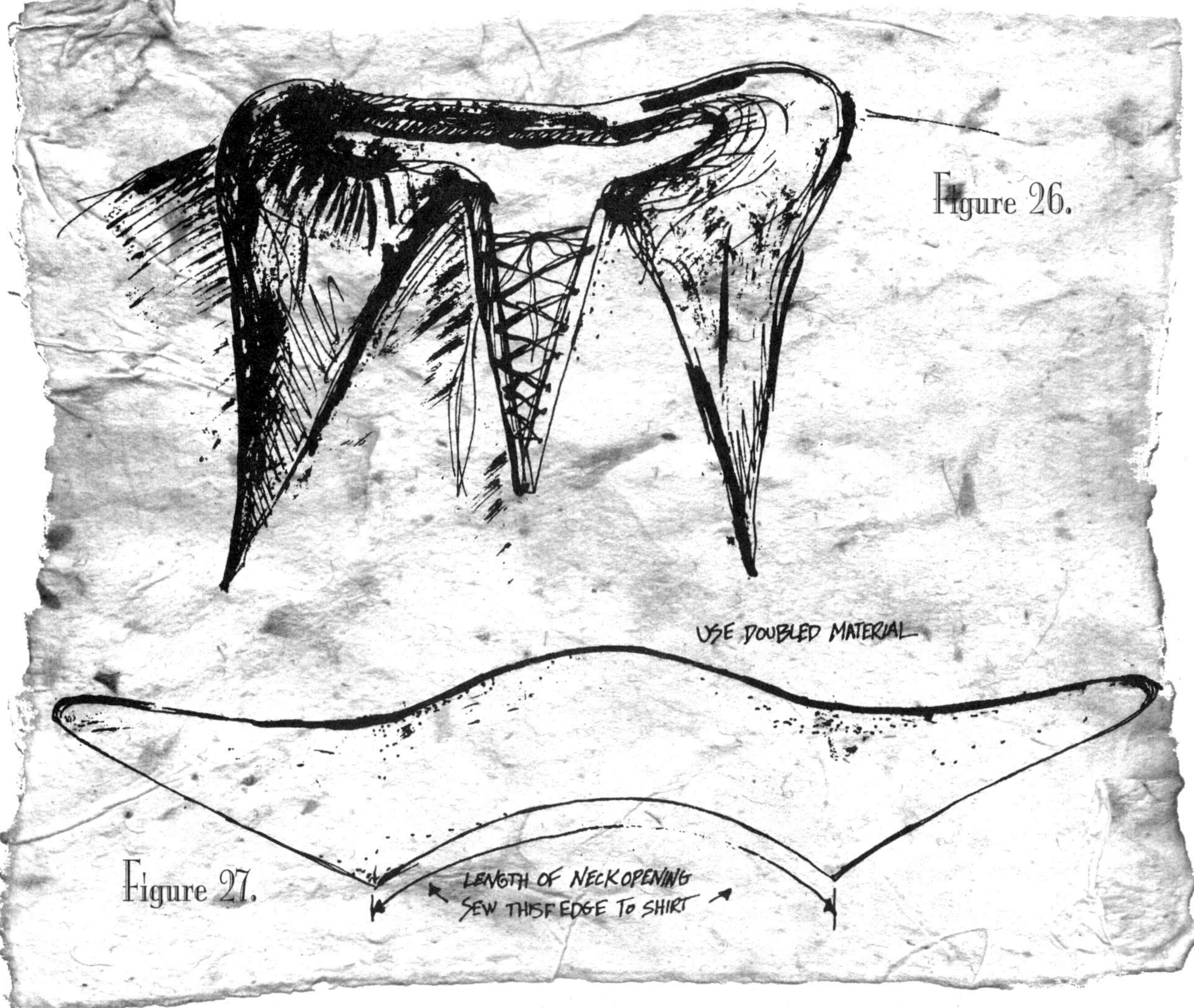

Figure 26.

Figure 27.

the intended effect of the shirt, further helping to reveal your character's personality. Best of all, the shirt costs you under $10 in its simplest form. Experiment with color, fabric, and style to adapt the shirt to different scenarios. The choice is up to you.

In Conclusion

The designing and making of costumes, or the building of a wardrobe for your character, is a fun way to add a little more personality to her, and it may give you a perspective of what her existence was like. You can make clothing from different eras and learn how those fashions were influenced by the technological limitations of that time. In return, you can learn how fashion research has influenced human advancement since the beginning of recorded human history. All you have to do is read the history of the humble zipper to see the link between fashion research and the advancement of human technology and society. The principles used in developing the zipper have led to many offshoot technologies and allowed for humanity to reach beyond the very confines of this planet. Space suits wouldn't work without an effective means of sealing them closed against the vacuum of space. It's amazing how all these seemingly unrelated events tie into one another. You can trace back through fashion design and come up with new wardrobe combinations by mixing different material types and styles from different eras. Most importantly, you will have the satisfaction of knowing your character is making a statement for herself within the confines of the story, without the need of any physical or verbal effort on your part.

One thing you should always keep in mind, no matter how much enjoyment you derive from the costumes you wear, is that chances are what you're wearing is representative of a certain culture and time period. To the people who lived during those time periods, what they wore wasn't considered a costume, it was what they wore as a part of their everyday lives. It provided them with a sense of identity and status, as well as protection from the environment. The same should hold true for your character. Your character has a history and a set of traditions, regardless of the type of creature he represents. The clothing he chooses to garb himself in should have as much meaning to him as it did to the inhabitants of the time period his clothing represents.

Chapter Three: Makeup

Mirror, Mirror
On the wall
The face you show me
can't be so.
— Styx, "Mirror, Mirror"

This chapter discusses the importance of makeup in theatre, its history and relevance to the world of **Mind's Eye Theatre**, and simple techniques that you can employ to transform yourself into one of its inhabitants.

History

The use of makeup on stage and screen has evolved tremendously over the years and has even become something of an art form. An actor can convey a lot about her character through the disciplines she employs in her craft. However, there are some things that simply cannot be conveyed without physically altering the actor to suit the part. This is especially true today, when audiences expect to experience realism in what they see during a performance. How would you, as an actor, portray someone racially different from you? Or, how would you convey the alien substance that is slowly mutating your body into something horribly grotesque? Barring surgery, the only alternative you have is to use makeup effects to create the illusion of the physical nature your role requires. Makeup is a powerful tool in this respect, and can be used to help you portray the unique qualities of your character in a **Mind's Eye Theatre** story.

In the early days of theatre, actors wore simple makeup to enhance their appearances and project their facial features to the audience. This became even more important as indoor stages gained popularity, and it is still an important part of theatre today. The stage is a harsh environment, with hot, intense lighting that washes out your facial coloring and your features by lightening the contrast of your skin tones. Makeup accentuates and gives contrast to your features, making them discernible to your audience. In addition to overcoming these environmental difficulties, makeup allows you, the actor, to lend believability to the role you are portraying. You can use makeup to help you communicate age, race, disfigurement, or any of the idiosyncratic features common to humanity. Or, you can use it to alter your appearance to resemble the features of a historical or fictional character. Basic makeup techniques have always been, and will always be, an important skill for all actors to develop.

As the art of movie-making developed, so too did the art of makeup and the importance it played to this budding industry. Unlike stage actors, movie actors no longer had to worry about speed. They had much more time to carefully apply their makeup and work on the details. This led to experimentation with just about every type of material that

could have been conceivably used as makeup at the time. Dry clay set with lacquer and collodion-filled cotton balls molded into shape directly on the actor's face were some of the techniques used in the early days of movie making. Some of the most popular early movies were ones that required quite a bit of modification to the appearance of the actor portraying the role. The original *Hunchback of Notre Dame* was a classic movies of this genre. *Frankenstein*, in 1931, brought makeup to new heights with Boris Karloff as the monster. From that point on, horror became a mainstay in movie making that continues to do well, even today. The most memorable of these movies are the ones with the most remarkable makeup effects. Think of the times you've been to a movie where the makeup effects were really good and how they influenced how you felt about what you saw. You may not have even liked the plot, but the characters looked convincing enough to make you believe the "reality" of the scene. With proper makeup techniques, your character can make the same impact on other players during the course of a game.

The world of **Mind's Eye Theatre** has so many diverse character types within it that it would be a shame not to explore some makeup effects that can help bring them to life. True, it can be a laborious process at times and you may ask yourself, "Why should I go to all the bother of making myself up for an event?" The answer to that question is up to you. However, there is nothing like actually seeing yourself physically transformed into something alien. You can give your skin the opalescent sheen of a vampire or a hint of the bestiality lurking within a Garou. More importantly, you can use makeup to help reinforce and define your character. If you are portraying a Nosferatu, you can give yourself a twisted visage that immediately tells others who you are. As with costume design, you can also experiment with incorporating makeup techniques from different time periods into your character. Your Kindred may remember ancient Egypt fondly and thus have a predilection for using kohl to line her eyes. The possibilities range from the outrageous to the sublime. All you have to do is decide to what degree you wish to take your character's physical representation, and then employ the proper makeup techniques to achieve the desired result.

In the end, makeup can be one of the most fun parts of portraying your character in a game. Character development gives you the motivation and nuances of your character, and your clothing can speak volumes for your personality. However, makeup truly does make the character real in a visual way. There's nothing like interacting with someone made up to be a Crinos form Garou during a game to relay the macabre nature of what you are doing. Makeup is a means to express the subtle twist that reality takes when you put on your fangs, sallow your cheeks, or add fur to your face, and proceed to portray your character as if nothing unusual is going on. Just playing around with altering your appearance in different ways is fun in itself. Having a reason to do it in public is even more so.

Terms and General Knowledge

In its most basic form, we use makeup every day to improve upon our looks, or at least to alter our appearances in accordance with the local traditions. Shaving can even be loosely interpreted as a way of altering your appearance from its natural form. The point is, we all have had some experience with makeup, whether we watched our mothers use it when we were young, or use it ourselves. Because of this, we are all familiar to some degree or other with the terms used to describe makeup and the application of it. However, to successfully make yourself up for an event, it is a good idea to familiarize yourself with some specific terms associated with makeup and the tools used by makeup artists. The following terms are ones that will be used throughout the rest of this section, so take some time to read through them. A good working knowledge of these terms will act as a basis for you to converse and share ideas with your fellow players.

Kinds and Uses of Makeup

Base — The first layer of makeup, used as a "base" which supports the effects you wish to create. It can be stick, powder, or street makeup, but all should be blended into the hairline and down the neck into the shirt line. Base should look as natural as possible and not caked on, assuring a professional look.

Street Makeup — (Base type) Everyday makeup that can be bought at most department stores. It is used to even skin tone without any drastic change to your appearance and is applied with the fingers, then blended with a sponge. This type of makeup can be made a little thinner with the addition of water, giving it a lighter, more natural-looking color. Street makeup can be removed with skin cleanser and water.

Pancake — (Base type) Thicker makeup that's applied using your fingers or a sponge and is blended with a sponge. Pancake is used to change skin tone and cover flaws. It can be bought at most commercial stores. Pancake makeup must be removed with cold cream.

Stick — (Base type) Stage makeup is highly resistant to sweating, etc. Basically, it stays put once you put it on. It is used to change skin tones and cover flaws. To apply, dot over the skin by placing the stick directly on the skin and twisting. Blend the dots together with a sponge. Stick can be found in theatrical supply shops, specialty catalogs, and to a limited degree, in department stores. Stick must be removed with cold cream.

Shadow — Every highlight has a shadow. Shadow is thick cream stage makeup used to create wrinkles, bags under the eyes, sagging jowls, double chins, stubble, etc. Shadow is applied with a brush and blended with a sponge or the fingers. It can be purchased in theatrical supply shops or through specialty catalogs and comes in various shades of brown, black, purple, green, etc. Eyeliner can be substituted, but it does not hold up as well and is more difficult to blend.

Highlight — Every shadow should have a highlight for contrast. Highlight is a white creamy makeup that is placed above shadow lines and blended up. Highlight and shadow are used in combination to create the illusion of three-dimensional features such as hollow checks, etc.

Cold Cream — A cleanser found in any department store that is used for the removal of makeup. Hand apply cold cream and remove as much of it as possible before washing the rest off your face. The drain may clog if too much cold cream is washed down it.

Spirit Gum — A solution such as gum arabic in ether used for the application of facial hair or appliances. It can be found in theatrical supply houses.

Surgical Adhesive — Found in medical supply stores, surgical adhesive is liquid skin adhesive that can be used as an alternative to spirit gum for the application of latex appliances.

Mastic — Mastic is similar to spirit gum and can be used for the same purpose. The only difference between spirit gum, mastic, and surgical adhesive is cost and sensitivity to the skin.

Appliance — A pre-molded feature, ready to be attached to the face or body to create an effect. "Appliance" is a generic term that refers to any such attachable feature.

PAX — An aerosol spray-on makeup used for complete coverage and color change. PAX makeup can make your skin bright metallic silver, gold, or any base color or hue. It's very durable and adheres very well, but can only be removed through lots of scrubbing with soap and water. PAX is safe for most people to use. Only well-stocked theatrical supply houses carry PAX.

Latex — Latex is an artificial rubber compound that comes in pre-molded features, which are attached with spirit gum or liquid latex. Latex is applied and then covered with makeup for the desired effect.

Liquid Latex — The liquid form of latex rubber, when applied with a brush, can be molded with the fingers to form scars, cuts, moles, etc. As with latex, cover liquid latex with makeup after application to complete the effect. Do not store liquid latex in freezing conditions, and remember that it cannot be shipped during the winter months because of this, so plan your orders accordingly.

Morticians Wax — Found at your local theatrical supply house or morticians supply store, morticians wax is a moldable, flesh-colored wax used to create features. It readily adheres to the skin and is relatively durable if not subjected to a lot of movement. It is more readily available and more reasonably priced than latex.

Nose Putty — Found at theatrical supply houses, this is a flesh-colored putty that can be molded to create features like morticians wax and then applied to the skin with mastic or spirit gum.

Fur and Crepe Hair — These can be bought at a theatrical supply store and cut to create mustaches, beards, fill-in hairlines, etc. They are applied with spirit gum and will remain in place for very long periods of time if applied properly.

Powder — Loose powder should be dabbed, not rubbed, onto the face. The excess is then brushed off to set the makeup and remove the shine. Opalescent powders are also available for special makeup applications.

Sponges — Can be found at any cosmetic store. Sponges are used to blend makeup.

Stipple Sponge — Looks like a sponge, but is made of plastic. It is used to create texture and stubble (with shadow makeup). These can be found at any theatrical supply house.

Brushes — Makeup brushes used to apply shadow, highlight, lipstick, etc., that come in different sizes. They can also be used to make thin lines or fill in large areas. They are found at theatrical supply houses, or you can improvise and use fine art brushes, available just about anywhere.

Bunny Brushes — Very soft brushes used to brush excess powder off the face when makeup is completed.

Hypo-Allergenic — Term used to denote products designed to prevent or reduce the chance of an allergic reaction. It is a good idea to determine your skin's sensitivity to any product on a small area before applying it to large areas of your skin.

Getting Started

Prior to using any form of makeup on your face, it is important to know the proper application and removal techniques, ensuring the best results. Also, the proper use of makeup will minimize any adverse effect it may have on your skin. Improper use of makeup, and the failure to follow the proper removal techniques, can cause skin blemishes. The skin is the largest organ of the body and is often the most neglected. It is important to take proper care of it and exercise common sense when using any product on the skin. Remember, a **Mind's Eye Theatre** game can last a lot longer than many plays and will demand a lot more from you physically throughout the length of the game.

Before applying makeup, be sure to thoroughly cleanse your face. Use a gentle facial soap. You don't want to trap any dirt under the makeup you apply. Trapped dirt will cause problems with your complexion over a period of time. Men should shave to provide a clean palette with which to begin. Stubble left on the face will cause problems with shadowing and texturing. After washing and/or shaving your face, pat your skin dry with a clean towel. Apply a moisturizer to your skin prior to applying makeup. Applying moisturizer makes it easier to remove the makeup later on. The moisturizer keeps the makeup from penetrating and clinging to the pores. People with excessively oily faces should not use a moisturizer, or the makeup may not adhere to the skin and then will slide off over the length of an event.

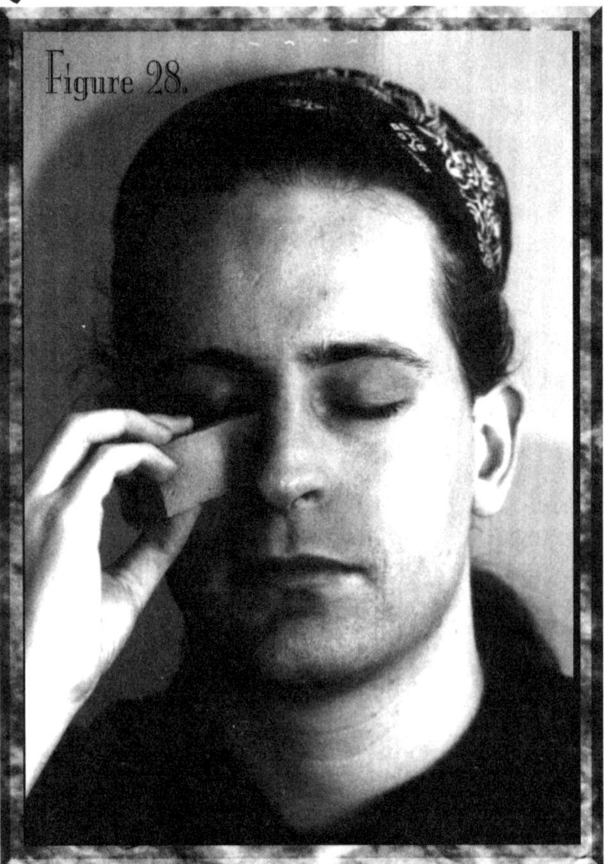

Figure 28.

Basic Makeup Application

Girl we've got work to do.
Pass me the paint and glue…
…When one knows the world is watching
One does what one must
Some minor adjustments, darling,
Not for my vanity,
But for humanity.

— Bette Midler, "Perfect Isn't Easy"

The following description is a generalized account of the steps involved with a typical makeup application. The sequence presented here is the same for almost any basic application, and should be used as a basis for all the following makeup descriptions. Practice the application of different makeup types on yourself before you attempt to make someone else up. Complicated or involved makeup applications are tedious for anyone to undergo. No one likes to be stuck in a chair for an hour or so, especially when being told to look up, or hold your head like this. Remember the person in the chair, and take the time to make sure he is comfortable.

You begin the makeup application with the base layer. In the same manner that an artist prepares a canvas for painting by applying a coat of white over it, the base prepares the face for the application of the rest of the makeup or appliances. Apply the base evenly over your face using the appropriate method for the type of base you are using. Next, begin adding shadow to the base layer you've just applied. Base makeup can make your face appear flat and

Figure 29.

one-dimensional. In order to create dimensions, you need to create shadows. Create shadows using the shadow and highlight makeup applied with a brush or sponge. Starting with the tip of the nose, place shadow lines down the sides of the nose (see *figure 28*). Make sure the lines are straight, otherwise you will end up looking like you have a broken nose. Blend the shadow lines down the side of the nose. Now, apply highlight between the shadow lines and blend it with the shadow lines. Blend the highlight up the nose and into the forehead, and down to the tip of the nose (see *figure 29*).

Now proceed to the cheek area. Place shadow lines directly below the cheekbone and blend down. You can find the cheekbone by sucking your cheeks in or making a "fish face." Place highlight above the shadow and blend up (see *figure 30*). Blend along the line where the shadow and highlight meet, so there is no "hard" color change. Making sure that your base is blended into the hairline, under the chin, and down the throat and neck to the shirt line is very important to ensure a seamless and realistic application of makeup. Also, pay attention to blending the shadow and the highlights you apply. There should be no visible lines where the makeup starts or ends, a mistake all too many women make when applying everyday street makeup. You can avoid the dreaded "pancake face" look by using a sponge and carefully blending any sharp lines. Remember, even if you are trying to produce a drastic shadow effect, your face is not etched from stone, so there should not be any sharp lines or crags in your makeup. Thick makeup is not necessary. The thicker your makeup, the more likely it will crease, cake or crack where your face moves or stretches.

From these basic steps, you can develop looks for different character types. Experiment with a variety of color tones and texture applications for the different types of characters. Garou are more swarthy, so use more rustic colors in their base application and shadowing. Cheek shadowing for Kindred should be done with gray, thinned shadow. Highlighting may not be necessary because the skin should already have a pale white base. Once you have this basic makeup application down pat, use it as a foundation upon which you can create illusions.

Basic Makeup Illusions

Wrinkles

Wrinkles should be made with the smallest, thinnest brushes you can find. Before you begin to apply wrinkles to your face, you should get to know its natural contours and tendencies toward wrinkling. Look in a mirror and squish and squint your face to wrinkle it up. Note where the wrinkles naturally occur, then relax your face. Take your thin brush and create a sharp point or edge by completely covering the brush tip with shadow makeup. Apply the makeup in thin lines along the natural wrinkle lines of your face. (*See figure 31*) The thinner the line, the more realistic the effect. A thick application will ruin the effect and look obvious. Wrinkles shouldn't jump out at you, they should seem natural and subtle. Create lip wrinkles by pursing your lips and following those contours created. Forehead wrinkles are defined by raising your eyebrows. Wrinkles are basically valleys and mountains. Shadow should be used in the valleys of the wrinkle and highlight, (*See figure 32*) should be used on the mountain top, or top of the wrinkle.

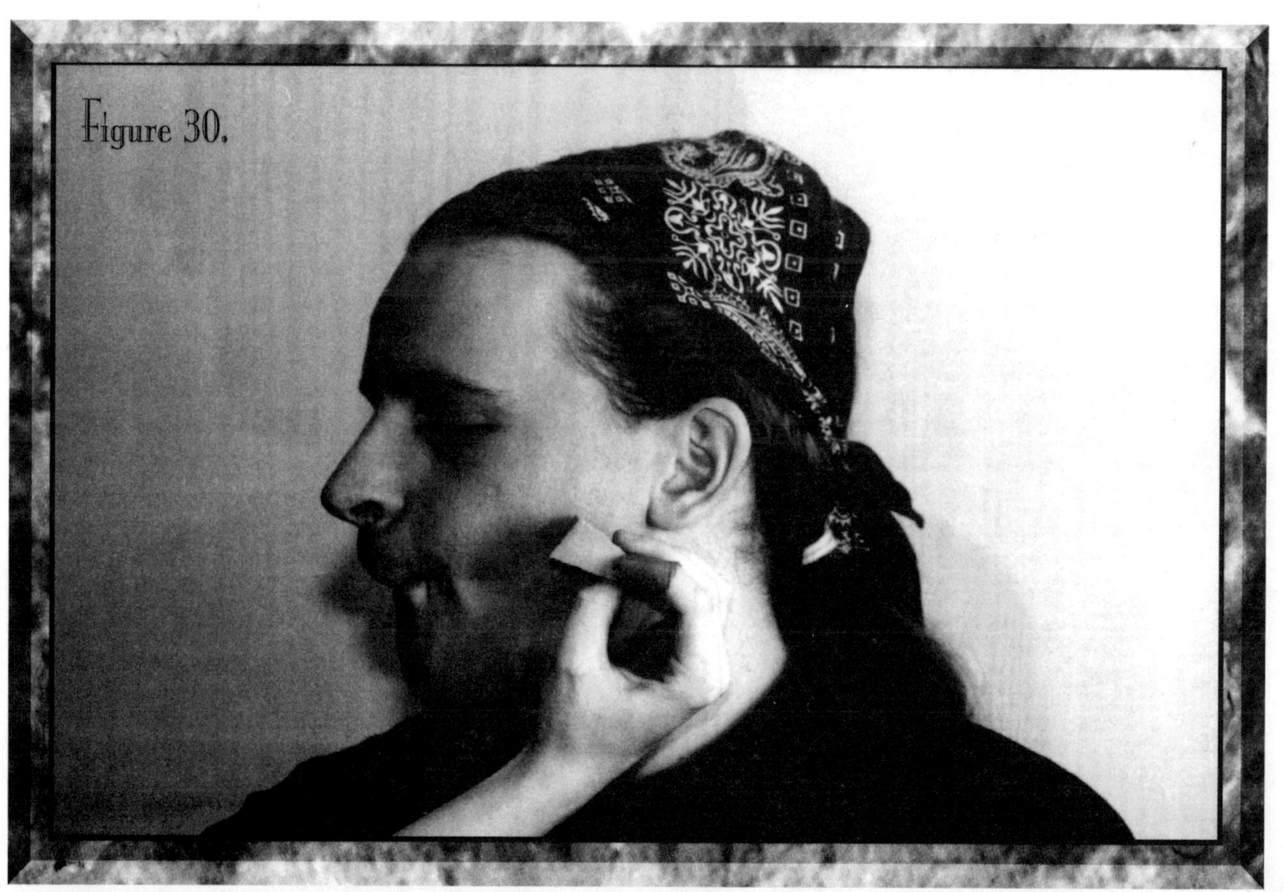

Figure 30.

Hollow Cheeks

As with wrinkles, hollows are created by following the natural tendencies and contours of your face. Suck in your checks and apply shadow along and throughout the hollows created. Use a large brush to blend the outer edges of the shadow you applied and add highlight above the cheekbone. Hollow checks should be darker under the cheekbone and slowly blended out and down.

Bags Under the Eyes

First, determine the natural location for bags under your eyes. For the best effect, bags should fill the area where they would naturally occur. For some people, determining where bags occur is relatively easy. If you are having a hard time determining where bags would occur in your face, take your fingers and feel below your eyes for the top of your cheekbone, immediately below your eyes. There should be a hollow spot. This is the area where blood naturally collects when you are tired, or have suffered a trauma. Bags are not a solid dark color. They are usually darker toward the inner corner of your face. In progressive situations, bags can be made worse and worse each night to suggest lack of sleep, failing health, or stress. Use purple shadow makeup to create bags, with a little highlight just above the shadow if you want to give the bags a puffier look; some people simply get dark circles under their eyes, while others actually get a small amount of puffiness as well (see *figure 33*).

Bruises

Bruises are very mottled in appearance and are rarely a solid color. Use a lot of purple to denote a fresh bruise. Slowly make green, then yellow more prevalent as the bruise "heals." Bruises are usually darker in the center, at the point of impact, then lighten toward the edges (see *figure 34*).

Final Touches

With all of the effects that have been described, powder is the essential last step. Powder tones down the colors and lessens the shine. It helps set the makeup and gives it a more natural appearance. Moderation is the key to all of the makeup techniques mentioned in this chapter. "Less is more" is the key to good makeup application.

Advanced Makeup Illusions

Once you have the basics of makeup mastered, you may wish to experiment with appliances or with moldable applications such as nose putty or liquid latex. It is important for you to have a good grasp of the basics before you proceed to this point. You may be quite good at molding features from morticians wax. However, if you don't know how to cover the application and make it seem a natural part of your skin, you're going to end up with a well-sculpted lump of wax, which just happens to nearly match your skin tone, on your face. Mastering the basics of shadowing, highlighting, and blending will make all your applications look believable, even on close inspection.

Figure 31.

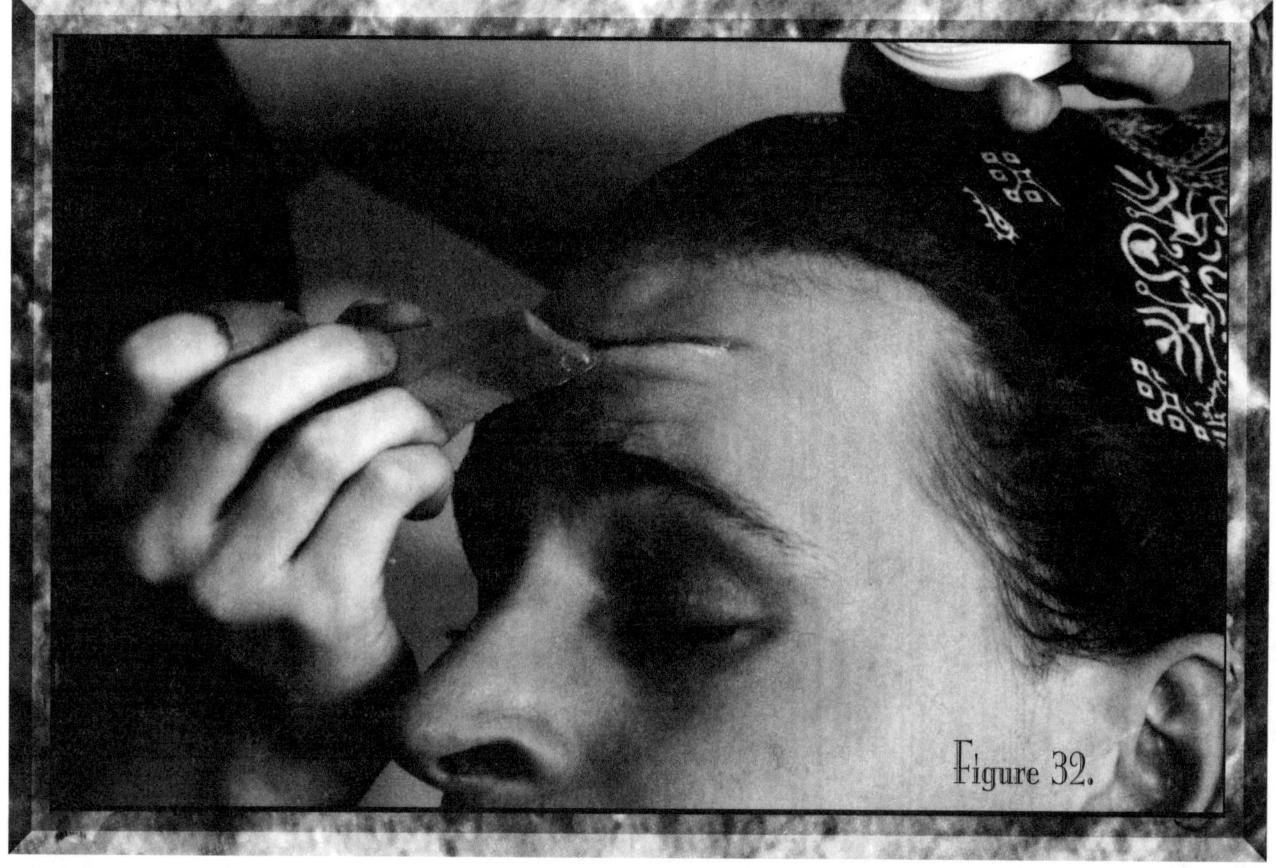

Figure 32.

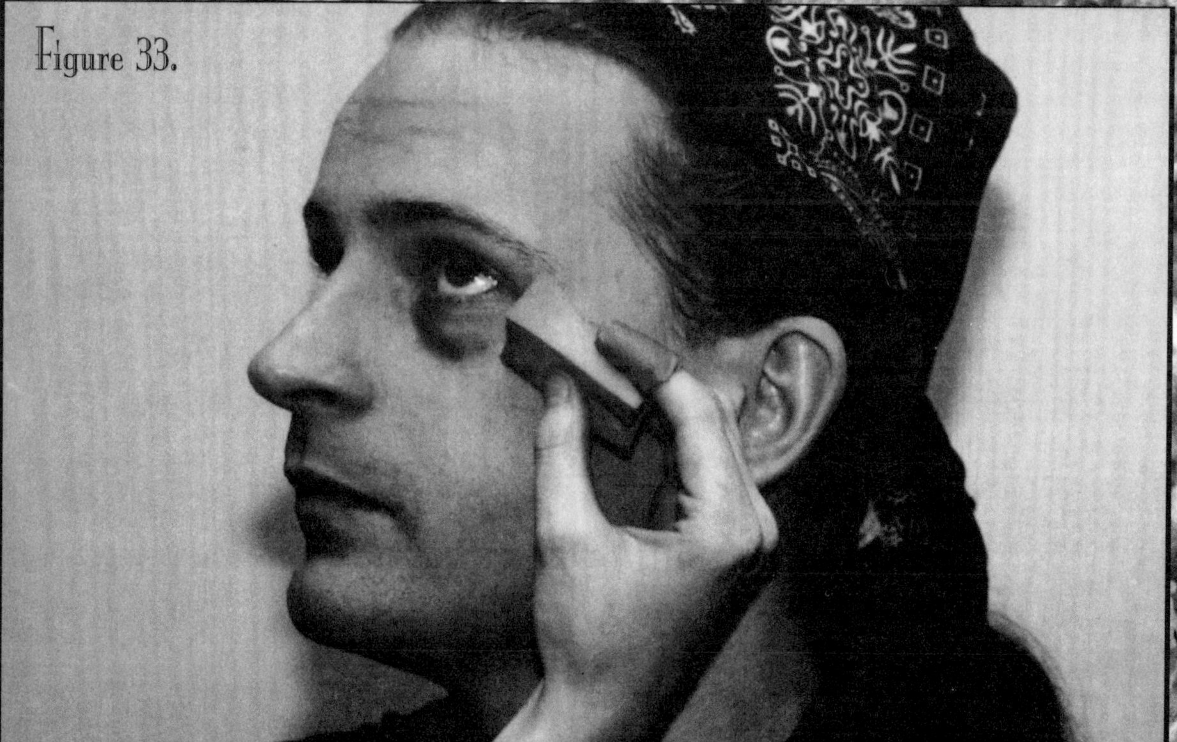

Figure 33.

Figure 34.

The following techniques will take some practice and a little time to master. Read through all the examples and determine which technique you want to experiment with first. Then, go out and purchase the supplies you need and experiment with the products to familiarize yourself with their characteristics, such as: drying time, storage, mixing, or any special handling instructions. Some people find that one application works better than another for them. It depends chiefly upon the skill and patience of the person applying the makeup, and the patience and skin type of the person being made up. You may find that people with very oily skin, or the tendency to sweat, will be limited to certain makeup techniques. The only way to determine this is to practice ahead of time and let the person run around with the makeup on for a little while. This will give you a chance to see what wear and tear does to the makeup in everyday use. This process also gives you the opportunity to practice touching up the makeup during the day. Such maintenance is something that you are going to have to do, regardless of how well you initially apply the makeup. Properly repairing any complications that arise throughout the day is a little-realized aspect to makeup that shouldn't be overlooked.

The following techniques include the use of liquid latex, mastic, spirit gum, nose putty, crepe hair and regular makeup techniques that have been mentioned earlier. We recommend using those products that require you to create all of the appliances yourself, only because many of the pre-molded appliances tend to look fake. This is because they are designed mostly for stage and film use, and not for the up-close and personal approach that a **Mind's Eye Theatre** game demands. Good effects can be achieved with pre-molded appliances, if you take the time to feather trim the edges so they "disappear" when adhered to the skin. Remember that the "less is more" approach is best followed with all of these techniques. The best effects are ones that show no lines. The appliances should not look attached, they should look as natural as possible (granted, pointed furry ears and fangs are not considered natural, but you get the idea here). You should also keep in mind that this makeup will be worn for a long period of time. If the makeup is uncomfortable after an hour, then in seven hours it will be unbearable. In such a case, you may have to go back to the drawing board and change your approach.

This section of this book cannot possibly cover all the different techniques developed over the ages for makeup. Again, as we have done in earlier chapters, we refer you to the local library to research more advanced makeup ideas. Research is a crucial part of any project you undertake. Even a woman's book on makeup and beauty can give you a better understanding of makeup application. Employees of a theatrical supply house may be able to explain a few more subtle techniques that have not been covered here. If there is a theatre in your local area, try talking to the makeup coordinator. He may let you in on a few tricks of the trade, or even recommend some courses you could take, depending on how serious you are. These are all good sources of information, but remember that none of them are designed for the up-close and personal nature of a **Mind's Eye Theatre** game, so go lightly with the makeup applications. Also keep in mind that stage applications are designed to combat the effects of bright lights on the faces of actors. At most games and conventions, the lights will not be as bright. When you are applying the makeup, try to duplicate the lighting that you will be in so that you know exactly what it will look like. Fluorescent lights make your face look one way, while 100-watt bulbs have a different effect on you. Natural sunlight will affect you differently than indirect light. The more light you will be exposed to, the more important it is to blend your makeup and use more color, and dark shadow becomes less important. The darker the room, the more you will need to focus on light and shadow, and the less on specific coloring of shadows or bruises.

Scarring

This is a relatively easy way to create realistic scaring and stitches. You will need some liquid latex, a disposable brush, a glass plate, and tissues. Brush some liquid latex onto a plate on an area about the final size you wish to make the scar. Tear some pieces of tissue and roll them up to make the line of the scar, and to make the lines of the stitches. Or, form a ring to mark the entrance wound from a bullet. Remember, do not make these lines too big or too thick, or they will look fake. Think thin; minimal marks and lines work best. You want this application to be subtle. Next, place the tissue forms on the latex you just brushed onto the plate. Make sure that this latex is completely dry (it should be clear). Once you have placed the tissue on the latex, lightly brush more latex on top of it. Make sure you do not brush more latex beyond the edges of the first layer of latex already on the plate. Let the first layer dry and apply a second layer, then a third. Once the latex has dried, brush some loose powder onto the wound (the powder you use to set your makeup). Then begin to peel the whole thing off the plate. Dust the back of the wound as well, so that it does not stick to itself. When you are ready, use spirit gum or mastic to apply the wound to your skin. Pay special attention to the edges when you apply the scar. You want a smooth transition from your own skin to the wound. If the edges have rolled up, or are not stuck down properly, it will not look right. Next, brush a thin layer of latex around the edge of the wound, to help it blend into your skin. Think thin and light as you apply the liquid latex. Once this last application of latex has been applied, you can then begin to apply your foundation makeup, like you would normally. Treat the wound as a part of your features, and apply the foundation over it. Make sure that you give the wound some color. Once again, the age of the wound will determine the intensity of the color and what color you choose. The newer the wound, the darker the colors; more red and purple. The older the wound, the lighter the colors; pink maybe a little yellow.

Add-On Features

Nose putty can be used to achieve several desired affects. These changes are not limited to the nose, but they are limited to places on the body where the skin does not move a great deal. For example, the forehead or along the tops of the knuckles are bad places, as the putty will eventually loosen itself from the skin with continued movement. Before using the putty, knead it in order to soften it. You can then begin to mold it into the shape you desire. The putty can be used to change the shape of the nose, eyebrows, cheekbones, chin and ears, or it can be used to make wounds. Some makeup artists recommend applying a little crepe hair with mastic or spirit gum to the skin where you wish to apply the putty. This acts as an anchor and helps the putty adhere to the skin. If the body part that you are applying it to is already hairy, then you may not find this necessary. You can use either makeup remover or grease to thin the putty. This is something that you will need to do around the edges of the putty so that you can blend it into your skin. As with the latex applications, you want to be careful not to make the putty fixture look fake. Be a minimalist; you only need to hint at the physical change. Once you have applied the piece of putty to the body, and have smoothed the edges out, apply your base makeup and any other makeup necessary to make the piece look real.

A wound can be created with the putty by applying a small amount onto the body. Then, apply your regular base makeup over the putty. Using a thin stick, like a blunt pencil point or the end of a brush, make a crease or depression in the putty to simulate a cut or a bullet entry wound. You can then apply fake blood for a fresh wound, or other shades of makeup depending on how old the wound is. Play with the putty and explore all the different effects you can create from your imagination. The more you practice, the better you will become.

Makeup and Character Types

So, you've mastered the basics of makeup application, and have even experimented with some advanced techniques. Now what do you do with all this information? The makeup applications that follow are guidelines for creating the illusions of the different creatures that you might portray during a **Mind's Eye Theatre** game. As with all things in this book, take the ideas that follow and experiment with them, developing a unique look for your character. Garou and Kindred offer a lot of challenges to any makeup artist and will be the two character types explored here. A look for other creatures can be developed from the ideas discussed previously.

Garou

Of all the inhabitants of the World of Darkness, Garou present the greatest challenge to the makeup artist. First, there are three major forms to deal with: Crinos, Lupus, and Homid. On top of that, there are metis, the interbred and deformed Garou, and Black Spiral Dancers, who may be physically affected as a result of being tainted with the Wyrm. Lupus form requires the most drastic makeup techniques, and wouldn't be feasible to portray in the live setting of a **Mind's Eye** story. Homid form has already been touched upon under basic makeup techniques. All you have to do is give your character a touch of bestiality, or swarthiness, to hint at your character's nature. Crinos form lends itself most well to experimenting with makeup. It is more or less the transitional stage between the two other forms, and allows you to experiment with incorporating aspects of both. True, you're not going to be able to increase your height significantly, unless you can fashion stilts that will give you the towering height of a Crinos form Garou. However, you can re-create almost every other physical aspect by combining some of the techniques described earlier and some of the new ones described below.

You can build up your facial features to give yourself a more animalistic look using some of the techniques described earlier in the chapter. Crepe hair, which is basically wool that has been dyed and braided, is very curly, so it works well for facial hair and will give any Garou a finished furry effect on the face, hands, arms and chest. To apply crepe hair, start with a clean, makeup-free surface. Applied hair will not adhere well to a made-up surface, and will most probably loosen and fall off during an event. After you've washed your face, start the application of the hair. First, un-braid the hair and pull it apart. You will want short strands about 3 inches long to start with. Using a comb, brush the hair out to help separate the strands and give the hair body. Trim one side of the hair to even it out. Only trim one edge of the tuft of hair. This is the edge that will be applied to the skin. Depending on where you want to apply the hair, you will trim the hair

Figure 35.

Figure 36.

Figure 37.

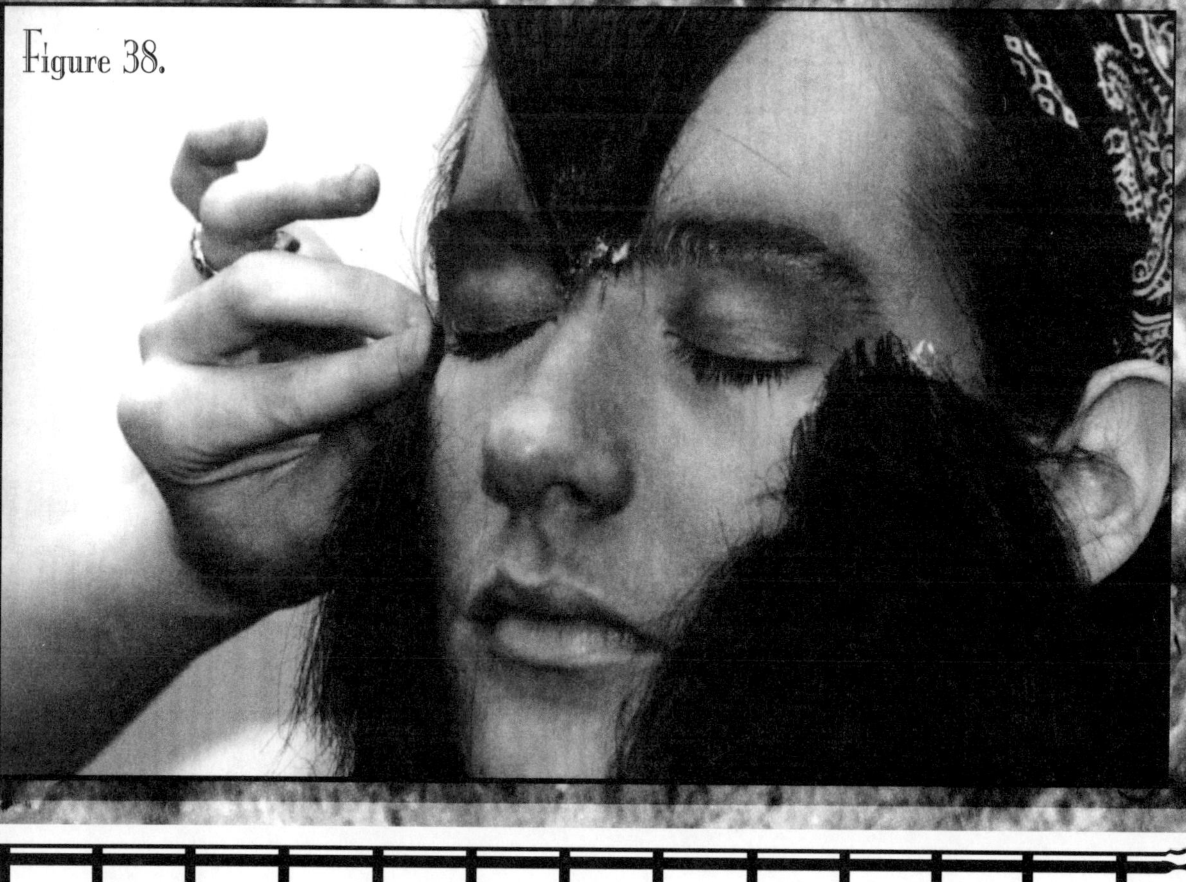

Figure 38.

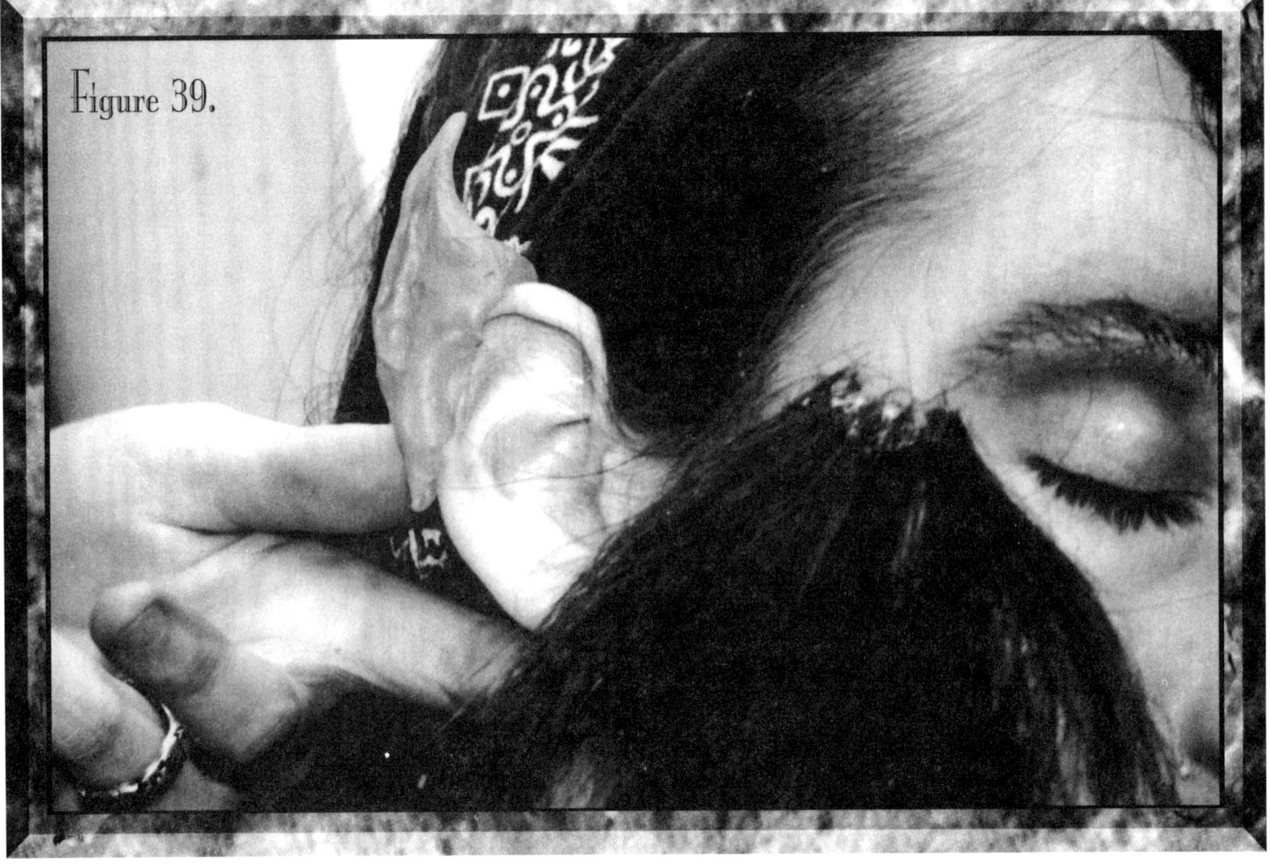
Figure 39.

Figure 40.

either straight across, or at an angle. For example, if the hair is being applied to the face, cut it at an angle so that it hangs down from the face (hair does not normally grow up). Then apply some mastic to the skin and gently press the hair into the adhesive. Layer the hair as shown in *figures 36 -38.* Start at the bottom of your application and work up to fill in necessary areas. After the hair has been applied, trim it to achieve the desired effect. When applying fake hair, it is better to start off with a shaggy look, then trim it down. It is very hard to add more hair to an application once you have finished trimming and styling the area, as it has a tendency to look added on and will ruin the illusion of real hair. In order to make the hair more realistic, choose a hair color that matches your own. A blond person is going to look very odd sprouting black hair. Of course, you can always dye your hair or wear a wig. Applying hair takes some practice and a lot of patience in order to achieve satisfactory results. An easy way around the hair application mess is to purchase pre-cut and backed hair pieces and adhere them to your skin. However, these are less convincingly real than applying crepe hair or fur. The results that you achieve by applying the hair yourself are well worth the effort.

You can apply nose putty or morticians wax to your features to make them more animalistic. Use nose putty to build up your ears and make them pointed. Fill in some of the ear ridges to change the overall shape and look of the ear. (*See figure 39*)Do not put the putty into your ear canal; use only on the upper ridges of the ear. You can build up the nose with either nose putty or morticians wax to make it appear blunter and more canine. Hair can be applied to either application in the manner described for skin application. The hair may not adhere as well to the morticians wax, and may have to be pressed into it with a small toothpick. Nose putty is something that you may want to play with before you do your first public appearance, and as with most makeup applications, practice helps you learn what works or doesn't work for you. It may be fun to have a group of your friends who are interested in makeup design get together for a makeup ideas bash, where everyone gets a chance to play with the materials and experiment with different alterations. The more you play with the products, the more you will learn about them.

Pre-molded latex applications, as mentioned earlier, offer a decent means of altering your appearance. Before applying them to your face, you must feather trim the edges. What this basically means is that you must trim the edges to a narrow edge with a sharp knife, so that the edge will not be as defined. This will help you achieve a more desirable effect, but it also requires the use of a sharp instrument. Be careful if you wish to modify your appliances in this manner. After you have trimmed the appliance to the shape you want, use a thin application of liquid latex to blend the appliance onto your features.

After you have made all the modifications to your features using applications or appliances, then go ahead and apply your makeup over them as you would your normal features. Consider the modifications that you have made to be your new features, and make them up as such. Apply a base over everything to even out the skin tone, and begin to add shadow and highlights as described under basic makeup techniques. This is where you refine the look of your character and reinforce the illusion you have created for her.

Kindred

Kindred offer up a myriad of clans, each with their own distinctive beliefs and look. The most distinctive of any are the Nosferatu and the Samedi. The appearance of the vampire has been documented in many works of literature over the years. Too often, however, people believe that just because a Kindred is undead, she must look dead. This is not necessarily true. Most Kindred feel an obligation to maintain the Masquerade, and this means they must learn to hide their differences from others. As a vampire, you might want to explore the ways in which your true nature can peek through.

Vampires are bloodless creatures that can suffuse themselves with the rosy look of life after a good feeding. However, most of the time, they are paler than the average mortal. This paleness can be achieved a number of ways. The simplest way to achieve paleness is by simply dusting your face with powder and then brushing it off. This method is very effective in creating a natural look, but sweats off easily. Another method is to use highlight makeup exclusively, applying it thinly with the fingers. The advantage of using highlight makeup is that it has staying power. It works well with any skin tone and looks very natural. Another method of achieving paleness is to use clown makeup as a base. This has even greater staying power than highlight does, but is hard to work with and is not very subtle. Clown makeup is very thick, very white and has a tendency to wipe out facial features. The trick is to use clown makeup very lightly, and use powder to set it. Make sure that you don't forget the other, exposed areas of your body when lightening your complexion. Any makeup job loses its believability, regardless of how well it's done, if you neglect to cover all the exposed parts of your body so that they match.

Kindred aren't ghosts. You don't need to look dead white. As a result of lack of blood, the natural color of the flesh reveals itself. The edges around the eye are pink and the lips are very pink in their natural state. Use pink eyeliner to achieve this look. Apply the eyeliner to both the bottom and lower portions of the eyes. Another thing to keep in mind is that the makeup application should not mask the contours of your face. If you ever have seen an albino, you will note that even though they are devoid of natural pigmentation, their flesh still has natural shadows and contours to it. Some shadowing may still be required. Apply the shadow very, very lightly to add contrast to your features.

One last method for achieving paleness is to use PAX makeup as a base. If you can find a pearlescent white or pearlescent peach color, you can play with what might be the ultimate in Kindred makeup. By applying the PAX first and then applying light layers of foundation on top of it, you can achieve a very luminescent, bloodless appearance. It will definitely take some practice to get the desired effect with this approach, and remember that PAX requires a great deal of scrubbing to remove. So, be prepared to spend some time with this technique before unveiling your final product.

The clans Nosferatu and Samedi offer many opportunities to play with advanced makeup techniques. Achieve the Nosferatu look of mottled, pockmarked skin by using a stipple sponge and lightly dabbling shadow makeup all over the face. You can also use liquid latex, brushed onto the skin and formed with the fingers, to create the effect you are looking for. Apply liquid latex in thin coats over the skin and wrinkle it up to create torn flesh. Apply it more thickly and create scars. Warts can be made by rolling a little liquid latex between your fingers to create the wart. Then, using mastic or spirit gum, apply it to your face. Apply your base makeup as before and make sure you add color to the wart, a little darker than your foundation or a little pink. Moles can be done the same way, just make them brown. If you don't want to be bothered with the 3-D effect, give yourself a mottled look by applying your base and then using a stipple sponge to apply a darker color, either a darker brown , red, or purple. Give this application more depth by using several colors and shades at once, starting with a shade closest to your base color and building from there with lighter and darker colors. When using this technique, you will want to use some yellow tones as well.

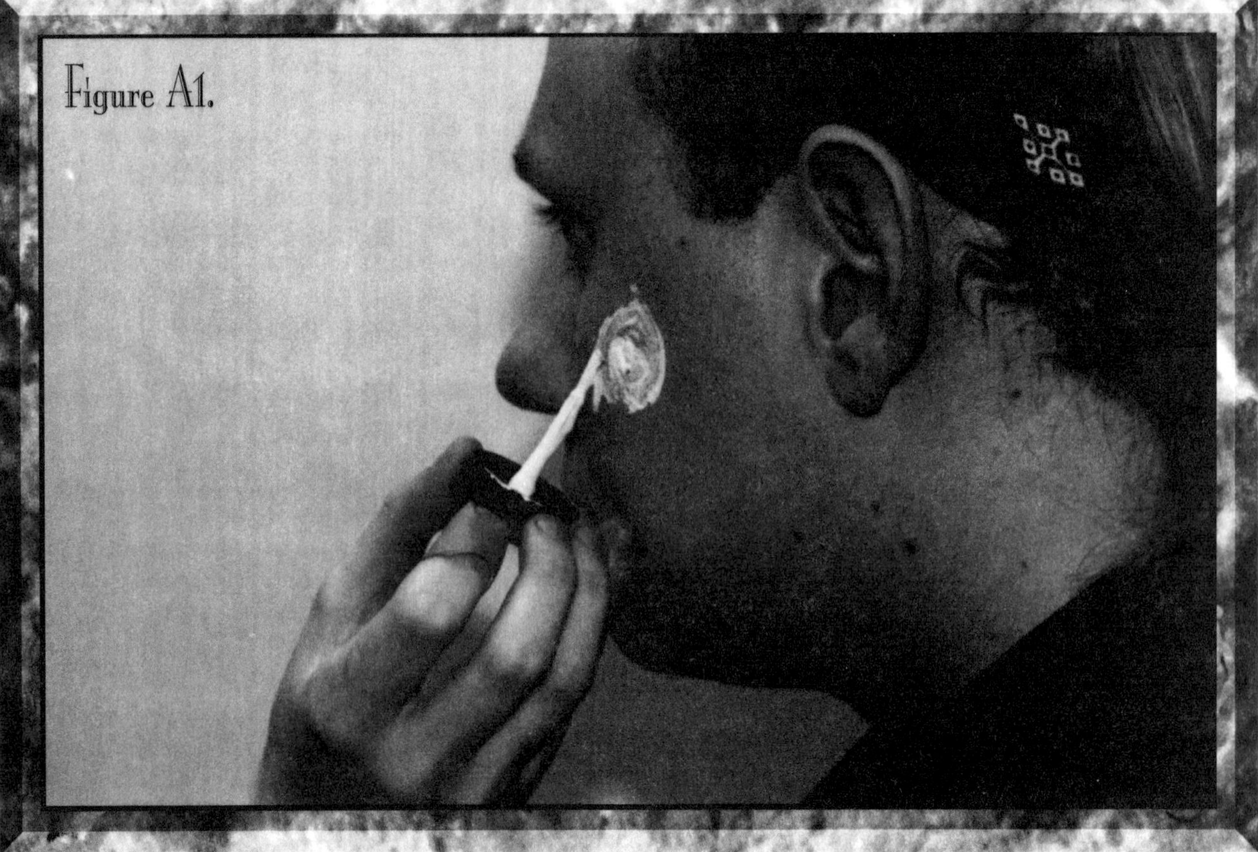
Figure A1.

You can also use nose putty, morticians wax and pre-molded appliances to alter your appearance to resemble a Nosferatu or Samedi. You're only limited by your imagination and willingness to endure tedious applications. Don't be afraid to explore some really way out ideas. Both the Nosferatu and the Samedi are known for their offensive smell. You might want to experiment with some unusual fragrances, like concentrated myrrh, or even just an extra dash of cologne, for that added level of noxiousness.

Fangs

Fangs are the most readily identifiable feature of all vampires, and some Garou may have a hint of bestiality about their canines as well. Once, the only type of fangs available to buy were the plastic ones from novelty shops. Now, with the current popularity of vampires, more and better sources of fangs have arisen. Novelty shops and theatrical supply houses now sell individual fangs that you can trim to fit and apply to lengthen your canines. Some dental technicians are now making extra money sculpting very realistic fangs. Of course, they will probably cost you an arm and a leg. However, they are worth it if you are serious about getting appliances that match your natural tooth color and fit without impeding the natural movement of your mouth and muffling your speech. All you have to do is call around to some dentists in your area to determine who could do the work for you. You can make your own fangs using moldable plastic supplied at craft stores. The plastic becomes soft when boiled and can be molded directly to your canines to form fangs before it cools. Read all directions carefully and use caution. The plastic is hot when it first comes out of the boiler, so be careful. The plastic comes in a variety of hues so you can come up with a reasonable match to your own tooth color.

The trick to fangs is subtlety. Unless it is your character's choice to have unusually long fangs, you should not feel it's necessary to have fangs that jump out and greet people when you speak to them. Remember, Kindred are trying to maintain the Masquerade. Try smaller or slimmer fangs at first, then work up to a size that you thinks conveys the idea of something being odd without being too obvious.

One Step Beyond

There are so many little things that you can do to add that extra touch to your makeup job if you have the resources. You can experiment with liquid latex to create various effects directly on your skin. Pre-molded latex appliances are available for you to use and come in a variety of shapes and designs that can be trimmed to fit your face. You can even go so far as to research the making of plaster molds and create your own facial appliances. This gives you the advantage of creating a look unique to your character that conforms to your face. The only disadvantage to this is the cost involved. Creating latex molds requires knowledge of different chemical compounds, which are not inexpensive.

Colored contacts are another way to add to the realism of your transformation. Visit an optician to purchase simple colored contacts, which enhance or change your natural color. You may have to look a little harder for special effects such as cat's eyes, solid black, glowing embers, etc. If you do find a source for these specialty lenses, make sure you get some information on their services. Some manufacturers make colored appliances for people who need to have an eyepiece manufactured to match an existing eye, and may not have experience making lenses for sighted people. It is possible to finally track down the pair of lenses you've always wanted, only to find out that they are opaque, or impair vision too much to be useful. Be sure that your supplier knows exactly what you intend to use the contacts for so they can be made properly.

Figure A2.

As stated before, smell is another area that can be explored to some degree. On stage, an actor is far away from her audience, so adding to that dimension of her character would be useless. Nosferatu and Samedi are known for their stench, which adds to the repulsiveness of their characters. This is in no way suggesting that you smear some disgusting concoction of refuse over yourself in order to become one with your character. Some things can get out of hand, and you have to keep the sensitivities of your fellow players in mind. There's no sense in grossing everyone out before the game even starts. What we suggest is that you go to a fragrance shop and ask for things that have strong, unusually pungent odors that you can use in a sachet. Don't be afraid to explain what

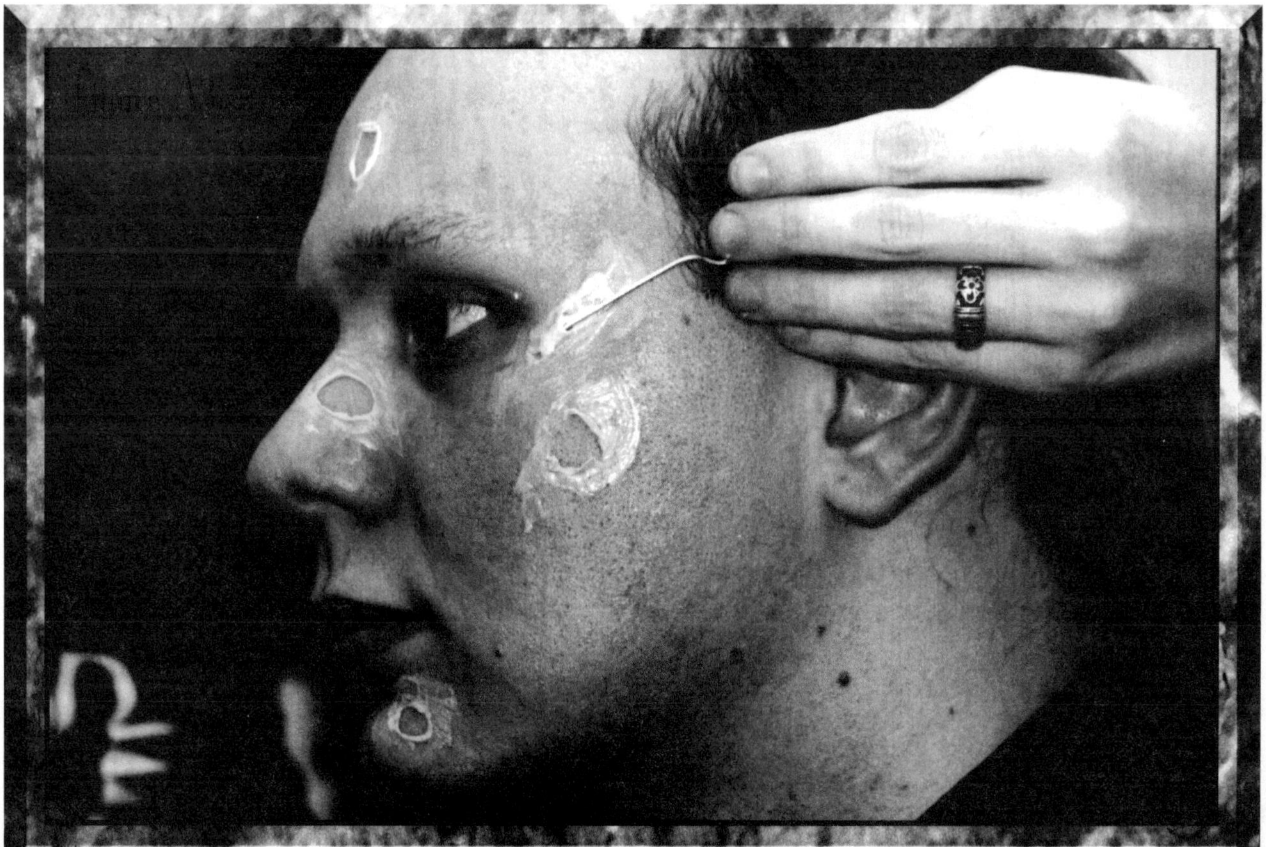

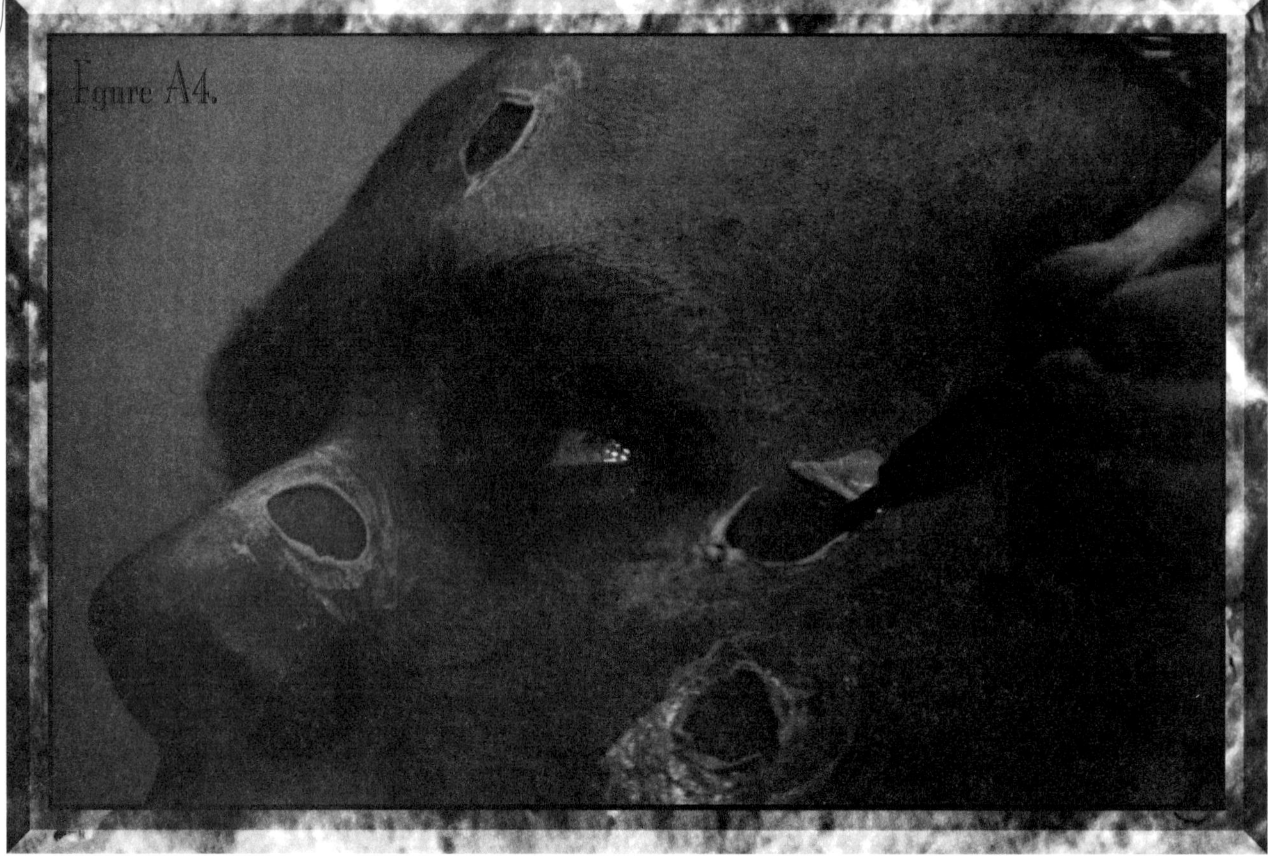

Figure A4.

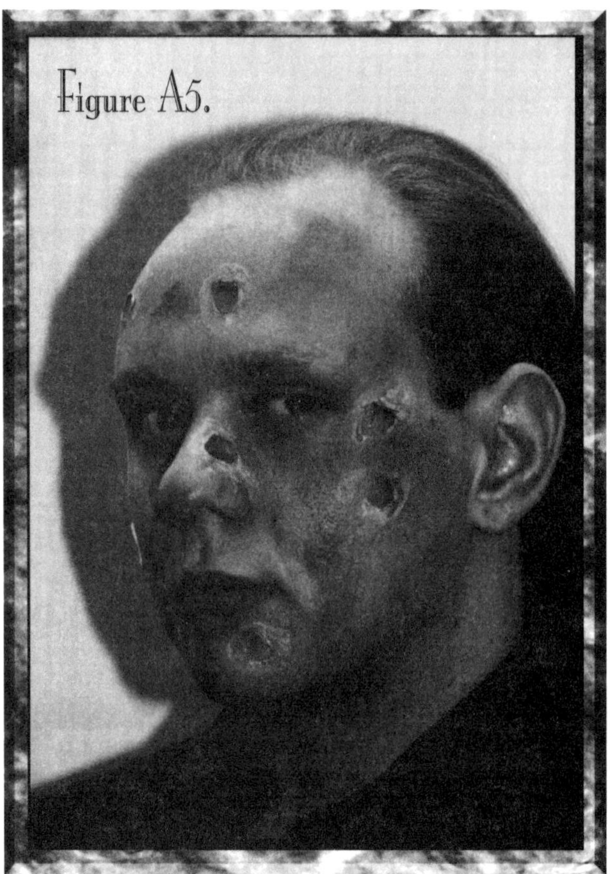

Figure A5.

you want to use the fragrance for. The advantage of using fragrances is that they are usually safe to keep around, and you can control the amount of fragrance released by keeping a little extra in an airtight container, and renewing it as needed. Remember, the odors you choose should not be overpowering.

Conclusion

Makeup allows you to add an extra dimension of reality to your character. It is one of the best ways for you to project your character's demeanor to another player in the story. The actuality of carrying on a conversation or interacting with someone so totally immersed in his adopted personae that he even looks the part, can literally drag you into the story. The player has now become a living, breathing representation of the creature he is playing. Imagine how intense a game consisting of players completely made up in character, and immersed in their characters, would be. You have to explore and play with different techniques to achieve this goal. You must strive to affect as many of the senses of those around you as possible to bring the reality of the moment home to them. You can control the senses of sight, touch and smell to influence those around you into believing in your character. There are so many little things that you can do. Take each of the ideas in this chapter and think of ways that you can expand upon it. As with everything else in this book, the most important thing is for you to have fun learning new techniques.

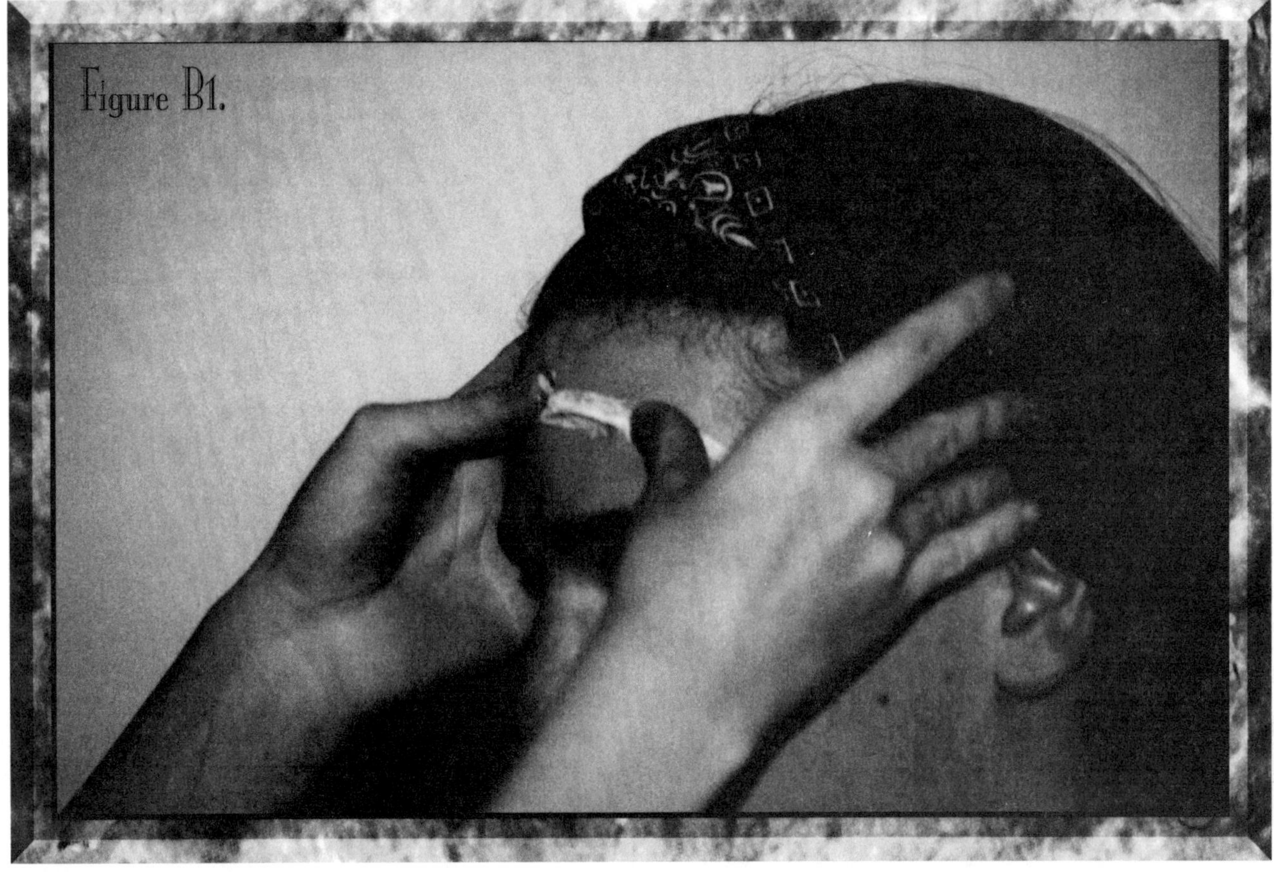

Figure B1.

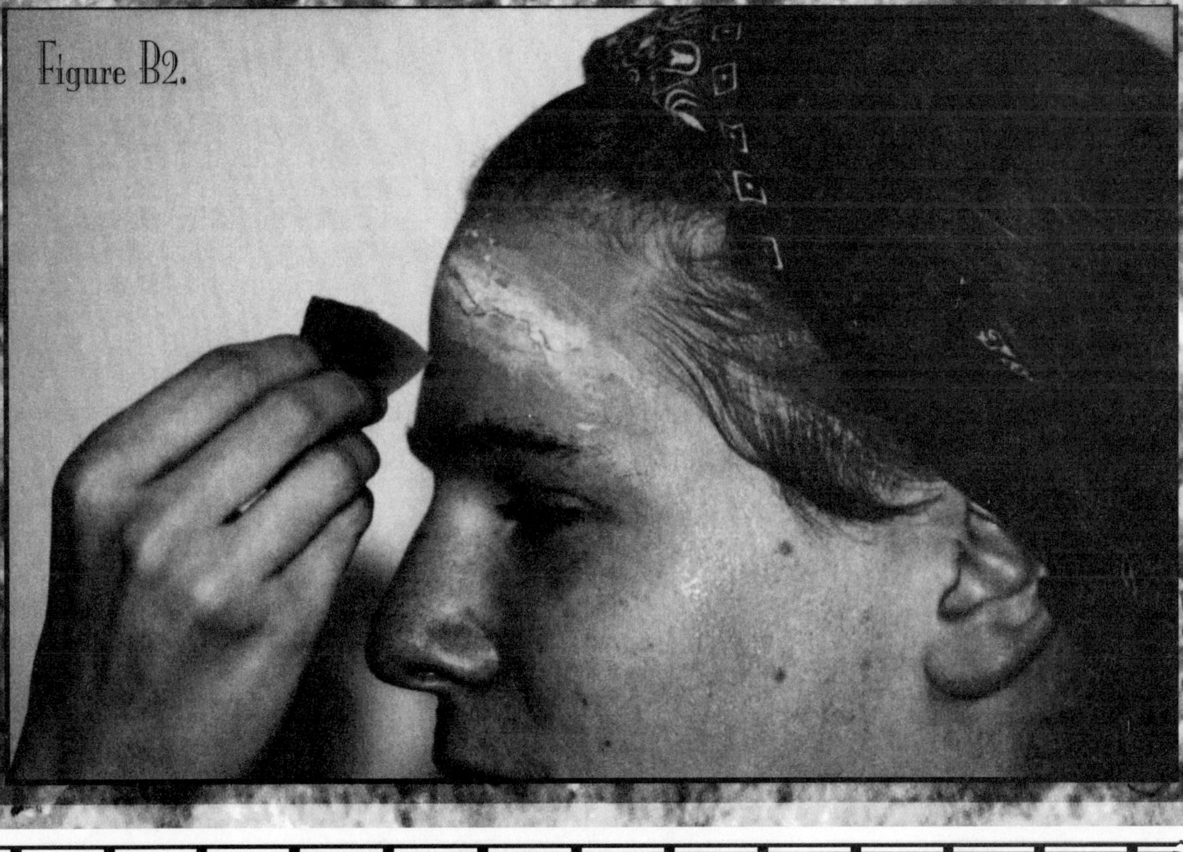

Figure B2.

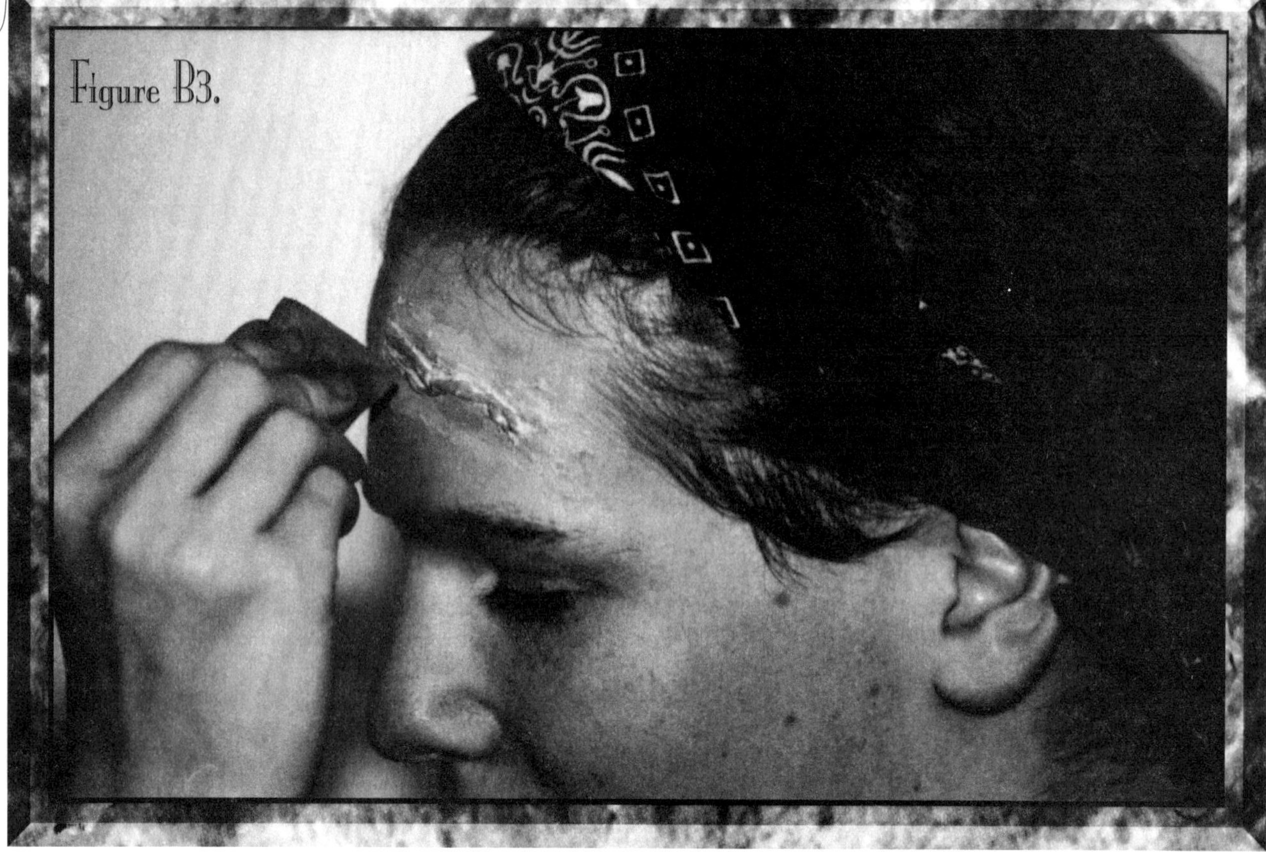

Figure B3.

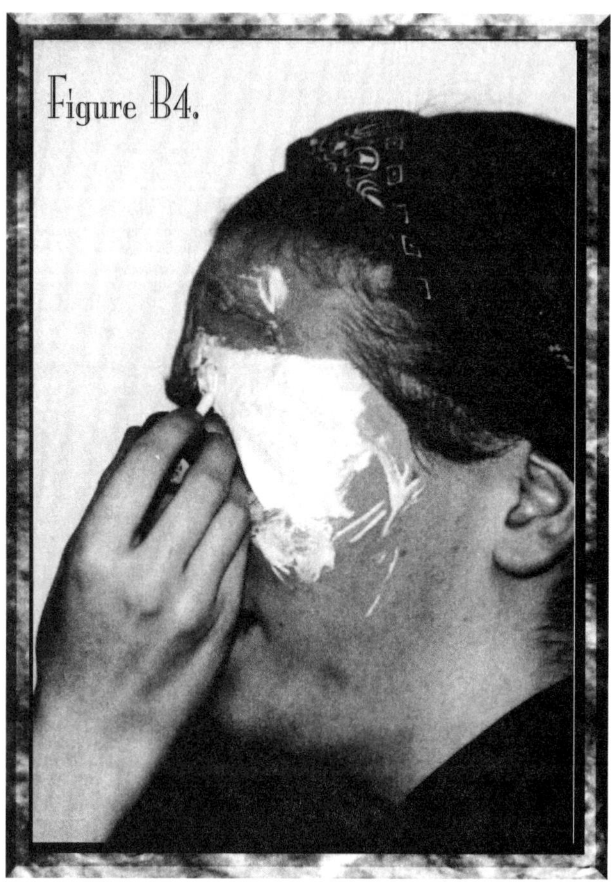

Figure B4.

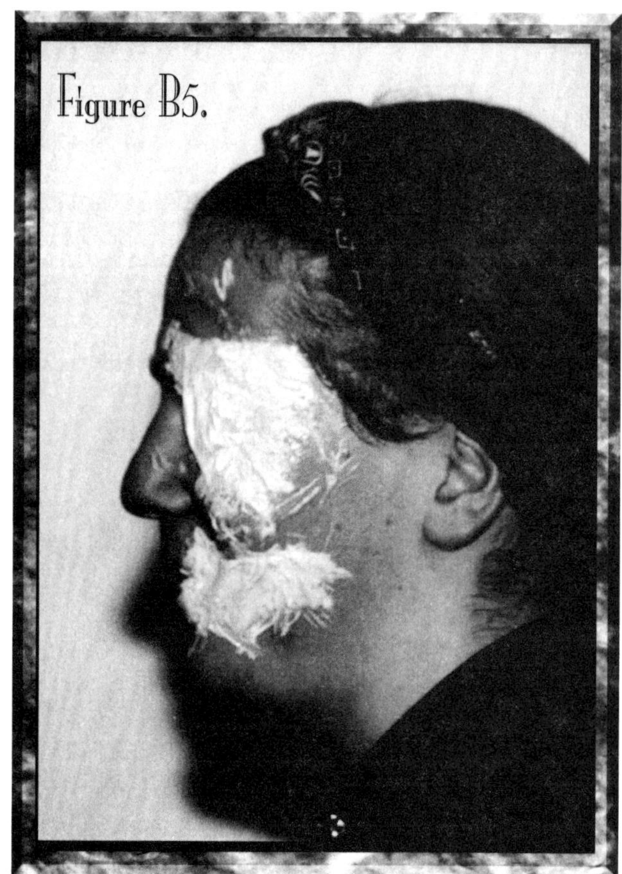

Figure B5.

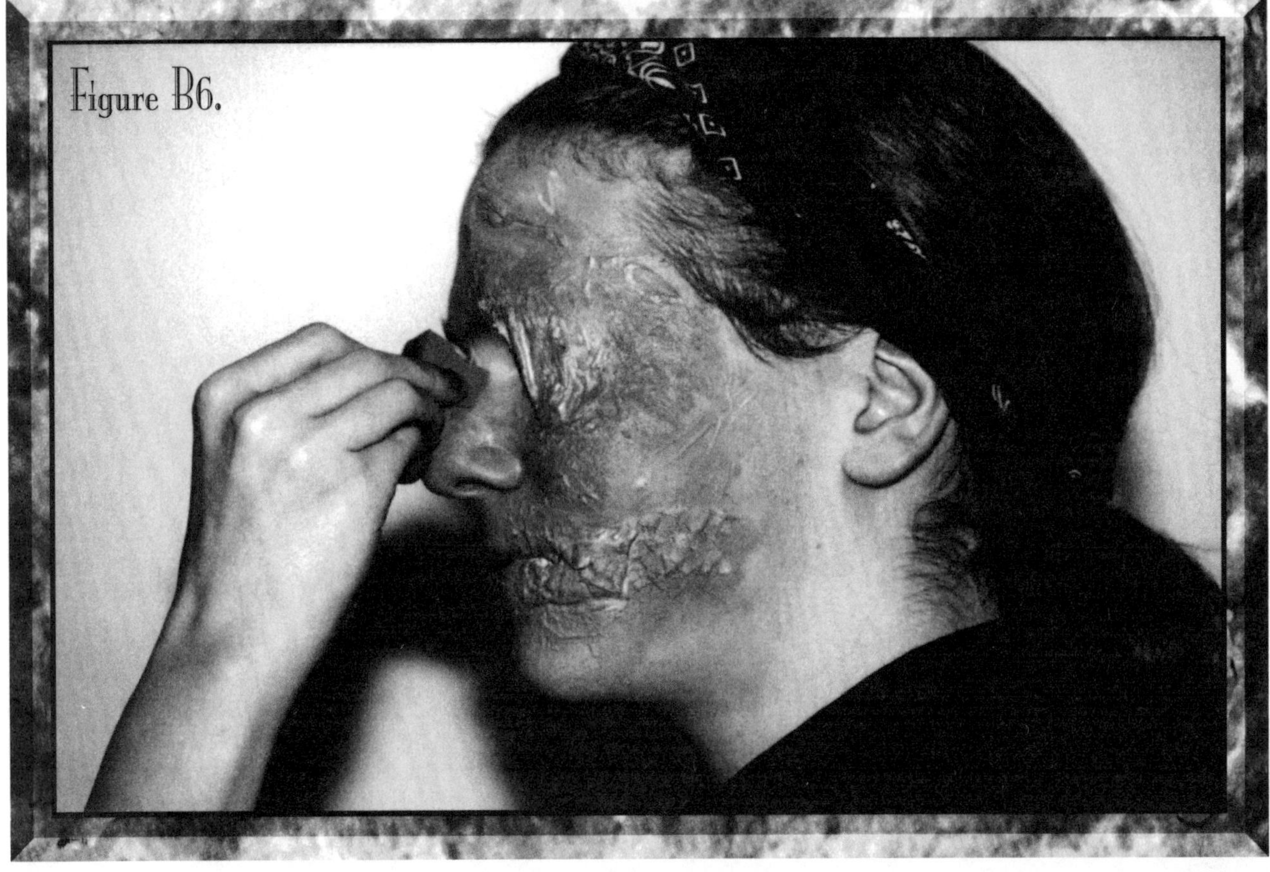

Figure B6.

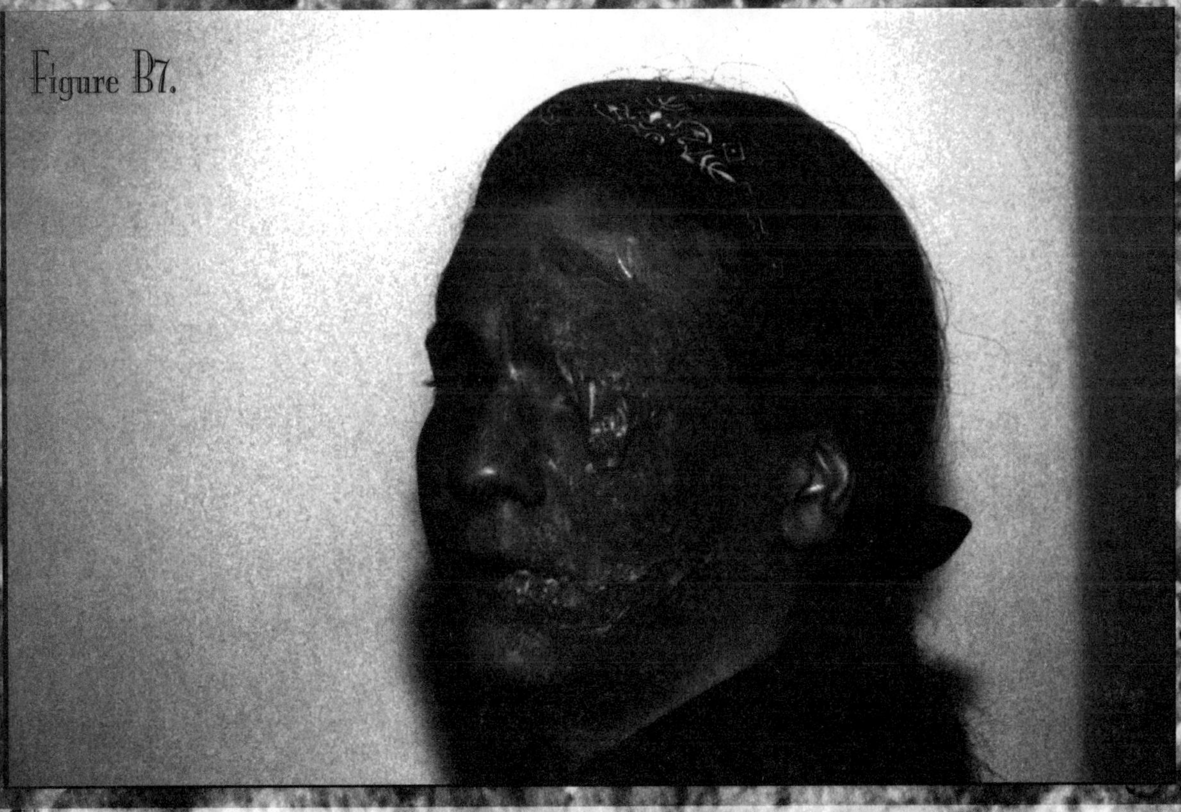

Figure B7.

0240
0286

Chapter Four: Personal Props

In this chapter, we will discuss many different techniques for designing and creating your own original props.

The Rules

Rules are not always boring and condescending. The code of conduct found in **Mind's Eye Theatre** prohibits the use of fake and real weapons, including stakes and clubs of any sort, and anything used to represent a weapon — use only your imagination. Things can get out of hand when real props are used, and can give other people the wrong impression. This rule really is for your own safety. Please keep it in mind. If you really need to play with a gun or other weapons in this game, use an item card. Within the game, it is just as effective, and the only real damage it can do is give someone a paper cut.

Of course, there is one exception to this rule. Props that resemble weapons may be used only if they are essential to the plot, and only if they are used solely by the Storyteller to visually enrich the game and are never brandished. Remember, "resemble" is the key word here. In the current state of the world, sometimes the only thing we can do to help a bad situation is to make a conscious effort not to add to it. This is one of those times. We're not asking you to gather round in a circle singing "Kumbaya," we're simply asking you to exercise a little common sense in this matter. Also, remember that anything you use to represent a weapon must look fake, even from a distance, so there are no misunderstandings or mishaps.

For example, a replica of a murder weapon, such as a knife or a stake, found at the scene of the crime, or in the suspect's possession, etc., may be used if it cannot be mistaken for the real thing. So, when creating these visual game boosters, remember that they are meant to do only that — enhance the game. These representations are for appearance only — strictly cosmetic. There are plenty of ways to represent weapons that will add to the game without being mistaken for the real thing. Item cards are the safest and simplest, and can be found in the back of this book, or you can choose to create your own by using index cards or something similar.

Sure, going to any toy store and picking out a suitable replica from the myriad of snazzy, plastic weapons is one way to go about it. If you want a physical manifestation of a gun for a game, look around for the more harmless types, such as rubber band or suction-dart guns. They are much less likely to be mistaken for, or even replaced by, a real gun. And, there's that toy company that makes all their toys, including some excellent missile shooting weapons, out of that soft-yet-rugged, foam-rubber material. We highly recommend their full range of safe projectile toys.

If you want to represent a gun, but don't have the time or budget to hunt out the right toy in a store, making one requires only very basic supplies: scissors and cardboard. Gun shapes can be cut out of a flat piece of poster board or thin cardboard. For a simple but more three-dimensional gun, all you need are two empty paper towel or toilet paper rolls, scissors, and glue or tape. One tube is used as the barrel, and the other is cut into a handle and glued on to the barrel — no mistaking this thing for a Walther PPK. To get a little more involved, make one long cut down the side of one tube, and roll it down to the size of your choice, cutting off the excess cardboard, and glue it shut (use hinged clothespins to hold it in place while the glue dries). The handle can be sized down the same way, and contoured by getting the tube damp enough to carefully mold against the inside of your fingers, or a bicycle or knife handle, as shown. This works with any thin cardboard or poster paper, provided the material you use isn't too wet or too dry, so be patient with it. Once dry (if you used up your patience on the molding part, use a hair dryer), you can paint it any way you like. There are some great new spray paints to choose from if you don't have the time or the ability to create a work of art. High-gloss metallic gold or silver spray paint can be used for the barrel, if that's the look you want, and it's usually the same price as regular-colored spray paint. If you look around in hardware or craft stores, you can find things like marbleizing and fleck-stone kits, which imitate the look of real marble or stone, to use on the handle. At around $12 to $15 a kit, they look great when used properly.

The other weapons most commonly represented in these games (as exceptions to the above rule) are stakes and knives. For the budget-conscious, making a stake or a knife out of ordinary household objects is an inexpensive option that also allows you to get more creative. Using soft materials such as paper or foam rubber is your best bet, as they are much safer than other, harder materials.

A quick mock stake can be made using any shade of brown construction paper, or even a manila folder or envelope, and scotch tape. Simply roll it into a narrow cone, tape along the seam (to avoid the risk of paper cuts), and fold or crumple the wider end into the cone. If you have a bit more time, hide the tape under the outside edge of the paper, and stuff the cone with crumpled paper to make it stronger. You can easily vary the look of the stake to suggest its origins. For instance, if a character hastily grabbed the leg of a broken chair, after following the instructions above, fold some parallel edges into the length of the cone and cut the wider end of it to get that splintered wood look. If it was snapped off a tree, or out of a pile of firewood, for example, crumple and/or paint the outside of the cone accordingly. There are all kinds of ways to create the look you want.

If you want to use something a little less flimsy than paper, foam rubber is probably elaborate enough to make a fake stake or knife, and aside from being extremely flexible, might be easier to find than you think. If $3 to $15 is more than you want to spend on foam in a craft, fabric or hobby shop, use an old seat cushion, egg carton foam, or any piece of flexible foam you can find. Some fabric stores sell scraps of foam for less than one entire slab, so ask a salesperson. You can shape it and paint it any way you like with scissors, a razor, an X-acto blade, or an electric knife. Borrow an electric knife from a friend if you can. They are very handy to have around, and can aid you in creating great-looking foam props with just a little practice, but usually cost about $20 in good hobby shops, department or cutlery stores. Keep an eye out around Mother's Day, Easter, Christmas, and back-to-school time for sales on electric knives.

Any kind of foam rubber will dissolve if you use ordinary oil-based paints on it, and some water-based paints have harmful chemicals in them that will do the same thing. The safest paint for foam rubber, or any type of foam for that matter, is the kind specially formulated for foam. You can find it in most craft or hobby stores, or save yourself a little time and ask an employee. Unless you're using the spray paint, use the tip of another scrap piece of foam rubber dipped in the color of your choice to paint your prop. Paint brushes can be used for special, smaller details or highlights, but using a scrap piece of foam is a bit quicker, and achieves the same results. Also, read the labels on the paint cans to avoid using too much, and check to see what the manufacturer suggests for application.

Again, you can vary the look of the stake depending on where it originated. For example, give a paper or foam stake the tree-branch look by first coating the entire piece in medium-brown paint (let one side of the stake dry a bit before finishing the other for less of a mess). Then, dip a wide-toothed hair pick or comb into black or dark brown paint, and drag it along the length of the "stake" in a rough line to create the shadows made by the bark of a tree. If you want the branch to look as if it's been sharpened at one end, use a lighter shade of brown paint (or just mix some dark brown with a little white), and coat the pointed end about one-fifth of the way up from the tip. Paint the center of the wide end with the same color to show where the branch was cut or broken off the tree.

For a paper knife, you might use light gray or metallic silver paper for the blade, and colored paper for the handle. Cut a piece of thin cardboard any shape you desire and either paint it (any high-gloss silver spray paint will do) or glue metallic silver paper over it. For the handle, start with an empty toilet paper roll, and depending on how big the knife in question is, slice it once down the length of the tube, and fold, mold and glue it into a square big enough to hold in your hand and decorate it the same manner as the gun handle previously mentioned. For smaller handles, use a box the size that toothbrushes come in and cut it down to the right size. Be as ornate as you like with the decoration on both the handle and the blade. Look through the cutlery or weaponry section of catalogs from any major department store for inspiration if you don't already have a design in mind. For the engraved look on either knife or gun handles, use a thin marker or a pencil, and make any pattern, picture, or original design, or photocopy a real one, actual size. Then tape or glue the paper copy to a piece of properly sized and shaped cardboard, and decorate it with anything from metallic paints to crayons.

Toy knives are also available at any toy or hobby shop. Plastic and rubber knives are now conveniently available in many shapes, sizes, colors and styles. As mentioned in the beginning of this chapter, these should only be used as props to visually enhance the game. The exception to the safety rule exists so you can physically represent something in the story, such as a murder weapon. There might be a knife lying in the gutter a few yards from the scene of a crime, or placed in a baggy as evidence for the police, but it should never be picked up by any players and waved around in a threat-

ening manner, even if it is a pink neon water pistol. So choose wisely, have fun, and bear in mind just how far your imagination can take you and the other players in your game.

Another useful prop is fake money. If the need to purchase something, such as a weapon, transportation, information, etc., arises during the course of the game, play money, in some form, is good to have around. Photocopying real money is not recommended, as it can cause confusion. Certain people, and most law enforcement officials, tend to get a little nervous when they see large amounts of what looks like money being exchanged between two individuals off in a corner at some social gathering. Make sure any play money you use is considerably larger or smaller than real money if it is any shade of green or light blue. Money borrowed from a board game is all right, but you risk some of it getting torn, spindled or mutilated, and there may be copyright laws in your way if you intend to photocopy it.

For a limited budget, one alternative is to draw up your own custom-made bills on any piece of paper and photocopy that onto colored paper. If you really want to have fun with it, put a different, interesting picture in the center of each denomination. Pick seven of your favorite cartoon or comic book characters, celebrities, authors, politicians, velvet Elvis paintings, whatever you want, and go nuts. If your artistic abilities are limited, however, any simplified representation of money on index cards, or rectangular pieces of paper, will do just as well. On the other hand, if you just want to get on with things and play a game without hauling out the crayons, play money is available at toy and hobby shops everywhere. For more affluent characters who find carrying large amounts of cash through the city streets a burden, credit cards, with space to record the current balance on them, can be made in the same way.

Personal Items

Choosing a personal item or prop for your character is a lot like picking out just the right gift for a close friend. It must visually project something about your character. Things like amulets and walking sticks are discussed here as well as in the costume section of this book, because they are as much a reflection of your character's personality as any other personal prop. For example, an ancient amulet may have a special significance to your character, placing it under the category of a personal prop. On the other hand, if your character is simply fascinated by small, shiny objects, they may be merely jewelry or part of your costume. If an embroidered patch on your jacket is a signal to other characters that you are a member of a specific gang, it can be considered a personal prop. If it's just something that was on the jacket when your character got it, it is part of your costume. Basically, any item that is significant to your character in the game, anything from an ancient goblet to a stuffed animal, is considered a personal prop.

If your character has been created for you, an item card representing personal items may be all you need to have, or all you are able to get together, depending on how much time you have before the actual game starts. Item cards can work just as well as the real thing — sometimes even better, especially if the item in question is, say, a 40-foot long bus. We're focusing on smaller versions of personal items here, as they generally are much easier to obtain and carry around with you during the course of a game. Anything too large to hold in your hands, keep in your pockets, or strap to your body in some socially acceptable way can be represented with an item card as a matter of convenience.

If you get a pre-written character in enough time, making or finding at least some of your personal props should be relatively easy. You can make an object that resembles just about any rare or unattainable object if an item card isn't enough for you. However, be sure to hold on to your item cards and personal items list, just to keep the records straight. As an odd example, a personal items list on a character sheet might consist of a red, leather, spike-heeled pump filled with multicolored candle wax from rituals past, a green Irish coffee mug from the 1925 St. Patrick's Day parade in Philadelphia, a rare commemorative Civil War spoon, and a fountain pen that was custom-made for F.D.R. These items subtly reflect that the character carrying them probably knows something about the occult, knows where to find a good party, and has had certain influential political acquaintances in her past. For a different character, these props might mean the character just likes to collect odd trinkets. If strange items were assigned to your character, and you feel an item card won't do them justice, but can't imagine where to find exotic articles of that nature, don't panic. These are really not very difficult to represent in a game. You can use a red sneaker, a travel coffee mug, a plastic spoon and a pen you borrowed from a friend, and it won't lessen your character, or your game, one bit. If your character knows what they represent, they will hold up just the same as an item card. These and any props you

use for a game are only to add to the visual reality of it all. Attach the item card to the object if there are any questions as to its authenticity.

Any personal items you have written up yourself should be thought of in the same way — they are a visual reflection of your character's personality. They are, like costumes or makeup, a way for other players to distinguish your character from the rest at first sight. Remember, most Kindred have been around long enough to develop good, or intentionally bad, taste. Chances are your character has collected at least one or two personally valuable items during all that time, like an ancient, sentimental bauble from before her Embrace, or maybe something she recently found that has some deeply rooted psychological meaning for her. It all depends on your character's own persona: her self-image, her disposition, her past and current influences in all aspects of her existence. The factors that influenced why you picked out those shoes you wore yesterday, however meaningless they may seem, are the same kind of things to think about when you decide on any personal item for your character. If you wore those shoes because they were the only matching pair you could find when you got up yesterday, this is indicative of your style. Remember, most of these characters go through the same mental processes as we do when deciding what to carry around with them night after night.

There is no need to skimp on your initial ideas because of financial reasons, either. You may only need to check your closets, attic and basement to find suitable representations. There are also many other places you can look, depending on how particular you want to get. Suppose you just can't seem to find the old relic in your attic that would add just the right touch to your character. For the best deals on vintage items, check your newspaper for a list of yard sales, and rummage through every pile of junk you can find. Antique stores are great, too, but can be pricey, and you usually can't haggle. If going from sale to sale is not something you want to deal with either, check out your local Goodwill, Salvation Army, or thrift shops and rummage through those piles of junk in the corners — you can find some of the most interesting items there. If you can't find exactly what you were looking for, pick out something similar and alter its appearance.

The following is a brief list of a few props that are commonly associated with the major clans. One or two examples are given for each clan listed, but a character may use a prop listed under a different clan if it suits her.

• **Brujah** — Any personal items these Kindred carry around with them will most likely reflect their personal strength and individuality. Even the most sensitive members of this clan are aggressive in their own way and possess the power to summon others of the clan to their side. Each individual's obsession with his own personal convictions, whether he is a philosopher or gang leader, is constantly on display. They will do anything within the boundaries of those beliefs to assure their individuality and freedom from any oppressive or conformist powers in their sights. For this reason, weaponry seems like an obvious choice for a personal prop. As you cannot wield an actual weapon in a **Mind's Eye Theatre** event, use an item card for any kind of weapon, from a pair of brass knuckles to a howitzer.

The Brujah consists of many varied individuals. Consider what your character would want or need to carry with her each night that would reflect her own diverse image. If she is an extremist in her cause, as most Brujah are, chances are she would be fully prepared to enter any setting the story threw her into.

• **Gangrel** — The Gangrel are not usually loaded down with too many personal items. Survival in nature is their main concern. They are nomadic, so they only carry what is absolutely necessary. They do not consider it necessary to live in the city, so they travel almost constantly. These are all things to consider when deciding what kind of personal item your character requires.

Camping and survival gear could be very useful to these nature-loving Kindred. A backpack or custom-made duffel bag might contain camping and hunting equipment, such as a crossbow (on an item card) to aid in slaying animals for food during a trip through the countryside. Any Army/Navy surplus store should have piles of satchels to choose from, and usually for a lot less than in a sporting goods or department store. A simple bag or backpack can be made with a few strips of material. One piece of material serves as the sack of the bag, two and a half times as long as it is wide (the dimensions, small or large, are up to you), and a few long, thin strips of material for the straps, 4 to 6 inches wide, and long enough to hang over your shoulders however you please. With the material inside out, fold it almost in half, leaving enough of a lip for a flap to close it with, and pin the edges together every 2 or 3 inches to secure the fold. Sew the bag up the

sides, either by hand or with a machine, removing the pins as you go along. Turn the bag right side out, and simply sew on the handles any way you please. The handles can be folded once lengthwise, pinned to secure the fold, sewn up, and turned inside out. You can then add pockets, snaps, Velcro, padding on the shoulder straps, symbolic patches, whatever, to the bag.

A character carrying certain kinds of traveling equipment immediately gives the impression that he is ready to pick up and move at any given time. Keep looking around in that Army/Navy surplus store near the camping gear and miscellaneous sections for those little extras that will help define your character's need to move, such as walking sticks, and hiking and rock climbing gear. Of course, you don't need to spend money on the expensive versions of these little extras. The cost, care, and practicality of something like a steel grappling hook attached to a length of professional rock climbing rope is probably more than you need to deal with at this point in your character's life. It is a lot cheaper, simpler, and certainly more sensible to have cardboard or foam rubber representations of certain items in your bag. Even if all you can come up with is a pair of ice tongs tied to your belt with a length of thick yarn, the point will be made, and you'll have saved yourself a lot of trouble and money.

• **Malkavian** — Due to the…eccentricity of Malkavians, a personal prop can be literally anything from a gold-plated candelabra to a helium-filled balloon. Here is where you can really scour the flea markets and yard sales for that odd item that will give your Malkavian character just the right *je ne sais quoi*. Be sure to check through all accessible attics, basements, closets, toy boxes, state hospitals, and trunks overflowing with miscellaneous items first. You might come across something even better at no cost.

Some Malkavians have a certain knack for picking up the strangest things during the course of a game, however, and an item card just doesn't cut it for some of these peculiar objects. For example, let's say a particularly bored Malkavian who had no one to play with, named Dr. Dead, strolled over to the Philadelphia Zoo and picked himself up an Indian elephant for a brief excursion around town. (Remember, we're talking about a game scenario here; we wouldn't want you to think that someone got bored at an event, picked up his stuff and actually went over to the zoo, picked out his favorite animal, and walked around Philly with it.) Anyway, in this case, holding a 2" x 3" item card up in the air doesn't do the elephant justice. You could find a larger piece of paper or cardboard and a pen, pencil, or marker (you can probably ask your Storyteller for some of these materials) and either write the words "INDIAN ELEPHANT" on it, or sketch a simple drawing of one on it. Either way, the other players won't have to get close enough to read the fine print on an item card to know that you have an enormous pachyderm following you around. This would make your fellow players happy, because anyone who got close enough to find out what was going on would probably find herself the victim of the prank.

• **Nosferatu** — One of these unsightly, information-hoarding sewer dwellers need only meet with another of his kind to unlock the secrets of the city. They will speak with other Kindred if they must, but have the power to easily slip away from any dangerous situations. Because of their vast knowledge of the city streets, and everything underneath them, a map of the city's power grids or plumbing systems might be useful. Anything from a street map you buy at a gas station to a fictional map drawn up by hand or printed out on a computer will suffice. Despite their warped visage, they have the power to alter their appearance with the Mask of a Thousand Faces power. Just holding your finger to your chin as a sign to other players that you have changed your appearance may not be enough anymore. You have the option of wearing a different mask every time you use this power. Party supply stores usually have a large variety of face masks for costumes of all kinds year round. Even that head shot of your favorite celebrity on the last issue of *People* magazine, or one of those great exotic faces out of a *National Geographic*, cut to fit your face, with a piece of covered elastic to hold it on to your head, is a definite reminder to the other players that you have changed your appearance.

The rats that live in the sewers can alert the Nosferatu if there is an intruder. Some of these rats have been taken in by Nosferatu and made into ghouls. Should your character require one, there is an assortment of fake rubber rats awaiting your perusal in novelty shops and toy stores. If you don't think your hard-earned money should be squandered purchasing one, even though the price is usually under $3, any old bundle of fake fur with a string for the tail will get the point across.

A Nosferatu might have a scrapbook of sorts, or a little black book to keep all of his information together. Lucky for you, the general public's recent obsession with organizational accouterments gives you an incredibly wide variety of just this kind of thing to choose from. The stationery section of a bookstore, supermarket, drugstore, office supply store, or department store will carry the little black book variety, and usually for less than a dollar. Almost any variation you can think of, all the way up to briefcase-sized organizers, complete with calculators, clocks, and a pocket for your portable phone, is available for anywhere from $5 to $95. Of course, any pocket-sized notepad and a pencil will serve the same purpose just as well, and you can probably find these lurking in the junk drawer of your home or office.

• **Toreador** — The search for, creation of, and preservation of beauty is what the Toreador are known for. The search arouses their senses. The creation stirs their souls. The preservation is what they are dedicated to. Beauty in song, on canvas, in print, on film and in thought is the one thing they need to survive, and usually the only thing that captures the focus of their attention. A wise person once said, "Take a picture, it'll last longer." It's a simple thought, and maybe a bit childish, but it is something to consider when deciding on a personal prop for a game. Still cameras can be found virtually everywhere these days, with prices ranging from $7 to well over $500. Those "disposable" cardboard cameras come in a variety of styles, and will only run you $10 or $12, maybe less. They can be found in gas stations and professional camera shops alike, and they actually take good pictures. Video cameras can also be used to create music or performance videos, and can provide you with a recording of the actual event for years to come. Many video cameras, as well as a nicer variety of still cameras, can be rented from camera shops if you don't have one or can't borrow one from a friend. Tape recorders are another handy device, and are a bit more common in most households.

Paint brushes, technical drawing pens, a tube of paint, or other tools of the trade are good objects to have sticking out of every pocket. Some Toreador might even carry a sketchbook to capture their personal version of beautiful scenes they stumble across. Unless you want to produce some of your own quality artwork on the finer, more-expensive grades of paper found at any art store, we suggest looking for some of the less-expensive pads of paper in the stationery section of any drug or toy store, or simply using typing paper. If you don't have access to fine artistic equipment, check the nearest "Everything's a $1" store for children's paint sets, sketch pads and the like.

• **Tremere** — These magical, mysterious members of vampiric society have the occult at their fingertips. Their hierarchy largely controls their actions. Tremere will call upon any number of rituals to carry out the plans dictated by this hierarchy. Your character could use different magical and ritualistic artifacts for each story, depending on what her objective is. Tremere rituals tend to steer clear of top hats and magic wands, although a small, gnarled tree branch could come in handy. They use mystical, ancient magic to manipulate those who possess things they need. You don't need to start studying up on actual ancient magic rituals to find the proper occult items, nor do you have to wander aimlessly through the aisles in Harry's Occult Shop. Anything from an amulet to a goblet will suffice. These items are only to spark the imaginations of the other players, not to actually wreak magical havoc on them. Fish through your own or your sister's jewelry box (ask first), and explore craft, sidewalk, and yard sales and flea markets for old baubles that could pass as mystical; this includes antique brooches and plastic charm bracelets alike.

A walking stick, for example, is a magical artifact that could be represented by anything from an old table leg or broomstick to a tree branch. To get the old finish, paint or bark off the stick, use sandpaper and/or wood files, and create a fresh surface. Toppers for walking sticks, such as the common metal ball, can be found in most hardware and housewares stores in the section with hooks, doorknobs, and chair glides - the little metal caps you put on the bottom of chair and table legs, which are excellent tappers for the other end of the stick. Again, search antique stores, garage sales, thrift shops and the like. Novelty shops usually stock ominous-looking plastic items, such as skulls, even after Halloween has passed. If you want a unique top for the stick, but can't find one in the aforementioned locales, go to the toy store, or look over your old toys, and consider what a little high-gloss metallic gold or silver spray paint will do to that old action figure, rubber ducky or doll's head. As you will be holding the top of the stick in your hot little hands, make sure the paint won't flake off by applying a coat or two of clear shellac or polyurethane once the paint has dried thoroughly. Another alternative is Plasti-Dip, a colored, rubbery, plastic coating normally used to coat the handles of metal tools. Following the instructions on the can, either dip the item directly into the can to give it an even coat, or use a paint brush.

If you can't figure out how to make that cool plastic skull stick to the top of your custom-made walking stick, ask around in a hobby shop or hardware store because there are all kinds of bonding adhesives on the market these days. Any hardware store employee will probably be more than willing to help you pick out the right grade of sandpaper, solvent, paint or varnish for whatever you need to do. At the risk of sounding like a craft show host, a hot glue gun really works well for gluing objects with opposing surfaces together. If you can't borrow one, a small one costs only $5 to $7, maybe less if you hunt around. The glue sticks usually run about ten cents each in hardware stores (they might be more in art or craft stores, so call around first), and now come in a variety of colors as well as the original clear glue. The only drawbacks to hot glue are that it can be pulled off smoother, non-porous surfaces, and it is prone to melting again if it is kept somewhere too hot, like the trunk of a car in July. The trick to using hot glue on porous surfaces (what the salesperson may not tell you) is to dispense a little at a time, and press the two surfaces together until the glue cools a bit. The glue comes out of the gun in a thin, tube-like line, and while the outside of the "tube" cools first, the inner core can still feel hotter than the sun if you accidentally get it on your skin, so be careful.

• **Ventrue** — Let's not forget the characters who have everything. These founders of the Camarilla seek intellectual solutions to any and all problems. For today's Ventrue, portable phones, beepers, laptop computers and other technological toys of the sort are certainly acceptable, and easily available. Thankfully, technology has invaded toy departments, where you can find realistic-looking portable phones, computers, and in some stores, even beepers. These can be expensive, so if you're on a tight budget, cut and paste a simple replica together with poster board, shoe boxes, cardboard or any appropriate materials you can get your hands on.

Beepers can be represented by a garage door opener, or any small box (no bigger than a Band-Aid box) painted the color, or colors, of your choice, with a paper clip glued to one side so you can clip it on to your clothing. If you actually want it to beep at random, find one of those novelty keychains that responds to a hand clap or a whistle with a beeping noise, and put it in the box.

For portable phones, use the handset of any recent model of phone that has a numbered keypad on it, or make one. Take a small cardboard box (about the size of a candy box) and attach an old, collapsible antenna to the top with hot glue. For one of those nifty little phones with the mouthpiece that flips down, you could attach the mouthpiece with a thumbtack that splits apart at the stem, or a separate piece of cardboard that flips up like a box top. For a sturdier model, modify a couple of plastic audio cassette cases, using a hot knife to cut the plastic, and bonding glue to attach one to the other. Hobby shops, party supply stores, and craft stores usually carry buttons, beads, or small plastic blocks with numbers on them, which you can attach to either model with any glue to make a keypad. A simple square piece of paper with a few black dots drawn on it can be used to represent the ear and mouth pieces. To get a little more involved with the cassette case model, dismantle an old phone that doesn't work anymore, use the wires to fill up the cassette cases, and attach the keypad in the appropriate place.

• **Mortals** — Human characters in these games represent people from many different ways of life. The most common types seen in story lines are police officers, FBI agents, gang members and priests. As with any Kindred character, there are innumerable personal items that any one of these distinct characters might use. The different organizations that most human characters are involved in can be compared to the different clans of the Kindred. Each group has one main objective or idea that brings them together. Regardless of how individualized each member of a group may be, each one answers to the call of their comrades. Even the loners of the world will occasionally require some assistance from the nearest helping hand.

Some of the more obvious ideas for personal items can be taken from prevalent stereotypes. Law officials such as police officers and FBI agents might carry their badges at all times, usually concealed in a wallet of some sort. Toy stores carry novelty police badges, handcuffs,

and pistols with holsters. This is not another exception to the "No Weapons" rule - what you can do is whip your item card out of your holster, should the need arise during the course of a game. Making your own law enforcement paraphernalia out of cardboard or cloth cut-outs is simple enough if you don't want to make another trip to the toy store. As for the stereotypical gang member, you may want to take another look at the ideas under **Brujah**. For specifics on priests of any faith, check with the church of your choice. The more obvious choices for a priest include a Bible and a priest's collar. Without sounding blasphemous, any book can be used to represent a real Bible if you cannot obtain one in time for the game.

BLOOD

Anyone not directly involved in playing or Storytelling in a game should be left out of the fantasy of it all as well. If you are at an event held in a place where the general public is free to stroll by, John Q. Public may call an ambulance when he sees a fellow human being walking around with blood dripping out of her mouth. Hotels, school or college campuses, convention centers and the like are places where any unsuspecting member of the general public may, as stated, become unnecessarily frightened and concerned — this would be bad. Games like these are always much more fun if there are no ambulances rushing around, or police reports to fill out. Also, unless you make your own blood with a liquid detergent base, as we will explain, you run the risk of staining anything it comes in contact with, including furniture, rugs, paper, clothing (yes, even polyester has been known to stain), and unprotected wood or concrete walls and floors. Be extra careful with home-dyed, old, or delicate fabrics, as the blood may not come out, or spot the dye. If it stains something, it will more than likely stay a distinct shade of bright red when it dries (not dark brown like real blood), so even trying to tell people it's a coffee stain won't work.

Caution is advised here for several reasons:

1. Fake blood can and will unnecessarily alarm those not involved in a game, so be careful not to "scare the straights" once you've approved its use with the Storytellers.

2. Fake blood is not always edible. If you go out and buy it at a special effects or novelty shop, be sure to read all labels on and in the package, and ask the salesperson if it is digestible, then clear its use with the Storytellers.

3. Fake blood can and will stain clothing, carpets, upholstery, etc., so test a little bit of it on any endangered surfaces to make sure it will clean up easily once you've gotten permission to use it from the Storytellers.

4. Did we mention getting approval from the Storytellers before using fake blood? If you are not a Storyteller with specific plot-related reasons to use fake blood, you must clearly get permission from a Storyteller to use it at a prearranged time and place.

Making Your Own

The fake blood you can buy in stores generally tastes okay, but you never really know if it's palatable until it's too late. Ask a salesperson at a theatrical shop which type of fake blood they recommend for your price range. It is generally sold either in powdered form, to mix with saliva or water, or in a gel-like liquid in tubes. However, making your own blood packs can be fun, economical and tasty. We have personally tested most of the following ways to make fake blood flow, as well as the various recipes. Unless you mix the blood in a plastic container that you won't mind staining, use a glass cup, jar or bowl. Clean up any messes on clothing, floors, walls, etc., as soon as possible, preferably before they dry, to avoid stains.

It is a good idea to prepare fake blood over a sink and to spread newspapers or plastic wrap over the countertop or table you'll be working on to catch any accidental spills or splashes. Remember not to wear anything of particular value. With all of the following recipes, you may have to experiment with a small amount at a time to get coloring, thickness and texture just right, so be patient. Also, there is really no need to resort to ordinary household condiments for the look of real blood. The kind of blood we're dealing with here does not emit any strong, deli-like odor, either, so unless you don't care if the wounded smell like ketchup, we offer the following suggestions for fake blood.

This first mixture is ideal if staining fabrics is a concern, but only if you're not going to get any of it in your mouth or eyes. Choose a clear liquid detergent, such as Woolite, All or any of the new translucent detergents that are "free of harmful dyes," and check to make sure that it will not cause an allergic reaction on your skin (or the skin of anyone else it will come in contact with). Next, mix it with a little bit of water until you achieve the desired thickness. Add red food coloring and either a teeny bit of blue food coloring, or chocolate syrup, to make it darker. Of course, you're risking stains if you use a lot of chocolate syrup, so add a little at a time. When adding color to darken any blood, proceed with caution, because just a few drops too many of the wrong stuff can make it look more like used motor oil than blood.

The simplest digestible mixture is vegetable oil and red food coloring. As large amounts of vegetable oil will make you feel nauseous, it is best to use this mixture in smaller vessels, like gelatin capsules. Empty gelatin capsules, which are the only method you should use to produce smaller amounts of blood from the mouth, are sold at most drug stores. Fill one half of the capsule to the top, and slide the other half down on top of it to close it. Most of these capsules start to dissolve soon after the liquid is in them, and some may not be leak-proof, so fill them as you are about to use them (generally within ten minutes). They will also dissolve with the saliva in your mouth, but you can bite down on them for immediate results.

If you'll be using more than a few small capsules of fake blood, or if the thought of a small pool of vegetable oil in your mouth makes you gag, use corn syrup with red food coloring instead. It's sweet and water soluble. The consistency is thicker as well, so add a little water to thin it out. Anything thicker than the oil-based mix is not recommended for gelatin capsules. You can use a small amount of chocolate syrup along with the red food coloring to make it darker. For a truly vile mess, scoop in some chunky style peanut butter, or even jelly. In all seriousness, it will give the blood a more coagulated, crude, this-guy-is-spilling-more-than-just-blood look. If you use jelly, however, make sure it is either strawberry or grape, and remove or crush all recognizable chunks of berries first. Experiment with different amounts of each ingredient to get the consistency, texture, and even taste, you desire. Unless you use the vegetable oil base, you can thin any of these ingredients with water. Remember to start with a small mixture, and keep track of how much of each ingredient you use so you can re-create just the right mix each time you need more.

Uses for Blood

Depending on the circumstances under which you'll be using the blood, you can carry and dispense it in a number of ways, including a blood pack, a sponge, syringe, or a bottle. Using a blood pack is one of the more commonly practiced ways to go about showing bloodshed on the body. Either cut a corner off a plastic bag, or use a good-sized square of plastic wrap, poked down between the thumb and forefinger to form a pouch. Be gentle with these while you're making them, as well as when they're finished, because they are made to burst, and they will do so if they are not handled carefully. Pour the blood in carefully, making sure not to get any on the outside of the pouch, and leaving at least 2 or 3 inches at the top edge of the plastic to close it up. To seal it, fold the top shut, put it between two pieces of tin foil, and briefly apply a hot iron to melt the plastic shut. Or, gently twist the top of the pouch, fold it over, and use a 1 or 2 inch piece of tape to seal it as shown. The idea here is to form a temporary seal so it won't be too hard to break open when you want to use it.

A blood sponge is simply an ordinary piece of sponge soaked in fake blood. Wet the sponge with water first, wring out any excess water, then let it absorb the blood. Obviously, this is only meant to soak up the non-chunky variety of blood. If you have the time, test both the oil-based blood and the corn syrup-based blood to see which works better for you in a sponge.

If you really need to be drenched in this stuff, or want to create the illusion of blood spewing forth from an open vein, a blood bottle, or a syringe, is just the thing for you. Just fill up any squeezable bottle with a spouted top, or a plastic syringe, with either the oil-based or corn syrup-based mixture. The bottle you use can be from a cleaned-out antihistamine nasal spray bottle, Elmer's glue bottle, or contact lens solution bottle, each of which come in a variety of sizes. If you look in drug stores, you can probably find an empty bottle with a spouted top for sale near the soap dishes and other plastic travel items, for about $1. That way you won't have to pay more for the contents, or wait until you've used up the last of your saline, or wash anything out, to get the bottle you need. Test the bottle with water first to see if the hole in the top of the cap is wide enough for your blood spurting needs. To widen it, use the sharp end of a compass, scissors or a nail, and insert the object slowly into the opening to get it as wide as you want. Empty plastic syringes can be found in drug stores with a wide opening at the end, not a needle. Turkey basters are another less-expensive alternative, especially if you already have one in the kitchen.

If you're outside, or somewhere that can be easily mopped up, and you really feel the need to let the crimson fountains flow, use what's called a bota bag, or, a wine sac. The least-expensive versions of these can be found at a K-Mart, Wal-Mart, Ames, or the like, in the camping goods section for $7 to $20 each, and they hold a great deal of liquid. These are not the most durable bags you can get, but they will last quite a while if you don't toss them around too much. More durable, and more expensive ones (from $10 to $50 or more) can normally be found at Renaissance festivals, large flea markets, specialty camping supply shops, and in the merchant's room at most science-fiction, comic book, fantasy or gaming conventions held throughout the country. However, you may not want to fill an expensive bota bag with fake blood and minutes later have it covered in the red stuff.

There are many different ways to conceal a blood capsule, pack, sponge, or bottle on your body. These are a few of the most common:

1. Place a capsule in a pocket on your clothing so you can pop it into your mouth at just the right time.

2. Hide the blood pack, or capsule, somewhere at the location you'll be using it, or in the pocket of a jacket or overcoat you'll wear. It must be in some little nook that nobody else will find, and where you can inconspicuously pick it up just before bursting it. Cup the blood pack loosely in your hand just as you slap it on the "injured" part of your body.

3. For a blood pack, or a blood sponge, sew a pocket just big enough for a pack to the inside of the shirt or pants, or undergarment you'll be wearing. Line the pocket with plastic wrap to keep a blood sponge in it. At the moment of injury, burst the pack by slapping it, and pull and squeeze the pocket, as if you're in pain, to get all the blood out and spread it around.

4. Tape a blood pack, bottle, or syringe to a strategic location on your skin — use first-aid tape, and shave any body hair that is in the way. Be careful not to hug or bump into anyone else while you're on your way to the scene so the pack doesn't accidentally burst before you want it to.

Chapter Five: Sets

All the world's indeed a stage.
And we are merely players
performers and portrayers.
Each another's audience
outside life's gilded cage.
— Rush, "Limelight"

All the World's a Stage

Sets are used in theatre as a means to establish the mood of a scene, to support the actors by providing them with a physical entity with which to interact, and to provide a visual background for the audience. Since players in **Mind's Eye Theatre** games are both actors and audience, sets add a great deal of depth and realism to any game.

In this chapter, we will be covering set design and construction for events run in the average home, at hotels and even outdoors. Read over all the sections on set construction because even if a certain section isn't applicable to what you are doing, there may be aspects of it that could be useful to you. If you are holding an event in a hotel, for example, and skip the section on holding an event at home, you might miss ideas you could use, or expand on. There is an immense variety of materials and tools you can choose from to re-create the ideas presented here. Experiment with different materials and building products. The more you do so, the more proficient you will become at set design and construction. Study the way buildings and objects around you are assembled, and find ways to adopt these techniques for your own creations.

By definition, sets can almost be considered props. Both are used in theatre to aid the actor by giving her something physical with which to interact. Both are utilized to add to the overall illusion intended for a scene. However, where props are portable and more personal, sets are the actual space in which the events of the plot unfold. A set can be the prince's haven, a Garou caern, or the inside of a gothic nightclub. Any area where the action takes place in or is dependent on is a set.

As a set designer, you have the option of leaving the set in the background as a mood enhancer, or making the set an integral part of what the actors are doing. Is the mountain in the background simply part of the scene, or are the actors climbing it? You must decide to what degree you want your sets to be a part of the action. In film, you may have a large budget to create or re-create specific settings in which the plot unfolds. You may even find it cheaper to pack up the whole film crew and shoot on location than it would be to re-create a scene in the studio. On stage, you have to find creative ways to relate the imagery the scene should evoke without going over budget. In a **Mind's Eye Theatre** event, the sets should provide a background as well as an interactive arena that adds to the story.

Set design, an art form in and of itself, requires knowledge of different trades and disciplines. Depending on the complexity of what you intend to make, you may find yourself learning a lot about carpentry, painting, drywall hanging, wallpapering, wiring, sculpting, drafting, plumbing, sewing, metal working, welding or any number of trades that you may have never imagined. This is why a lot of careful planning is essential when deciding to embark on building a set. It is very easy to start with simple ideas and have them grow to epic proportions as the project progresses. Control and patience are important disciplines to have. It is also a good idea to have an understanding of safe construction principles before undertaking really big projects or those that involve power tools. The sets you build may have to support the weight of people or artwork, and thus must meet basic safety requirements. If you are going to build something for your characters to interact in, or on, you must assume responsibility for their safety. As such, common sense is the most important factor in set design. Take the time to learn how to use tools safely. If you don't feel comfortable handling power equipment, get an experienced friend to help you. Never be afraid to ask for help if it will save you trouble later.

Safety

Always keep safety a priority, both for yourself and for the people who will be enjoying the scene you create. When designing and building a set, it is easy to overlook simple factors that can become dangerous — little things, like flammables (cloth, paper, etc.) located near candles, outlets, heaters, or smokers. Sure, that old lamp looks even better with that scarf draped over the top of it, and it adds just the right ambience to the room. Until, of course, the heat from the lightbulb ignites the cloth directly above it, setting fire to the lampshade and the curtain next to it. Be sure to leave a considerable distance between anything that emits heat and anything that melts, boils, or catches on fire when exposed to it. Warn your players where hazards such as candles are located, so they don't get too close and set their costumes ablaze. Also, ensure that lamps, candles, heaters, and other things that might spill, shatter, or stain are placed on a stable surface. You can't predict when accidents will happen, but you can prevent them from being too disastrous.

If you are involving larger effects such as theatrical lighting, smoke machines or large sound systems, watch out for hazardous electrical overloading. Whether you are setting up an event in someone's home or in a rented space, such as a hotel, make sure that electrical equipment you plug into an electrical outlet will not blow out a fuse somewhere in the dark recesses of the basement. Some likely culprits include:

• All computers and accessories — printers, hard drives, etc.

• Larger-than-normal stereo systems — over 55W power consumption.

• High-wattage lamps — especially any theatrical lighting.

• High-wattage electrical appliances — from hair dryers to battery chargers.

• Any electrical device with a power cord that's thicker than that of an ordinary lamp or alarm clock — approximately 1/8 inch.

If power cords are strewn across doorways or in other hazardous locations, there are several things you can do to avoid accidents. If the cords are long enough, and there is a doorway nearby, you can run them over the top of the doorway with tape or hooks, depending on how the owner of that particular doorway feels about it. Or, if it won't be damaging to the carpet or the floor, and if you get permission from the proper people, you can put them underneath the carpet or a large throw rug. If this approach is unacceptable at your location, try securing them to the rug or floor, depending on the type of carpet or flooring, with tape that is at least 2 inches wide. Use clear packing tape, which can be found at any office, hardware, housewares or drug store. Masking or duct tape is not recommended, as it can be very difficult to remove, and leaves a sticky residue on nearly every surface. Tape the entire length of the cord to the floor any place where someone might trip on it or snag their foot on it You don't want the valuable electronic item at the end of the cord to get yanked across the room. If you know the room is going to be dimly lit, or particularly smoky, or you just want to be sure your players know what they're walking over, put small pieces of brightly colored tape in a dotted line over the initial layer of tape, so it stands out more. If the floor is dark, use white tape, and if the floor is a lighter color, use fluorescent tape or anything that does not blend into the color of the floor. A prominent sign with "Caution — Power Cords Below" or "Speed Bump" written on it, hanging on a nearby wall at eye level, is another way to call extra attention to power cords in the line of traffic.

At Home

PHENOMENAL COSMIC POWER…
…iiiddy, biddy living space.
— Robin Williams, *Aladdin*

There are endless possibilities for what each scene in one specific story could look like. We will give you some ideas for a few of the more commonly created scenes at **Mind's Eye Theatre** events, which you can use and expand upon. First, we will explain how to change certain rooms of a house into a Kindred's haven, a nightclub, and city streets. We will take a room in a house that has been professionally decorated, right down to the designer light switches, and give you a few ideas on how to transform it into a haven most Kindred would look forward to crashing in at the end of the night. Then, moving to the living room, we will clear out the clutter and make way for a nightclub. We will then help you turn lifeless hallways or spare rooms into dark, mysterious city streets. Remember, if each room represents a different place in a city, it should not only look different, but should sound different through background noises or music, and even smell different by burning candles or incense. All of these elements stimulate the senses, and create a unique atmosphere for every location.

Don't worry, there is no need to repaint the walls or tear up the carpet to alter the look of a room; even drastic changes can be made without doing anything permanent. You may actually only need to make a few simple changes to a room for it to suit your needs. Keep in mind that while a room's appearance adds to the visual reality of a game, it is not entirely necessary to put your house through radical changes every time you hold an event. Be certain, however, to remove anything that you fear might get broken or is simply not appropriate to the setting.

In the Bedroom

Wyatt, it's snowing in my bedroom!

— Bill Paxton, *Weird Science*

Suppose one scene occurs in the haven of the vampire prince of the city. Start with an ordinary guest bedroom, which has a bed, a desk, a chair, a bureau, and a bookshelf, in addition to some aesthetically pleasing lithographs hanging on the walls, which cleverly match the pastel carpet, drapes, wallpaper, and floral print bedsheets. What you now have to ask yourself is, "Would a vampire prince want to come back to this room at the end of every night?" If pastels and floral prints are appropriate for her haven, all you need to do is dust and vacuum. For dignity's sake, however, we will assume that she has been around long enough to develop good taste, therefore necessitating a stronger style, or at the very least, a better class of artwork.

Many Kindred have an unbearable fear of sunlight and therefore will go to great extremes to ensure that they are protected from the sun's deadly rays. A very authentic-looking stone coffin can be made relatively easily out of foam rubber. Craft stores usually sell large chunks of foam rubber, but you should shop around to get the best prices, or find out if there is a distributor of foam rubber in your area. Certain plastics factories manufacture foam rubber in large blocks and are willing to sell scraps to the general public. Carve out a simple coffin with an electric knife, and paint it as you choose with any paint that is safe for foam. To conserve on foam and paint, make the coffin bottomless. You can then stand it up in an open doorway and pull the old disappearing vampire routine for friends and family alike.

Figure 41.

Of course, not all Kindred harbor a great fear of sunlight, so a bed would suit them just fine. In this case, think of how the character would decorate the bed. Plain white sheets can be bought fairly inexpensively and then easily dyed any color you desire. Remember, if you do opt for the coffin look, you will have to move the bed into another room for the duration of the evening.

Now, over to the bookshelf, bureau and desk. If any of these flat surfaces are piled with poorly written paperback romance novels or thrillers, or some other form of literature you feel the prince would not think fit for kindling, replace them with books that are more to her liking. You don't actually need to find original copies of ancient volumes. Libraries and schools occasionally hold public book sales where you can purchase books cheaply. Also, don't forget yard and garage sales, thrift shops, and Goodwill for bargains like "a bag of books for a buck." Some of these books may have the look you want, and others may even address some appropriately obscure topic. In addition to books, desks and other flat surfaces can be adorned with items such as unlit candles, small sculptures, relics from the vampire's lengthy past and other objects, all of which can be found around the house, or at any of the yard sale and flea market kind of places previously mentioned. Burning myrrh-scented incense gives the room the smell of death, a nice touch for any vampire's haven.

Chairs, headboards, and windows can be draped with anything from old silk scarves to novelty fish nets, again depending on how the prince would want it. If she has sealed off the windows and the cracks under the doors to keep out sunlight, simply close the blinds, or cover them over with paper or cloth. If you want a dark, ominous look for the room, buy inexpensive lengths of material to cut into strips long enough for draping (at least 6 feet long). Old sheets can be used in the same fashion, but if they aren't yours, make sure to get permission before you cut them up. You can use sheets to drape over just about anything. Don't rule out pillow cases, either; they cover windows, tables, crates and boxes quite nicely. Hold up one strip of material to the window, or headboard, to make sure the ends fall at an equal distance to the floor and that there is enough slack material hanging between those corners to form a wide "U" shape. Tie a loose knot in the strip where it reached each corner, or point, that you want to attach it to the frame (see *figure 41*). Fluff the knot by pulling it out a little and separating the gathers. Using string, straight pins and any curtain rods, nails, hooks or blinds that are already there, hang the strip by the knot, and separate the material hanging in the middle to give it more body. Fabric stores, craft stores, and any store that sells curtains carry many different hooks, complete with directions, for creatively draping windows. If the hooks or nails supporting pictures on the walls are sturdy enough, you can drape material from nail to nail in the same manner.

It is easy to create various kinds of artwork for the walls of any room. For a portrait of a dearly departed relative, cut pictures out of magazines, or even use old family photographs that are stored in a closet or attic. Create a piece of artwork yourself, if you are so inclined, or photocopy one out of an art book. Pieces of art are wonderful props to use as places to hide clues or even as clues themselves. A photograph might prove to be a picture of the person whom the characters are seeking, or a piece of art might actually be part of a riddle or puzzle.

The Living Room

No, you don't really need to fill your living room with smoke, blaring music and a fantastic light show to create the mood of a nightclub — but it would help. We've set the nightclub in the living room because it usually already contains some of the major elements of a nightclub. Many clubs, and most bars, have a television set in full view of the main room with a news or sports channel broadcasting continuously. If you tune the tube to one of the all-music channels, that takes care of the music aspect as well. If you have access to a VCR (if you own or can borrow or rent one), pop in a mixed tape of varied, suitable videos, and it will have the same effect. Or, if you don't want to be bothered, and if you don't want your players zoning out of the game to watch the latest video, put the TV on any old channel, turn down the volume, and warp the pictures on the screen by putting some foreign object in front of it. As strange as it may sound, hanging wrinkled, colored cellophane, or even just a plain white piece of paper, in front of the screen subdues any broadcast and creates a pulsating light source. We do not recommend attaching anything directly to a television screen with tape or any other adhesive because it may damage the screen. Furniture such as couches, easy chairs, and coffee tables can be left in place and covered with different fabrics or sheets to give them a different look, as well as some added protection from the elements.

Lighting

There are many ways to create different lighting effects. Since we're in your living room, we'll start with common household lamps. If you don't want to get deeply involved in constructing something as spectacular as an altar of candles or a laser light show, the easiest thing to do is to remove the lampshade and replace it with something more suitable. You can make your own custom lampshades with almost any material: cloth, paper, tinfoil, colored cellophane, or anything that reflects light or allows light to pass through. Be careful not to cover the lamp with any type of flammable material. Light fixtures can become extremely hot after long exposure.

To construct traditional style lampshades, bend two wire hangers into any shape you want (circles, rectangles, dodecahedrons, whatever); one for the top, and one — you guessed it — for the bottom. Bend a piece through the middle of the top one, with a loop in the center to hang it on the lamp like the original lamp shade, or construct a piece of separate wire that will attach it directly to the lightbulb and not heat up the top rim of the shade. Make sure it is wide enough to leave at least 2 full inches of space from the lightbulb, or it will burn through. Cut a strip of whatever material you want to use to make the lampshade and then decorate it any way you like. Once this is completed, then attach it to the two wire frames. For a less-than-traditional style lampshade, take three or four wire hangers, attach the hooks to a top frame, keeping the triangular part the same, and hang several different articles of clothing, or anything else light enough for a wire hanger to hold up, on each one. Or, attach a length of cloth around a top frame long enough to cover the rest of the lamp to its base, or even cover the table it is sitting on. Anything that goes along with the chosen theme for the room, or stands out on its own while providing different lighting in the room, will effectively create a new and different atmosphere in any room.

The effects we've discussed are relatively simple, because there are limits as to how far you can go with lighting effects in the average home. Christmas lights and party lanterns (which are basically the same thing) are manufactured into some of the most interesting things, from ordinary blinking bulbs to plastic vegetables and animals. Scour novelty magazines and shops to find just the right ones. Keep an eye out for them in party supply stores and anywhere else party goods are sold. Any odd light source will add to the atmosphere of the room. Take a stroll through the lightbulb section of a major home supply store. Any colored bulb will visually draw the corresponding color out of anything it shines on, giving it a grayish hue, and therefore will aid in changing the look of any room.

Music

Music makes the world go round, right? So it can safely be presumed that if you don't have a sound system of some kind within the confines of your own house, whether it is a clock radio or a state-of-the-art sound system, you should at least be able to ask one of your players to bring along his boom box for the game. If the only thing available is a Walkman, you can buy extension speakers at most music, electronics or stereo supply stores from around $10 to $50, and they will hook right up to anything with a headphone jack. You won't get glass-shattering sound out of most of these smaller speakers, but they'll do just fine for a less-boisterous club or bar. Plus, as with all detachable speakers, you can hide them in inconspicuous places throughout the room to add to the ambience. If you really don't want anyone to think about where the music is coming from, carefully conceal the speaker wires, and hide each speaker in a dark, unnoticeable place like under that end table in the corner of the room, or behind the sofa (with the speaker facing up or out, of course), and toss a black cloth over it. The speaker wire, and any special jacks you need to hook everything together can be found at most music, electronics or stereo supply stores. Ask a salesperson for help in determining which wires are right for you. Let them know that you need to keep costs down for your project, and they will probably not try to sell you an entire entertainment center. If you decide to opt for a louder nightclub, keep your neighbors in mind and continue reading, because we will be discussing how to put these elements together for a larger club scene later in this chapter.

From Hallways To City Streets

The rhythm of the city,
Boy, once you get it down,
You can own this town.
You can wear the crown.

— Billy Joel, "Why Should I Worry?"

Any room in the house can serve as a town square or an intersection which includes city streets. We have chosen to deck the hallways because they are physically similar to city streets, with each doorway marking the passageway to another street or building. That little chair and table set up for the telephone in the hallway can represent a phone booth. The pictures on the wall can be turned into billboards or condemned building notices through the use of item cards. Statues or sculptures, if they are not exceptionally valuable, can be placed on top of sturdy pedestals or tables as landmarks. Try to remove home furnishings that would not normally be seen in the middle of a city street, such as throw rugs or an expensive vase on a decorative display table. However, there is no need to pull up the wall-to-wall carpeting or paint bricks and graffiti over the wallpapering. Your players are coming to your event with their imaginations fully prepared to ignore the fact that their city street has shag carpeting and a dropped ceiling overhead. Your assignment is to get them to stroll down a city street and take notice of what's there for their character, not just pass through a lifeless corridor on their way to a more interesting place.

Lighting can have a very dramatic effect on this transformation. To minimize the light seeping in from other rooms, hang sheer curtains in offending doorways to cut down on direct light without completely blocking the view of the other side. If you want to hang solid curtains, consider cutting slits or shapes in the curtain so there is some way to see what, or whom, you're about to walk into. Tension rods (curtain rods with rubber or plastic ends that are made to hang by themselves, without nails or hooks, in doorways) are available at a reasonable price anywhere you can buy curtains or housewares, and at most hardware stores. To emulate streetlights, hang a few flashlights (stock up on batteries) or a couple of those small clip lamps above doorways, or even use oil lamps hung on the wall (if you have any that are suitable for hanging), or set on top of a stable stool or table. If you don't have many small tables hanging around, use strong cardboard boxes, painted over or draped in the fabric of your choice. Since these are liable to wobble or be accidentally kicked across the hall, put a cinder block or a stack of heavy books in the bottom for weight. Depending on what part of the year your story is set in, you could even hang the appropriate holiday decorations on doors, windows or between the street lamps. Larger party goods stores usually have decorations for every major holiday on the shelves, or in stock, year round.

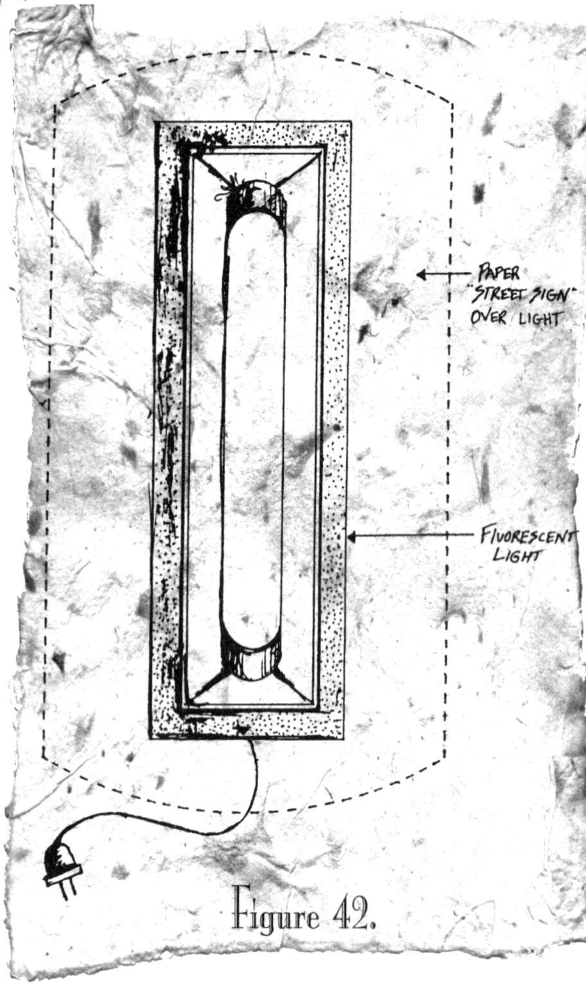

Figure 42.

Make storefront signs or house numbers, depending on the type of neighborhood it is, for the top or side of each doorway using anything from an item card to cardboard cut-outs. To make an illuminated storefront sign, use a fluorescent lightbulb in one of those under-the-cabinet countertop lights that doesn't emit a lot of heat, and draw up a design for the name of the store or business by hand or on a computer, on a white piece of regular paper, and hang it in front of the light as shown [paper taped to wall on either side of the light and on the top] (see *figure 42*). To make a light box sign, cut the bottom of a shoe box out for the sign to be taped or stapled into, or make the sides out of poster board and shape it any way you want, and hang that in front of the light. Just make sure that whatever light source you use does not put out too much heat, so there is no risk of burning the paper or the box.

If the street you are creating has trees planted in the sidewalk and you've got the room, borrow a plant from another part of the house or a friend and move it into the hallway. If you don't have access to foliage, some nurseries and larger florist shops rent large potted plants for a day or two for special occasions. Check your yellow pages under "Plants" to locate appropriate sources.

Take a walk down any street that closely resembles the one you have in mind for your hallway (during a safe time of day if you're envisioning a back alley), and note any little details you can re-create. Or, if you are located close to the city your game is set in, take a few friends with you for a day in town, and select a particular section to re-create as specifically as you can. If there is nothing quite like a bustling urban street anywhere close to where you live, rent a movie that is set in the city your game is set in (at least one movie has been made or set in every major city in America, even if it was 40 years ago), and pay special attention to every little detail the cinematographer recorded. Store windows can be represented with pictures drawn or painted on large sheets of newsprint, or on even larger sheets of paper purchased from rolls in any art store. It need not look like an exact replica of the store window you saw at Zipperheads on South Street last Tuesday. If you have the time and the talent to get that elaborate, go for it, but any painting or drawing detailed enough to be recognized as a store window will do. Anything you can do to make an area look different, or remotely interesting, will help to make the event that much more realistic to your players.

On Location

Major hotel chains usually have a number of banquet or conference rooms for rent. Plan to scout different locations in person, and well in advance, to assure you will get the most for your money and to scope out the possibilities for bringing in your sets. Depending on the size of your game, and your budget, you may also want to look into other rentable spaces, such as banquet and conference halls at your local fire halls, lodges, etc. (under "Banquet Facilities" in the yellow pages). Most of the business people you will deal with to rent these spaces have most likely seen a few strange conventions roll through town, but you will still need to explain to them exactly what these games are like, and make your players aware of the rules and regulations of the place you are renting. The owners want to be sure that their property will be protected from harm, and you want to be sure your players are, also. Explain the basic safety rules of the game to the people you are renting from as well. It will put them at ease to know that there will be no weapons, no stunts, and no harmful or threatening physical contact from any of your players. Also make them fully aware of the type of sets you will be bringing in. Most hotels and banquet facilities will let you borrow a ladder, or certain smaller office supplies, if they believe you know what you're doing with them and can be assured that you will return them in the same condition they were given to you.

The Nightclub

Can you hear this?
Do you want me to turn it… up?
— Judd Nelson, *The Breakfast Club*

Okay, now we can talk about large sound systems because there are no neighbors to wake when you have permission to put together a nightclub in a hotel. However, you must comply with any regulations imposed by the owners and staff of hotels and other rented spaces previously discussed. Riots have started over lesser things than a disc jockey being forced to turn down the music, so please follow any arrangements you have made with the owners regarding volume and time constraints. In most hotels, college campuses, fire halls, and lodge halls, you will be able to bring in bands and/or disc jockeys with little or no problem. If you don't have enough in your budget to call in the professionals, you can always put together a sound system with what you or friends have at home. Whatever you can't get through a friend of a friend of a friend, you may be able to rent from musical instrument dealers who rent equipment, or rental agencies (look under "Music" and "Rental" in your yellow pages).

A mixture of dry ice and water will produce an eerie fog for your nightclub, but there are certain safety tips you must follow when using it. First, do not touch dry ice with your hands, or let it come in contact with your skin. Use metal tongs in conjunction with protective gloves to handle it. Second, do not inhale anything emitted from the ice and water mixture. It is carbon dioxide, and it must not be breathed into your lungs. Make sure your players are aware of this fact, lest they decide to kneel down with a cloth over their head and breathe in the vapors. Third, do not put it in any plastic because it will crack the container. Use a cheap Styrofoam cooler or container, found anywhere party goods and picnic coolers are sold for under $2. Experiment with a small amount of dry ice at a time to see how much you should use, and how long it will last. If you have the budget for it, you can rent a smoke machine from a theatrical supply store that rents equipment (that's right, they're under "Theatrical Supplies" in the yellow pages), but be careful, as many of these leave a residue anywhere the smoke travels.

Large-Scale Sets

When constructing any setting, there are several basic considerations to remember. The first of these is strength. Will the object you build have sufficient strength and durability to perform in the manner you intended for it? How about in a manner you didn't quite intend? Keep in mind that things are often used in a manner they were not originally designed for. Will people be able to gain access to the setting? If you want to keep people off the set pieces, plan on making or renting rope stands similar to those used in banks and movie theatres. These give the piece a museum quality, adding to the illusion of great age. As an example of how things can get out of hand, when Disneyland first opened, the trademarked Cinderella's Castle, though massive, was not structurally sound on the upper levels because that part was meant only for display. Disney's security guards feared for their own lives when they had to remove a large number of overly enthusiastic spectators who had found their way up there to take pictures. If you don't want anyone touching or misusing your props or sets, make that perfectly clear to everyone, twice.

The second consideration is weight. Not only does the object have to be strong and durable, it should be light enough to be carried by a small number of people. In other words, if you cannot avoid making the object heavy, be sure you have an ample supply of people who will definitely be available on the days it needs to be moved to and from locations and storage spaces. Keep the people who will be carrying the pieces in mind, as well as their own personal physical limits. If you can only find two people to carry a piece that you know takes three to carry, don't risk getting hurt. For any event, it can be safely assumed that there will be at least a few players wandering around before the game. From our own experiences, we can tell you that they will usually be more than willing to help you set up for an event, and should be very cooperative in not revealing information you don't want everyone else to know before the game. If they can't help you, chances are they know someone who can.

Don't forget to take into account the size of the vehicle you will be using to transport the piece to the site, as well as ceiling heights, door widths, elevator and stairwell dimensions, and any other barriers that you may encounter. The general rule is that if any one piece is bigger than you are, you are probably going to have some problems lugging it around. This is why it is important to design your set in smaller pieces that can be assembled at an event location before the game starts. Design your sets with wing-nuts and other high-strength fasteners that can be easily undone. A good set design will take into consideration safety, strength, durability, weight, and portability. To be fully prepared in the event of an emergency, bring along the remainder of the paint, some brushes, a drop cloth, and anything else you think might be helpful in touching up accidental scrapes or scars on the set pieces you built.

The following projects will test your skills as a designer and a builder. You will be required to come up with innovative solutions to construction problems. A project like this will try your patience, develop a spirit of cooperation among those who build it, and help you to understand the true meaning of the words "limited budget." The materials used for some of the pieces that follow can only be bought at contractor's supply stores and can be costly. Most of the materials required can be found moderately priced at hardware stores. When you are calling around to hardware stores about the availability and cost of materials, try telling the salesperson that you are working on a set for a local theatre, and that you are interested in keeping costs down (it is easier than explaining the specifics of these events to them). Often, the salesperson will give you less-expensive alternatives for the materials you need. Call around to as many different stores as you can find and get an estimate on cost before making any solid, non-refundable plans for any project. You don't want to get everyone enthused about a great set idea you have, only to find out that it costs more than your budget will allow. So, let's grab our saws and wallets, and start building.

The Monolith

The monolith was part of a set we helped create and construct for the nightclub of a large event. Legend says that it was found in the deep desert by nomads who stumbled upon the ruins of an ancient city. Who carved the engravings on it, and how it came to reside in a Kindred nightclub, are still secrets. How it was actually made is a tale of seven nights of exhaustive work facing a very tight deadline, and will be explained in detail herein. It may not be as exciting a tale as the plots to come, but in the end it will be just as informative.

Space

You will need a large space, preferably the size of a garage, in which to construct the monolith. The individual pieces of the monolith make it hard to negotiate small stairways, and the taller pieces will not fit upright in rooms with ceilings 8 feet high or less. Make sure that you will be able to remove the completed monolith from the construction area.

Materials Required

Legend

(HW) - *Can be found at hardware store*

(CS) - *Can be found at contractor's supply house*

- Approximately eight 2" x 3" (Not 2" x 4", unless you want to pay more) by 8' pieces low-grade framing lumber, fairly straight. (HW)
- Four sheets 1-1/2" thick 4' x 8' extruded polystyrene foam insulation board. Do not use expanded polystyrene insulation board composed of small beads like those found in bean bag chairs. You need a smooth surface to engrave your designs in. (CS)
- A box of 3" finishing nails (HW)
- A box of 3" regular framing nails (HW)
- One gallon of flat black latex paint (HW)
- One quart of burnt orange or rust-colored flat latex paint (HW)
- One pint of dark yellow flat latex paint (HW)
- One can of flat black spray paint designed to be used with plastic foam. This can be found at any craft store.
- A large drop cloth, or several layers of newspaper, to protect the floors.
- One packet of paint texturizer (HW)
- Paint roller (HW)
- 4" brush (any cheap one will do) (HW)
- 1" brush (HW)
- Four or more tubes of construction adhesive (HW)

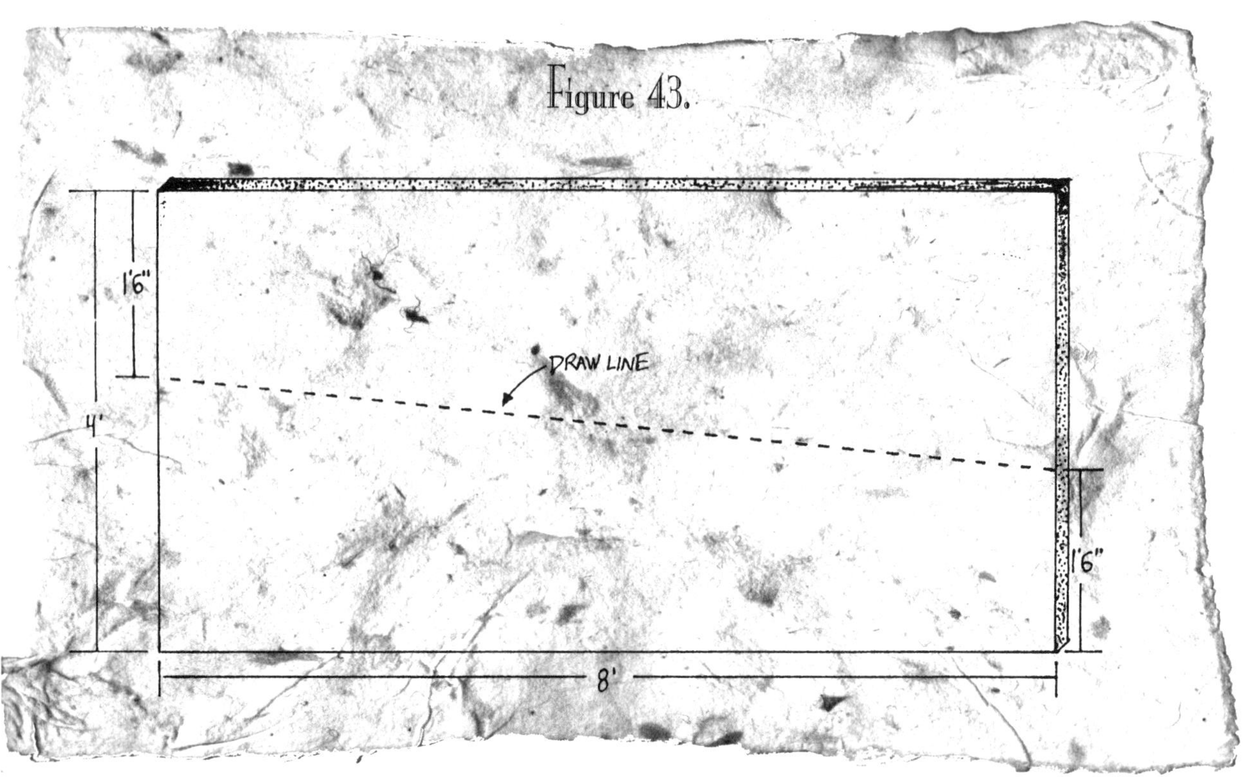

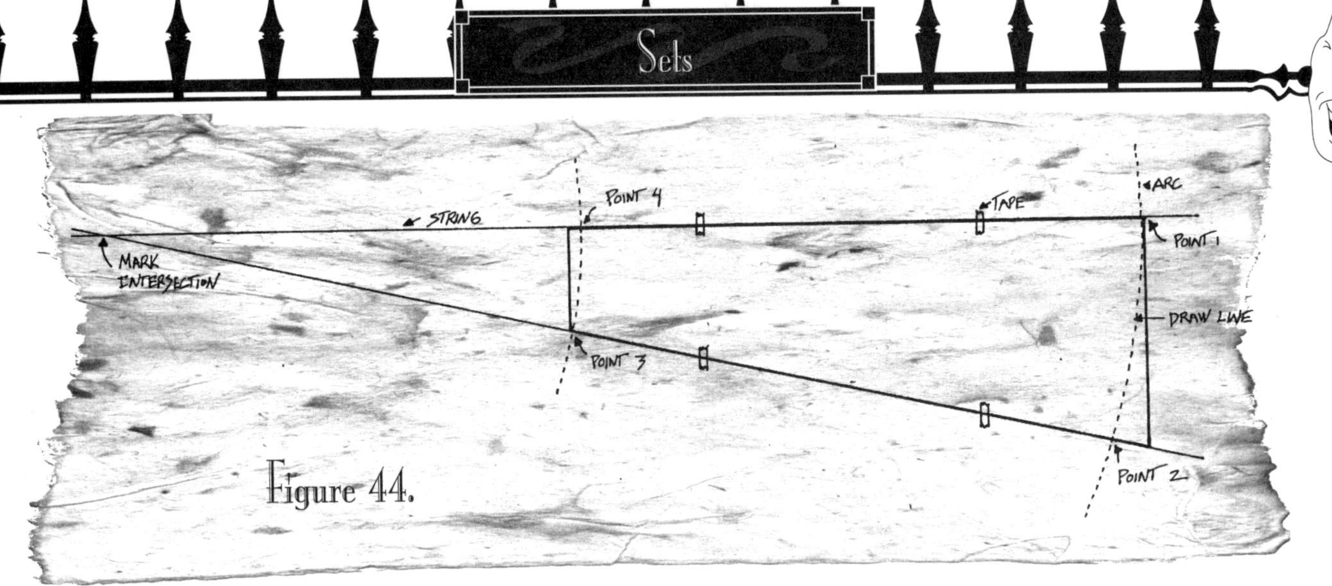

Figure 44.

• Four or more tubes of polysulfide or similar caulking. Do not use silicon-based caulking. You need a paintable caulk. Find the least expensive one you can. (HW)

• One small bag of plaster (HW)

• One sheet of 1/2" plywood (HW)

Tools you will need:

• Hand saw or circular saw

• Hammer

• Caulk gun

• Protective eyewear

• Filter mask

• Earplugs

• Utility knife

• Dremel carving tool with 1/8" rounded bit

• Black magic marker

• Straight edge

• Duct tape

• 1-1/2" putty knife

To Begin:

1. Lay out two sheets of the extruded polystyrene insulation board and draw a line diagonally 1' - 6" from the opposite short ends as shown in *figure 43* . Use the handsaw to carefully cut along the line you have drawn. Keep the line as straight as you can. The material is soft so it is easy to stray off the line or to hold the saw at a side-to-side angle. When you are finished cutting the two sheets, you should have four equal pieces. These will be your face pieces. They should appear lopsided at this point if you cut them right. The edges of the face pieces must now be evened up.

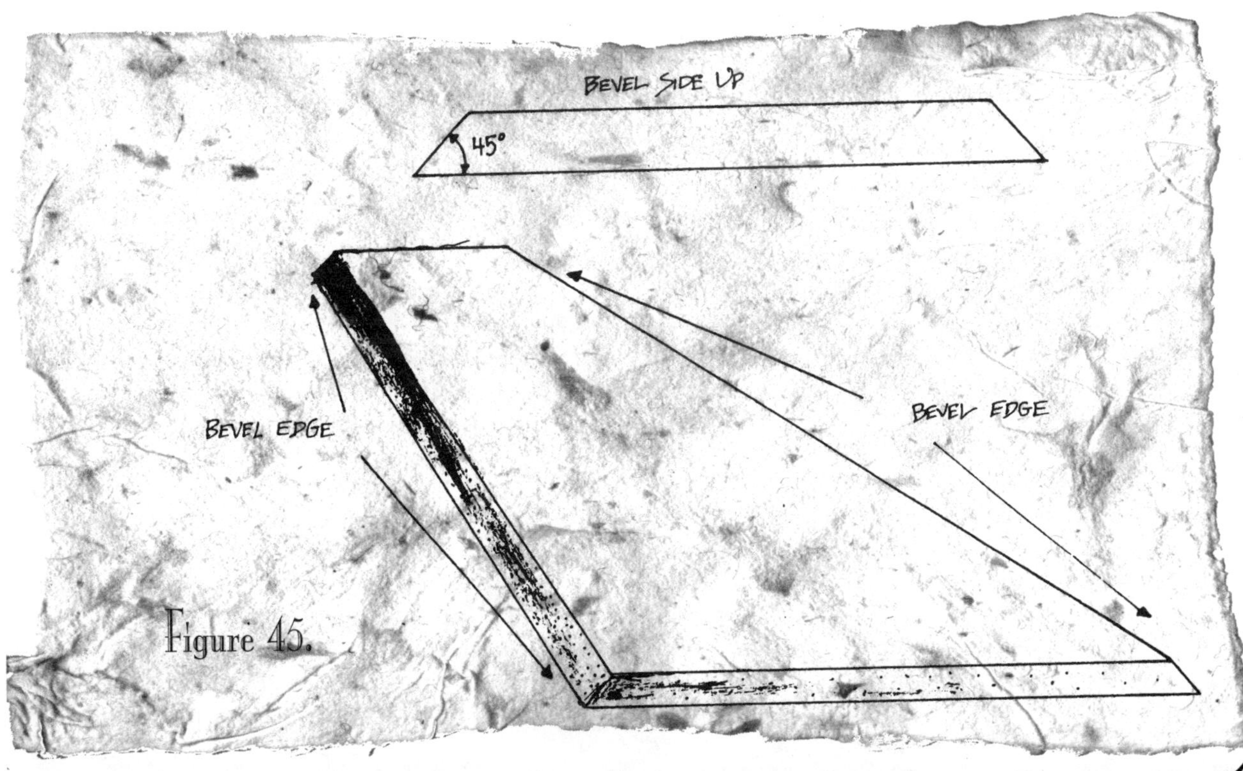

Figure 45.

2. Take one of the face pieces, lay it down flat on the floor, and anchor it with some tape. Take two pieces of string and lay them aside the two long sides of the piece. Extend the strings beyond the short end of the face piece until they intersect. Mark the point at which the two strings intersect. Anchor a third string at the point of intersection with some tape, or have someone hold it for you. Refer to *figure 44*. Hold the string taught and place it on point #1 as shown. Swing the string along an arc until you come to point #2. Use the magic marker to mark this point. Now pull the string to point #3 and swing it in an arc to point #4. Mark this point also.

3. Draw a line from point #1 to point #2 with the straight edge, and do the same from point #3 to point #4. Use the handsaw to cut along these lines. This will even up each side of the face. Use the face piece you have just completed as a guide for the other three, or repeat steps one and two over again for each remaining piece.

4. Trim the two long sides of each face piece at a 45-degree bevel as shown. This will allow you a maximum carving face.

5. Lay two of the face pieces flat on the floor, bevel (short) side up as in *figure 45*. Take four of the 2 x 3 pieces of framing lumber and place one on either long side of the two face pieces along the edges of the bevel (see *figure 46*). Mark where the 2 x 3s are to be cut. Take another 2 x 3 and make cross pieces along the top and bottom of the face piece. Cut the 2 x 3s and attach the long boards to the short boards with framing nails. You should have two pieces.

6. Take the two remaining face pieces and place them on the floor, bevel edge up, as you did in step five. Place the two 2 x 3 assemblies from step five upright on the edge of one of the remaining face pieces. Make cross pieces for the top and bottom and attach the two assemblies together using the cross pieces and framing nails (see *figure 47*). Place the open side of the assembly on the last face piece and make the last cross pieces. Be sure to number each face piece, and its corresponding frame piece, on the back so you can attach the face pieces to the correct frame pieces later. After nailing the assembly together, glue all the joints with construction adhesive to give it additional strength. Avoid getting glue on the outside of the frame assembly.

7. Set the frame assembly (monolith frame) aside for now and let it dry.

8. Take extruded polystyrene face piece #1 and trace your design or text onto it with the magic marker. Experiment with a piece of butcher's paper or newsprint cut in the same size and shape first to make sure the proportions of your design are correct. Transfer the design to the face piece and complete the three remaining faces as well. Make sure there is a space of 1-1/2" from the edge of the face piece to the start of your design. This will give you some room to trim the pieces, if necessary, when they are attached to the frame assembly.

9. Once you are finished tracing your design on the face pieces, begin carving your design. First, make sure that you are in a well-ventilated area and are wearing a filter mask.

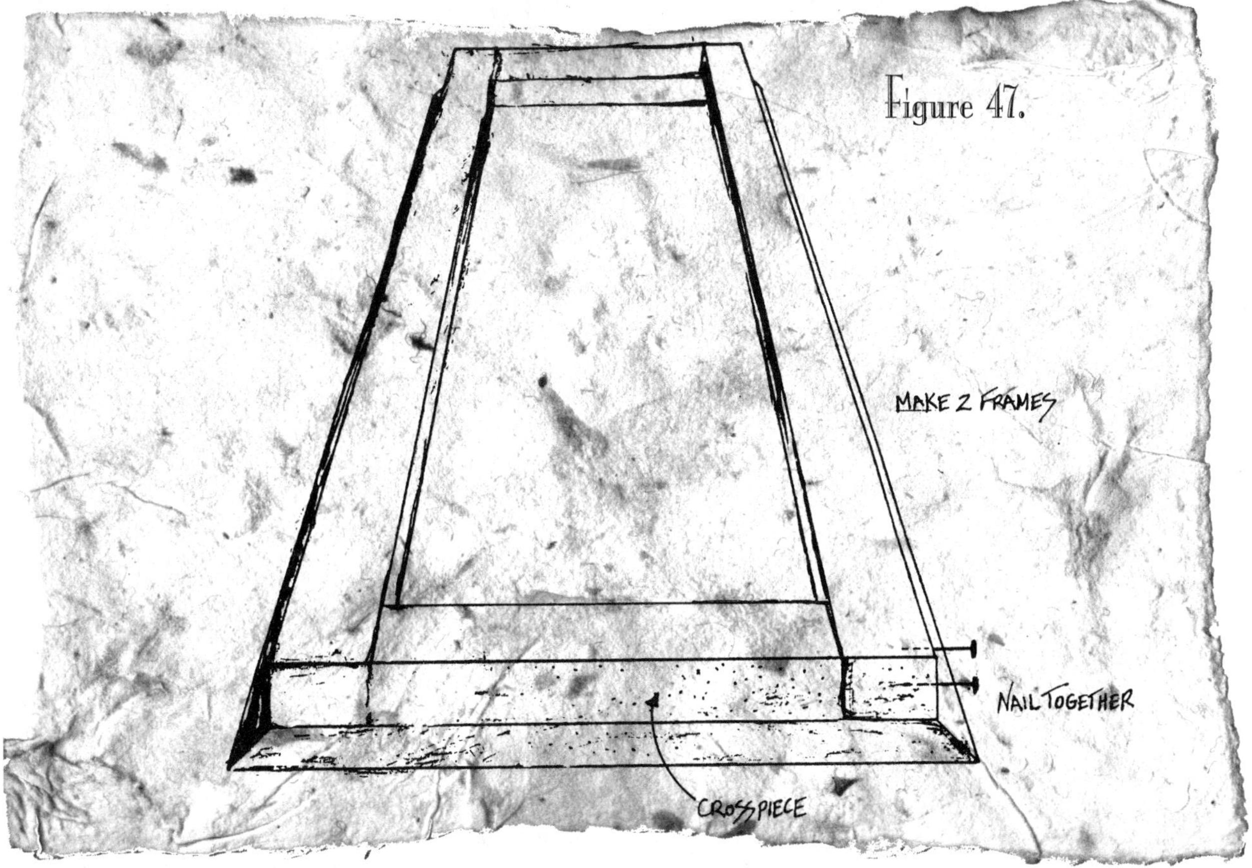

The heat generated from the Dremel tool can cause the insulation material to release noxious fumes, and the carving itself will produce a fine dust that you should avoid breathing in. Wear earplugs to protect your hearing from the whine of the Dremel tool. Practice on a spare piece of insulation board first to determine how much pressure you will need to apply with the tool when carving your design. The material requires only a light touch, and a little practice will increase your ability and allow you to easily carve your design.

10. After you have finished carving the face pieces, attach them to the frame assembly. Take face piece #1 and apply a generous amount of construction adhesive with the caulk gun to the back where it will come in contact with the frame assembly (side one). Apply the face piece to the frame and tack it in place with finish nails. Next, apply side three in the same manner. Then side two, and finally side four, as shown in *figures 61 - 65*. Staggering the application helps to keep the sides even. Don't worry if the pieces are not perfectly aligned. Trim the pieces as required to fit the frame assembly and do any final trimming with a sharp knife after the pieces have been fully assembled and have dried overnight.

11. Attach the four face pieces to the monolith frame assembly. Top the monolith with four triangular pieces beveled and trimmed to form a symmetrical peak. Glue the whole peak together with the adhesive and tack it in place with finish nails pushed in place through the insulation board. Allow the entire monolith assembly to dry overnight.

12. At this point, you can begin to assemble the base frame, upon which the monolith will rest. This is a simple box frame consisting of four upright pieces attached top and bottom to four pieces forming a square. To determine the proper width for the base, measure the final dimension of the bottom of the monolith and add 6 inches to each side. Assemble all the pieces with framing nails. Cap the frame with a piece of 1/2" thick plywood, trimmed to fit.

13. Take the remaining insulation board and apply it to the four sides of the base assembly. You do not need to bevel these pieces. They can be overlapped Attach the pieces with construction adhesive and tack them into place with finish nails. At this point, carve whatever design you wish into the faces of the base assembly.

14. Let all the pieces dry thoroughly.

15. After the monolith and base assemblies are thoroughly dry and ready for handling, trim the corners and any excess material from both with a sharp knife. Fill all the cracks with caulking and shape with a moistened putty knife. Hold off on caulking the base assembly and concentrate on the monolith for now. Try for a sandstone-like appearance. Make sure that the caulk doesn't sag or run, causing formations that look unnatural. Fill all the cracks and nail holes and shape smooth. Take this time to correct any mistakes you may have made in your carving. Allow the caulk to set for a couple of days.

16. When the caulk has set, place and center the monolith atop the base. Cut four strips wide enough to span the distance between the edge of the monolith and the edge of the base. This will form a pocket as deep as the insulation board in which the monolith will rest. Attach the trim pieces with adhesive and finish nails.

17. Remove the monolith and caulk all the joints of the base assembly and finish as you did the monolith in step 15. If necessary, use some plaster of paris to repair large areas that need to be filled.

18. Now you can begin painting the entire set piece to emulate the look of sandstone. First, mix the paint texturizer and plaster of paris with the gallon of flat black paint. The paint should have the consistency of thick gravy. Apply the paint to the carved areas of the insulation board first with the 1" brush. Work it into the carved surfaces as well as you can. Take your time and do a good job painting the carved areas. A good paint job will hide a lot of flaws in workmanship. After the carvings are filled, apply the textured, flat black paint to the rest of the monolith and base with the paint roller. Apply the paint heavily and evenly. The roller will ensure that no brush strokes are visible on your final piece and help give it a gritty finish. Apply at least two coats of paint.

19. Between coats of paint, check the carvings for any bare spots where the insulation board shows through. Use the spray paint to touch up any bare spots that you cannot reach with the brush.

20. Allow the entire assembly to dry thoroughly before going on to the next phase, dry brushing the pieces. The black base coat must be completely dry in order for the next effect to work properly.

21. Take the dark rust flat latex paint and dab a small amount onto the 4" brush. Wipe off the excess with a paper towel until only the barest amount is left on the brush. This is called dry brushing, and is used to apply one color as a highlight over another. Start working the paint in a back and forth motion, using light pressure to highlight the black. You do not want to cover the black, merely highlight it. Replenish your brush as often as you need to complete the entire monolith and base. Let it dry and touch up any areas that haven't been covered sufficiently. When you are satisfied, let the paint dry completely before proceeding to next step.

22. Repeat step 21 with the dark yellow flat latex paint. However, use this color even more sparingly than the rust color you applied in step 21. The point is to use the dark yellow as a highlight to the rust. Experiment in a small, out-of-the-way area first. If you do not achieve the effect you want with the monolith the first time, you can always go back to step 18 and start over again. However, we recommend experimenting on a small piece of insulation board before painting your setting piece.

23. Your monolith is ready for display.

Variations on the Monolith Design

There are many different approaches you can take in the construction and finish of your own monolith, depending on what effect and use you intend for it. This monolith was constructed with the intention of emulating a sandstone finish. By experimenting with other finishing techniques, you could make your monolith appear to be limestone, granite, marble, petrified wood, or just about any other type of stone finish you can think of. You could also change the design of the monolith and make it smaller or larger to suit your own needs. If the monolith will be protected from the general public, you might experiment with the possibility of eliminating the monolith frame assembly from behind the face pieces. This will make the structure considerably weaker, but also less expensive.

The Arch of the Kindred

The arch of the Kindred is another artifact of Kindred lore. Like the monolith, its origins are shrouded in time. Rumor has it that the arch was built by the Toreador as a gift to a powerful Brujah Elder, during the time when the Brujah were still philosophically inclined. The arch had upon its facade the carved images of each of the founding clans and represented the unity of Kindred in their unique existence in the world, forever apart from humanity. Strong and ageless, the arch has fallen into neglect, as have the bonds that linked the Kindred as brethren so long ago.

Construction

Space requirements and considerations for construction are the same as for the monolith. However, the arch will require more storage space when completed.

Materials Required

(See **Materials Legend** above)

- Two sections of cardboard concrete column forms, 7' long each and 18" in diameter. They are commercially known as either Core-Form or Sonotube concrete forms. (CS)
- Three sheets of 1" thick, 4' x 8', extruded polystyrene foam insulation board. See monolith. (CS)
- One sheet of 1/2" extruded polystyrene foam insulation. (CS) (HW)
- Approximately eight 2" x 3" (Not 2" x 4", unless you want to pay more) by 8' pieces low-grade framing lumber, fairly straight. (HW)
- One 2" x 6" piece of framing lumber (HW)
- A box of 3" finishing nails (HW)
- A box of 1" finishing nails (HW)
- A box of 3" regular framing nails (HW)
- One box of 2" wood screws (HW)
- One half-gallon of flat black latex paint (HW)
- One quart of dark emerald or sea green paint (HW)
- One quart of light emerald or sea green paint (HW)

• One pint of white paint (HW)

• One half-gallon of high-gloss, quick-drying polyurethane finish (HW)

• Two 4" brushes (any cheap ones will do, as you will need to cut a few bristles off one for marbleizing) (HW)

• 1" brush (HW)

• Open cell or natural sponges(HW)

• Four or more tubes of construction adhesive (HW)

• Half a dozen or so 3" foam brushes for use with polyurethane (HW)

• Two or more tubes of polysulfide or similar caulking. See monolith. (HW)

• One 4' x 8' sheet of 3/4" plywood (HW)

• One small bag of plaster (HW)

Tools you will need:

• Hand saw or circular saw

• Drill with power driving bit for wood screws

• Hammer

• Caulk gun

• Protective eyewear

• Earplugs

• Utility knife

• Black magic marker

• Straight edge

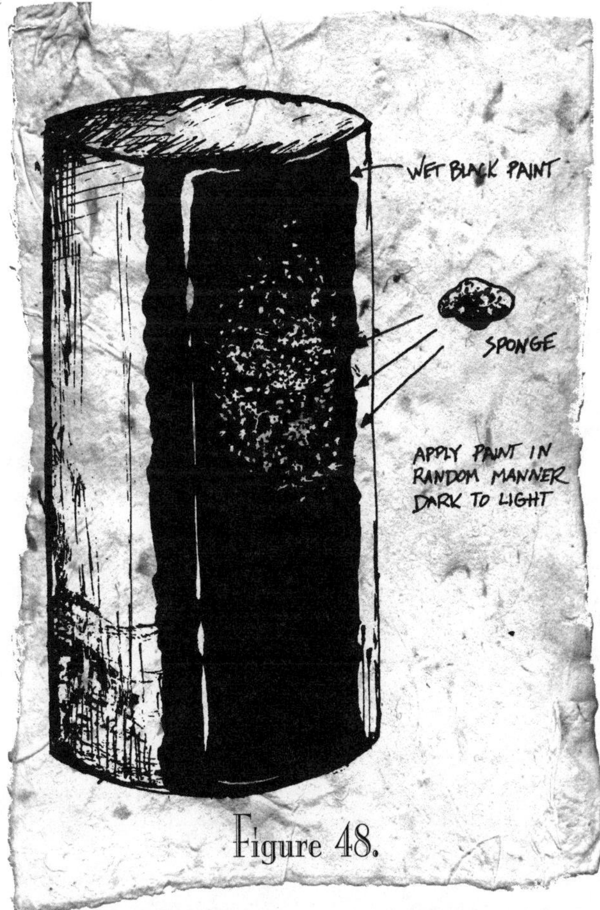

Figure 48.

• Duct tape

• 1-1/2" putty knife

• 400 and 600 grit sand paper, about six sheets each (HW)

To Begin

1. Place the two concrete forms upright on end. Sand the entire outside surface lightly with 400 grit sandpaper to form a good surface for paint adhesion, and to remove any industrial dirt. Wipe down with a clean dry cloth to remove all dirt and dust from the surface.

2. Paint the entire surface of the column forms with one coat of flat black paint, and let it dry thoroughly.

3. A. To achieve the look of marble columns, the following steps should be taken. There are many other options to choose from, however, so investigate these if you are interested.

B. Before you begin the marbleizing process, look at some of the many different patterns of marble at a tile store, or an art store (or on many of White Wolf's book covers), to choose which kind of pattern you want to simulate on your columns and archway. Take the time to test and perfect the following technique on a separate, large piece of brown paper bag or cardboard before you paint the actual column. You don't need to paint the top few inches of the column, because they will be covered over by the archway.

C. Apply a second coat of black paint to one quarter of the column at a time, and while still wet, apply the dark shade of green paint with the open cell sponge in an irregular dabbing manner. Smear the paint with the sponge a little bit in random spots so that the black paint mixes with the green, giving the mottled, blotchy look of marble. After wiping off any excess dark green paint from the sponge, repeat the dabbing process, only using less, with the light green shade of paint. Don't coat the entire column in one solid block of green. The idea is to carefully swirl and intermingle all four colors — black, dark green, light green and white — so they combine to create the detailed look of marble, not the look of something that just rolled out of a swamp.

D. To re-create the thin white veins in marble, you can use a very thin artist's brush, but some of the lines formed this way are unrealistically thick. Instead, we recommend trimming six or seven long bristles from the 4" brush, and holding them between your thumb, forefinger and middle finger so that the ends of the bristles are uneven. Dip the bristles into the white paint, and wipe off any excess drops of paint on the inner rim of the can, as you want to make thin veins, not gloppy lines. With the bristles in one hand, and the other clean, dry 4" paint brush in the other, make quick, erratic strokes (ragged, uneven lines anywhere from 1-6" long, some connected to each other) with the bristles in about one square foot of space at a time. Smear a few of the resulting white lines with the paint brush by gently pushing into the paint and twisting your wrist at the same time. Move right on to the next area before the black and green paint dries. Don't worry if you feel you've messed up. Remember that designs created in nature do not look alike, particularly not

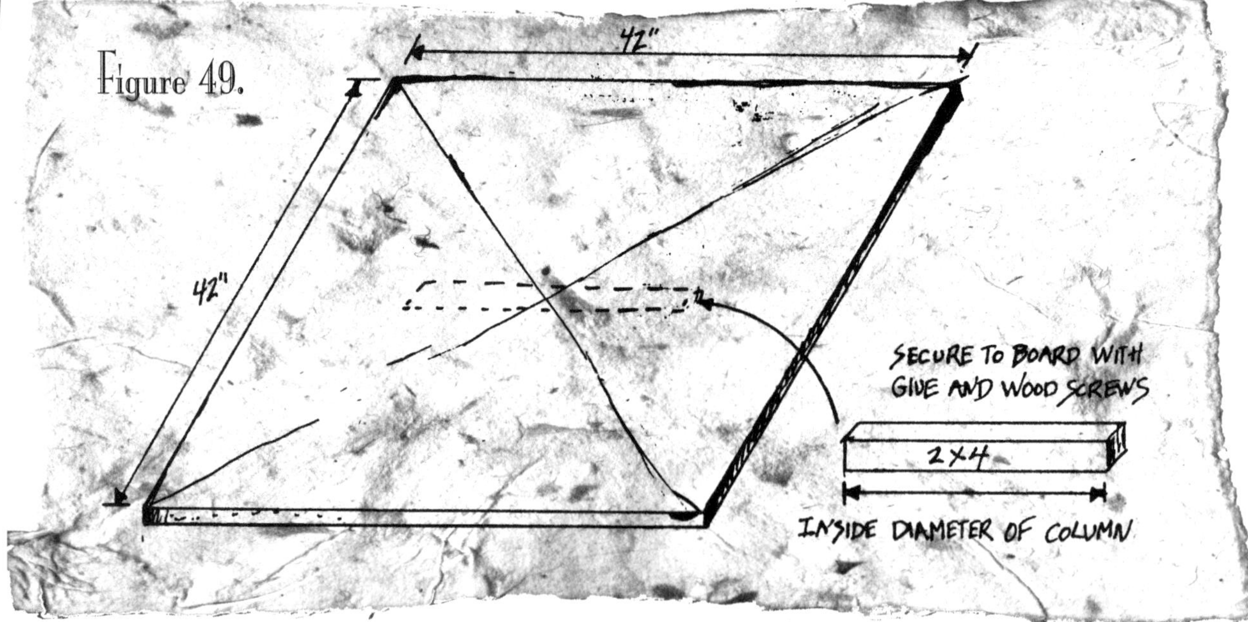

marble. You can always paint over any smaller "mistakes," but try to avoid any excessively thick layering of paints. Continue to paint the rest of the column in the same manner, one quarter at a time so the paint won't dry before you have a chance to work with it. Allow the paint on both columns to dry thoroughly.

4. Using a foam brush, apply a coat of polyurethane over the entire surface of the column. This seals and presses the finish and gives the surface the high-gloss look of polished marble. Allow the coat to dry and lightly sand the finish with 600 grit paper. This helps to even out the finish and make it smooth. Wipe off all the excess dust generated from the sanding with a clean dry cloth. Apply a second coat of polyurethane with a new foam brush. Allow this coat to dry and also lightly sand it with 600 grit sandpaper. Wipe this down, too. Apply the final coat over the surface of the column and let the polyurethane dry thoroughly overnight before going on to the next step.

5. Cut two pieces of 3/4" plywood to form a square, 42" each side. Strike a line diagonally from one corner to another and mark the point of intersection of the two lines. This is the center point of each square. Measure the inside diameter of the column and cut a piece of 2 x 6 this length. Mark the edge of this piece along the midpoint and apply construction adhesive along the narrow edge. Line the mid-point of the 2 x 6 piece with the center mark on the base piece. The piece should be adhered in the upright position, as shown in *figure* 49. Secure it to the base plate with 2" wood screws driven through the bottom of the plate. Cut two smaller pieces to fit on either side of the piece you just fastened into place to form a cross (*See figure* 50). The overall length of the two pieces placed on either side of the main piece should equal the interior diameter of the column. Glue and fasten these pieces in place as you did the main piece. Allow the adhesive to dry. Repeat this procedure for both base pieces.

6. Paint both bases flat black. Apply at least two coats.

7. Slide the columns over the base assemblies. The 2 x 6s should fit within the columns snugly. Secure the columns with wood screws driven into the end of each 2 x 6 piece. Make sure that the columns are standing perpendicular to the floor before fastening. When finished, set the completed columns aside until needed later.

8. You can now begin constructing the actual frame for the arch. Using 2 x 3s, construct two boxes that will slide over the top of each column. By placing the square frames on the inside of the four uprights as shown, you are creating an internal shelf that will keep the columns from sliding all the way through the boxes you are constructing. For now, refer to these two box pieces as column cap assemblies.

9. Use four 2 x 3s cut to 6' lengths to form the span of the arch. Create a rectangular tube using cross pieces cut to the lengths shown. Be sure to include a cross piece at the midpoint of each span, which will allow you to hang sculpture or other artwork from the arch. This assembly is the span piece.

10. Attach the span piece to the two column cap assemblies. Make sure that the span piece is even with the tops of the column cap assemblies and not with the bottom. Run cross bracing through the cap assemblies into the span piece to firmly anchor the pieces together. Use construction adhesive on all the joints throughout the piece for added strength. Your frame assembly is now complete. Allow the adhesive to dry thoroughly before proceeding to the next stage.

11. Begin applying the 1" insulation board to the face of each cap assembly. Use the construction adhesive as directed and tack the pieces in place with finish nails. Complete covering each cap assembly.

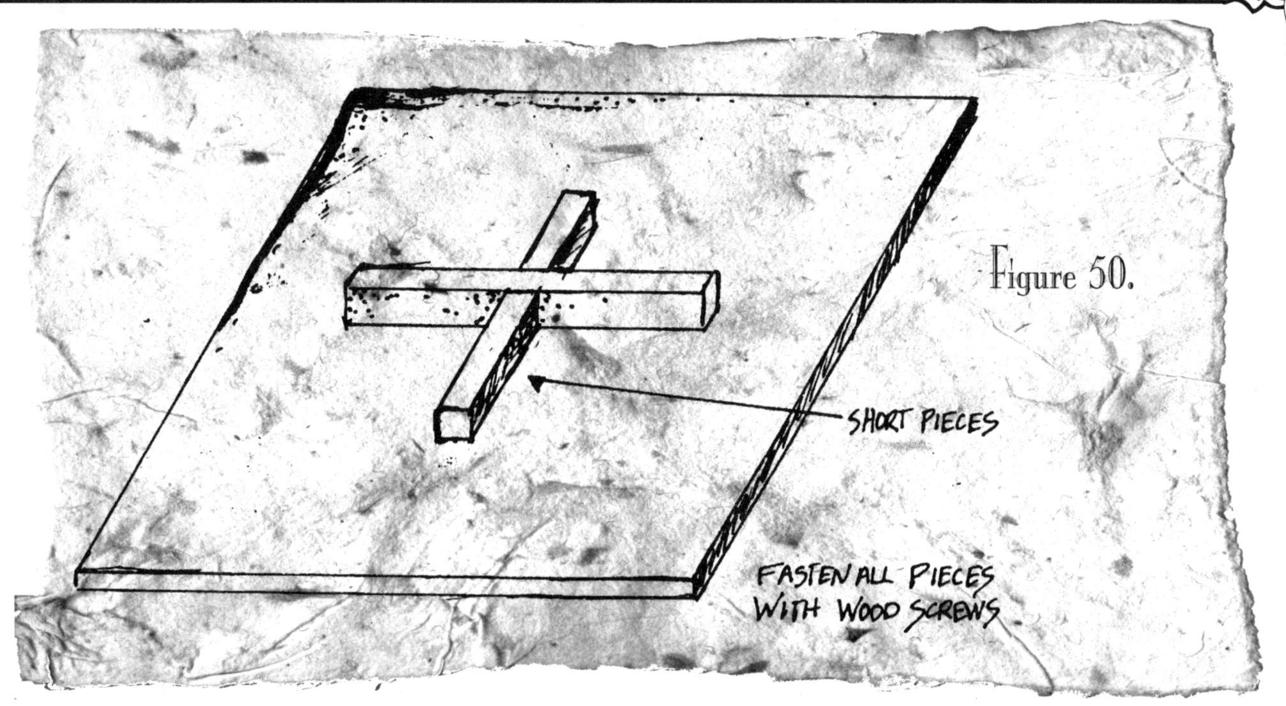

Figure 50.

12. The actual arch can now be formed using the 1" insulation board. Cut two pieces of insulation board to fit on either side of the span piece for the full height of the cap assemblies. Make sure the pieces fit snug and fill the entire area between the cap pieces. Keep one of these pieces in place and have someone trace the dimensions of the void under the span pieces and between the cap assemblies. Remove the insulation board and place it on a table marked side up. Carefully draw an arch from one edge of the span piece to the other within the area of the void space. Make sure to leave 1" of space clear along the top of the void to allow room for the insulation board used to form the arch. Using a sharp utility knife, cut out the arch. Copy the opening on the opposite side piece and cut the arch section out of this side also.

13. Apply the trimmed insulation pieces to the span piece the same way you applied the insulation board to the cap assemblies. Allow the adhesive to dry thoroughly.

14. Using strips of insulation 4" wide, begin filling in the area between the trimmed insulation pieces to form the bottom side of your arch. Use construction adhesive on each end and between each piece, and secure each piece with two finish nails pushed into either end. When you are finished, allow the adhesive to dry.

15. You now have to finish the bottom of each cap assembly. Position the column pieces so that they are aligned with each cap assembly. Cover the upper half of the columns with a drop cloth, newspaper, or some other protective layer attached to the top rim of each column, protecting the finish from anything that may drip or splatter from above. With the help of a few friends, hoist the arch into position and slide the arch down along the columns until it rests in place.

16. Use some of the remaining 1" insulation board to form trim pieces around the column under the cap assembly (see *figure 51*). Make sure that the insulation is not wedged up against the columns. You will want to be able to slide the arch off the columns with relative ease. Secure the trim piece to the bottom of each cap assembly with construction adhesive and allow it to dry before removing the arch from the columns.

17. Remove the arch from the columns and place it on the floor. Using the 1/2" insulation board, cut a series of 3" wide strips to use as trim work around each of the cap assemblies and at the top of either side of the span piece. Attach these trim pieces in the area with adhesive, and tack in place with 1" finish nails.

18. With the remaining 1" insulation board, cut a series of 4" wide pieces that will be attached to the arch piece flat side down to form the stepped-out molding at the top of the arch piece. Secure it in place with adhesive and 3" finish nails pushed into the insulation, and allow it to dry.

20. If you desire, you can create a keystone for the arch using the leftover 1" insulation board. Make sure that the keystone is tight up against the cross piece you installed at the mid-point of the span in step 12. This step ensures that you can hang objects from the keystone without damaging the insulation.

21. Place the arch back atop the columns and use a step ladder to reach it so that you can begin to apply caulking to all the seams and joints. Fill all the nail holes and correct any flaws at this time. Smooth the caulking with the putty knife. Mix the plaster of paris in a bucket and begin to apply it to the bottom of the arch. Use two or more coats to smooth out all the seams formed by the narrow strip used to fill in the bottom of the arch. Do not apply the plaster too thickly. It will take longer to dry if applied too thickly and will probably crack as it does so.

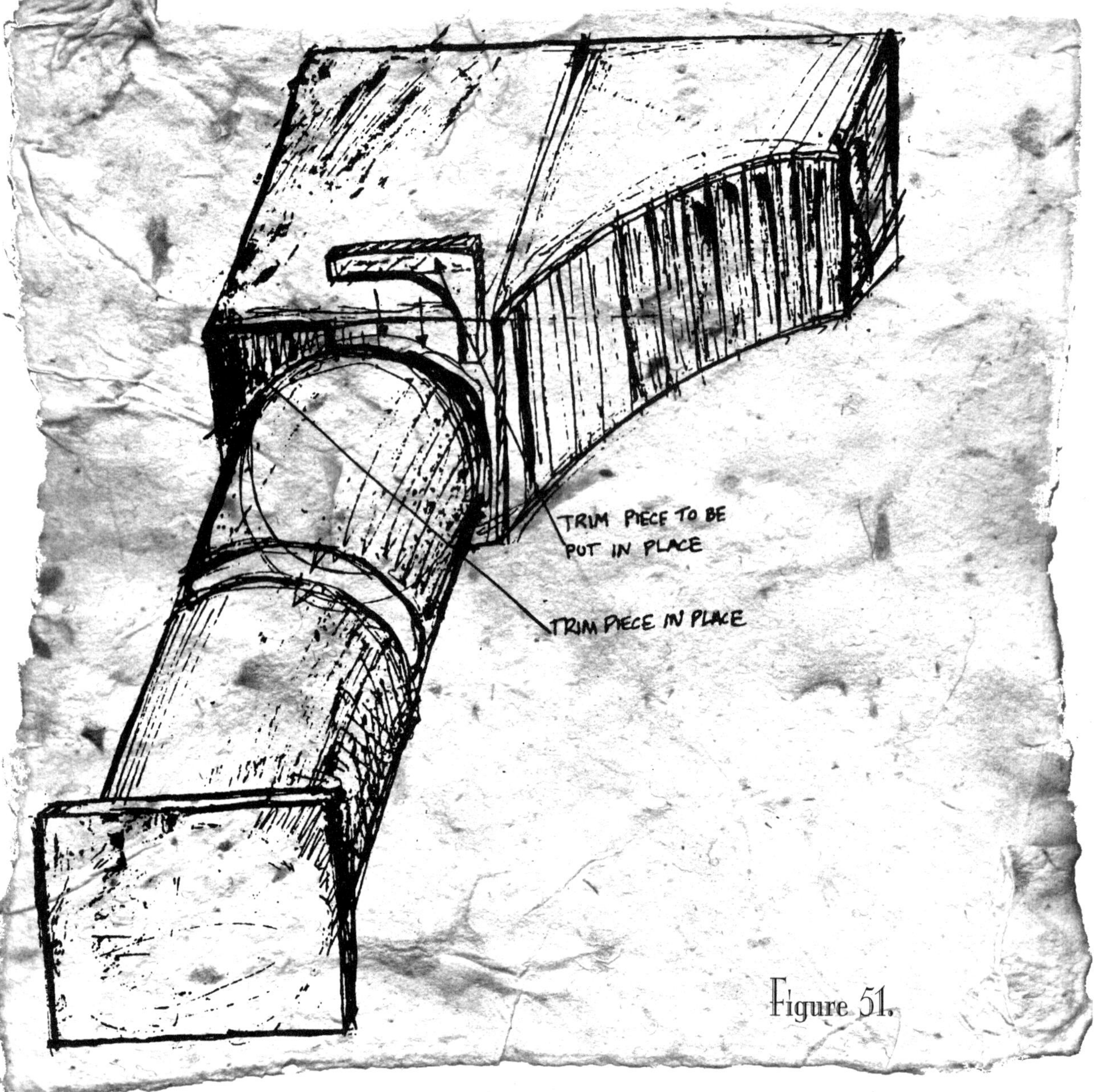

Figure 51.

22. Once all the caulking and plaster have dried, begin painting the arch. Start by applying one generous coat of black paint to the entire arch assembly, and allowing it to dry thoroughly. You can leave the arch atop the columns or place it on the ground for easier access. Remember that you have to paint the bottom of each cap assembly as well, and it may be easier to do so if you don't have to work around each column.

23. A. For the arch, we copied the appearance of black marble. To achieve this look, you will only need black and white paint. Remember to paint one small section at a time so you can work with the paint while it is still wet. Also, as you will only be using two colors instead of four, you may want to practice this technique before starting on the arch.

B. Start with the second coat of wet black paint, and with the few bristles in one hand (see step 3B), and a clean, dry 4" paint brush in the other, dip the bristles in the white paint. This time, you may leave more paint on the bristles so you can work some of the white into the black paint with the 4" brush. Use the same technique described in step 3C. Allow the paint to dry thoroughly.

24. You arch is now ready for display. Make sure that the columns and arch are stable. If the arch is wobbly, cut another piece of plywood slightly larger than you used before for the bottom plates of the column. Attach it to the base plates with screws driven up thorough the bottom of the new piece into the existing plates. Make sure that the screws do not stick up through the bottom plate and create a safety hazard. Remember, safety must always be your top priority.

25. As a finishing touch, use the arch to display complementary sculpted artwork. Be certain that any object attached to the framework of the arch is securely fastened. The insulation board has very little holding strength and you must provide a solid surface to hang any objects from.

Variations on the Arch

As with the monolith, there are many variations you could make on the design and construction of the arch. Unlike the monolith, however, the arch is a structure that must support its own weight. It is inherently less stable that the monolith and so care must be taken to ensure that it will remain freestanding on its own. Other than these considerations, the sky is the limit when it comes to the type of finishes and proportions that you could use. You could finish the columns so that they look like the ancient white marble columns of the Parthenon. If you are skilled at carving, you could even make the columns fluted. You are limited only by your imagination and your ability to sculpt the insulation.

Ideas for Things to Come

With a little creative thinking, you can create or re-create any effect you wish using common construction materials in ways that you may not have thought of before. Extruded polystyrene insulation is a very versatile material. Even though it is expensive initially, with a little planning you can minimize the amount required for a project. You can layer it to form any thickness and easily sculpt it to re-create whatever effect you wish. The monolith and archway are two examples of the use of insulation board, and both require a supporting frame. However, you can make entire projects from insulation board alone, such as a breakaway stone or wood table. However, always exercise caution when using such props. Breakaway props should only be utilized by narrators, and players should be warned of their existence, so that no one leans on the prop or accidentally breaks it before the proper time. Here is a quick overview of its construction for you to use as a guide.

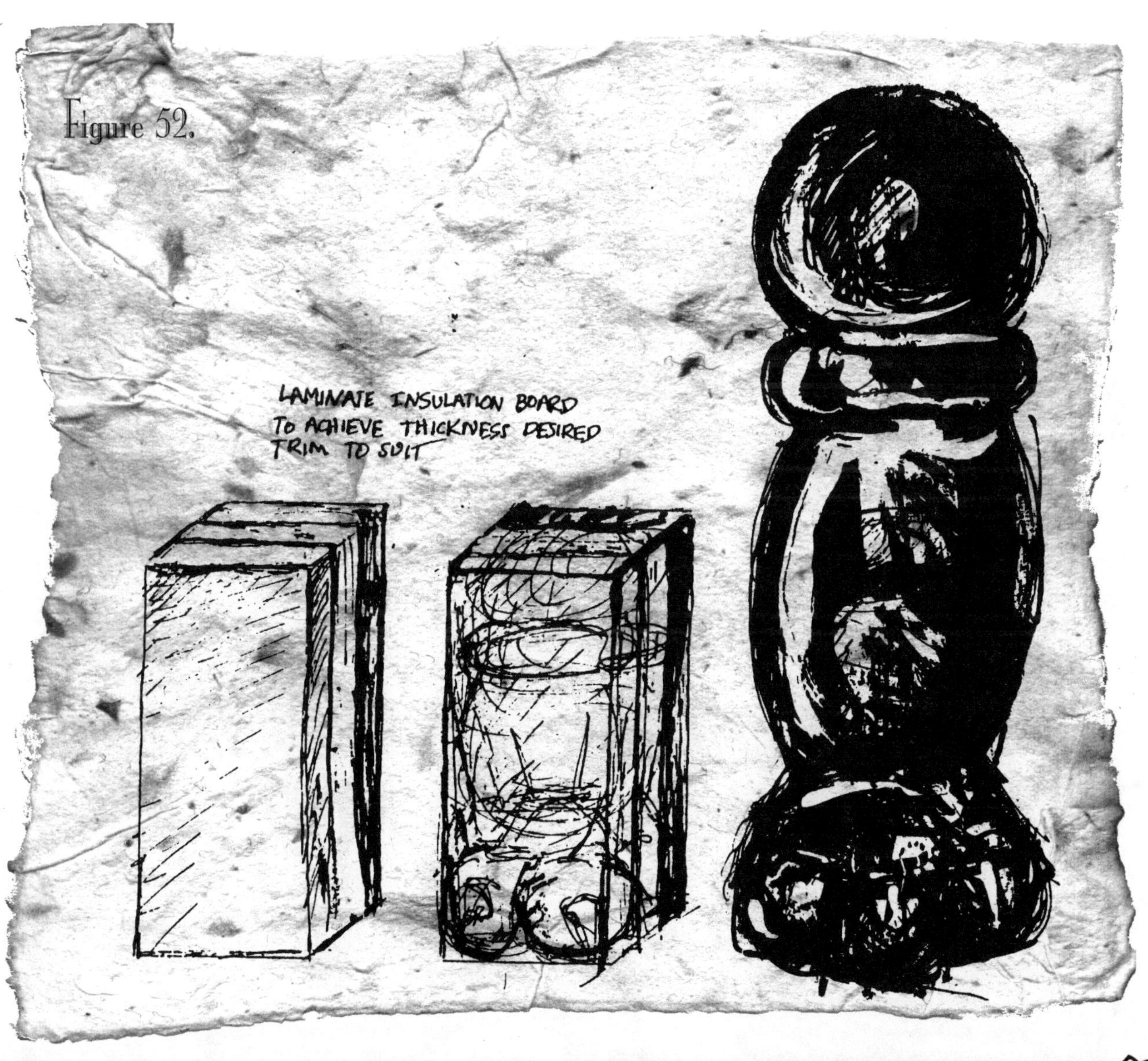

Figure 52.

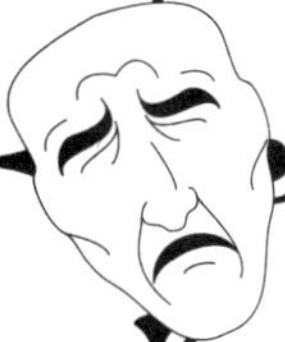

Materials needed:

- 4 sheets of 1" extruded polystyrene insulation board (CS)
- 4 or more tubes of constructions adhesive (HW)
- 3 tubes of caulk or a bag of plaster
- Utility knife

This is a long stone table with a top dimension of 3' x 8' and a height of 32". First, trim 12" off the side of one sheet of insulation board to form the top piece. Cut the legs from another piece of insulation board, as shown in *figure 52*. The design of the table legs is up to you. However, they should be in proportion to the mass of the table. You might have to glue two or more pieces of insulation board together to make the leg pieces thick enough. Be sure to allow for a cross piece in your design between the leg pieces so that they may stand on their own, as shown in *figure 53*.

Cut strips of insulation board 3" wide from the trim piece left over from making the table top. Adhere these to the bottom of the table top along all the edges to give the tabletop the look of a massive stone slab. Once the adhesive is dry, start trimming the leg and table pieces as required. At this point you can make decorative carvings in the leg assemblies or add whatever personal touches you wish. Fill all the voids and seal all joints with plaster of paris. If you are not going to use the table as a breakaway piece, you can use caulking instead of plaster. Caulking will flex and stretch if the table is broken, resulting in a mess of caulking spaghetti. Use the utility knife and score the underside of the table top where you wish it to break. Score to within a 1/4" of the surface of the table. Fill the scored line with plaster of paris. This will enhance the effect of breaking stone.

You can now finish your table in a stone, marble, or wood finish. To simulate a wood finish, stain and polyurethane the pieces the same way you would a wooden table. Follow the directions on the can of stain as you would do for any wood project. The porous nature of the insulation board allows the stain to penetrate deeply into the surface. Use a dark stain and cover the piece heavily to camouflage any flaws and joints. If you are planning to use the table as a breakaway piece and want to be able to use it over and over again, do not use the marble or wood finish. They are very hard to repair once they have been damaged. The stone finish is the easiest to repair, and so works well for this effect.

Once the table has been broken, you can reuse it by adhering a piece of 1/2" insulation board to the bottom of the tabletop under the area of the break. Fill the break with plaster and reapply the stone finish. Repair the cross piece if necessary by gluing the broken ends together again. If you are careful, you can reuse the table many times before it becomes too far gone to rescue. At that point, you could probably make something out of the scrap pieces. Never use finish nails or any other hard object to tack the table together. Use only "soft" materials when constructing and rebuilding this piece. You do not want to fall through a table, only to have something hurt you in return.

The table is effective when used in a staged combat scenario, lending credence to the power of the struggle taking place. A character being thrown onto a stone slab with enough force to break it is in for a lot of pain, and the character who made the toss is obviously potent. If the thrown character raises herself up again, unscathed from the toss, it's time to leave the fight. Even if the table is only to be used as a set piece, its light weight can be used to a character's advantage. Casually lifting a stone slab that appears to weigh hundreds of pounds is a feat that only the most powerful can do. You could write a scene into the plot where the character reveals himself in this casual display of strength.

Figure 53.

Outdoors

For some **Mind's Eye Theatre** story lines, there may be an area in the great outdoors near you that would suit your needs better than any private home or rented indoor space. Of course, the story should be one that is set outdoors, but will not require you to thoroughly transform any chosen space. Nature is ours to foster, not mutilate. When staging an event outside, we suggest you try to keep it simple. An outdoor event should not require you to set up a sophisticated light and sound system. If you want special light or sound effects, battery-powered flashlights, lanterns, and tape recorders ought to be as far as you need to go. Your players should not expect a sparkling yellow brick road twisting through the wilderness if it is not something you have made essential to the story, so choose your story lines accordingly. If the story line of your event can be set outside, there are simply not as many technical options to consider for the physical setting.

As with any indoor space you hold an event in, you must first get permission to use outdoor space from whomever owns the land you'll be using. This includes public parks of all kinds, school or college campuses, athletic fields and complexes, and anyone's back yard, no matter how big it is. There are certain legal limitations we all must obey. Someone else may already have something planned for the little nook in the woods you want to use for a game on the same day. Always find out who owns even the smallest bit of land you would like to use, and get their express permission first, so your players don't end up getting the hose turned on them, or having to spend the day in a police station for trespassing. Also be sure your players are fully aware of all of the preexisting boundaries, such as property lines and electrified fences.

Once you've confirmed a place, you can begin setting it up. Depending on the type of space you have obtained outdoors, and the story line, you will want to make it clear to your players that this is the place to be. Clues to a mystery they have to solve could be hidden in the ground, under an ominous mound of dirt you shoveled up beforehand, or concealed under one of the stones in the wall of an old (fake) well you have built up with stones or bricks, or even inside a hollow tree. You could have a roaring bonfire burning as your players arrive at the scene for a gathering of werewolves, if your location already has a fire pit, or you have the proper tools, know-how, and authorization to build one. Many minor, but effective, alterations like these can be made to the landscape without destroying it.

The Sky's the Limit...

Well, at this point, you are basically limited by your budget and your imagination as to how far you can go in adding believability to your events. You could make stone guardians for an ancient crypt, or a wooden coffin for your character's daily slumber. For chronicled events, set construction can give continuity to a game that may move from location to location. Look at your plot and determine which areas of your scenario are most often frequented by your characters. If you have a place where you regularly run a chronicled event and have access to a lot of storage space, you can begin to amass an entire city of sets for your characters to exist in. Start slowly, with a few pieces, and add to each set as you can. Plan ahead and stage the construction of your sets to give your characters one pleasant surprise after another. You could even hold contests between different clans, gangs, pacts, etc. to build a set for their hangout or haven. The prize could be a free game of whatever you wish to give your players for their efforts. The advantage of this is that it involves the players in creating their surroundings and gives them more of a sense of responsibility for taking care of their turf. The sky is the limit to what you can do.

Conclusion

So many ideas and so little space and time in which to express them. Hopefully, this book has inspired you to add a little realism to your games. **Mind's Eye Theatre** provides you with a system to act out a fantasy and share it with others. It gives you the means to get together with other people and have fun; to work together for a common goal. It doesn't matter that the goal of the story isn't real, because the goal of the game is real: to bring people together to cooperate and make fantasy a reality for a brief period of time. Maybe by cooperating on something this far removed from our everyday lives, we can gain an understanding of how we can get along in the real world. The ideas in this book are just that — ideas through which you can add a little more depth to your play and gain more enjoyment out of the end result. However, it will always be your decision to make the effort to have that fun and share it with others. Through teamwork, no obstacle is insurmountable, a maxim that holds true in the plot of a game as well as in life.

Notes

Notes

"White Wolf created its own universe of reference, a world that would make Batman's Gotham City look like Disneyland."

— *Dracula Monthly* (UK)

NEW FICTION BY:
ROBERT BLOCH
NANCY A. COLLINS
HARLAN ELLISON
ESTHER M. FRIESNER
RICK HAUTALA
AND 17 OTHERS

Throughout the world's history, mankind has been manipulated by shadowy, inhuman beings. Wars have been waged to settle vampires' secret feuds. Cultures have been created to advance mages' visions of Ascension. Enemies of the Earth have been laid low by werewolves as they prepare for their Apocalypse. This is the World of Darkness, a nightmarish place where mortals' thoughts may not be their own.

Dark Destiny is an anthology of original short stories. The premiere 1994 World of Darkness fiction release, this collection includes stories by Robert Bloch, Rick Hautala, Nancy A. Collins, Robert Weinburg, and others.

4598B STONEGATE IND. BLVD. · STONE. MTN. GA. 30083

The Wyrm devours the world
Garou fall beneath its coils
Only the strongest can survive
Only the greatest can conquer
When will you Rage?
RAGE
Werewolf: The Apocalypse
Trading Card Game coming
May 5 from White Wolf.
It has been said that as the Apocalypse draws nearer, Garou will fight Garou. Werewolves will war with their own kind, battling for dominance and glory. Now, the 13 tribes are gathering as they prepare to turn their anger inward — against brother, against sister, against packmate. And out of this trial by fire, only the toughest will survive to fight the Wyrm.
Rage is a trading card game of savage combat. Players pit their werewolves against each other in brutal war, using supernatural powers, summoning spirit allies and wielding mystical fetishes. The werewolf pack with the most Renown wins, whether through destroying creatures of the Wyrm or defeating the other player's werewolves!
Features:
• Over 300 collectible cards, illustrated in full-color by hot comic and game artists.
• A game for two or more players.
• Fast and furious game play using a new rules system which allows players to choose the length of their games.
• Designed by the co-creators of Jyhad™, RAGE is the second World of Darkness game to be translated into cards.
KAUF, 1994